From the Fund in Memory of
R. AMORY THORNDIKE — 1900-1972

WAYS OF ESCAPE

Also by Chris Rojek

CAPITALISM AND LEISURE THEORY

FORGET BAUDRILLARD?
(*co-editor with B. Turner*)

THE HAUNT OF MISERY
(*co-editor with G. Peacock and S. Collins*)

LEISURE FOR LEISURE
(*editor*)

SOCIAL WORK AND RECEIVED IDEAS
(*with G. Peacock and S. Collins*)

SPORT AND LEISURE IN THE CIVILIZING PROCESS
(*co-editor with E. Dunning*)

Ways of Escape

Modern Transformations in
Leisure and Travel

Chris Rojek
Senior Editor in Sociology
Routledge

Rowman & Littlefield Publishers

ROWMAN & LITTLEFIELD PUBLISHERS, INC.

First published in the United States of America in 1994
by Rowman & Littlefield Publishers, Inc.
4720 Boston Way, Lanham, Maryland 20706

British Cataloguing in Publication Information available

Library of Congress Cataloging-in-Publication Data
Rojek, Chris.
Ways of escape : modern transformations in leisure and travel /
Chris Rojek.
p. cm.
Includes bibliographical references and index.
ISBN 0–8476–7898–9
1. Leisure—Sociological aspects. 2. Travel—Sociological
aspects. I. Title.
GV14.45.R66 1994
306.4'812—dc20   93–33328
                                                              CIP

Printed in Great Britain

For T.D.
(1954–79)
– Who Escaped –
???

In the Rowman & Littlefield series

POSTMODERN
SOCIAL FUTURES

General Editor
Stjepan G. Meštrović
Texas A & M University

Contents

List of Illustrations

ACKNOWLEDGEMENT

The author and publishers wish to acknowledge with thanks the source of the illustration on page 193, and to state that they have tried without success to contact the copyright-holder. They will be pleased to make the necessary arrangements at the first opportunity.

Preface

The critic who complains that this book sometimes reads as if it doesn't have both feet on the ground has a point. For much of it was conceived, considered and executed in mid-air as I flew from city to city in Europe and the USA pursuing my responsibilities as Senior Editor in Sociology at Routledge. Although air travel is commonly associated with anxiety, I have always found it to bring me peace of mind. Up there one is, as it were, suspended from earthly cares. Looking down from above the clouds one cannot avoid thinking.

And I often think about the circumstances that led me into a career which I never intended to follow – but which, I should add, has in many ways been a revelation to me. As an undergraduate and postgraduate at Leicester University in the mid to late seventies I had experienced enough of the expansion in higher education and I was far enough away from the retrenchment of the 1980s to imagine that an academic career was viable. But the Thatcher adventure put paid to this as far as British sociology was concerned. Like many others of my generation, it took me a long time to get an academic job. In my case it was two years before I was appointed to a one-year fixed contract at the College of St Mark and St John, Plymouth. After that I was lucky to secure another fixed-term post at the Queen's College in Glasgow. At that time I was the only sociologist in this small college situated at the edge of Kelvingrove Park. Sociology was taught as a service stream to a variety of courses. From memory, I taught on eight different courses involving students at all levels of higher education: I taught sociology to business studies students working for Scottish diplomas, postgraduates in the catering industry on one-day release courses, undergraduates in Dietetics, Resource Management and Catering and Accommodation, postgraduate students training for a one-year qualification in social work, and mature students with family commitments who were studying for the certificate Qualification in Social Work. To make some extra money I also started teaching the old D102 course run by the Open University on one evening a week.

My job at the Queen's College was a fixed-term appointment. So I thought it expedient to build up my publications record in order

to prepare for the awful day when I would be forced to reapply for
my job. In just under four years I completed one book, began work
on another two, signed a contract for a fourth and published over
twenty articles in a variety of academic journals.

Gill Davies, the publisher of my Tavistock book *Capitalism and
Leisure Theory* (1985), saved me from this stooped existence by in-
forming me that a Senior Editor's post in Sociology had come up at
the venerable firm of Routledge and Kegan Paul. In truth I had spent
much of the previous eighteen months feeding her with sob stories
about the hard life or, if you prefer, my hard life in Glasgow. At all
events, to my surprise I was appointed to head the RKP sociology
list in July 1986 and I commenced my duties three months later after
having served my notice at the Queen's College.

As to why I selected leisure as a suitable subject for my energies,
I must confess to a degree of calculation. As a postgraduate at
Leicester I had been working on convergence theory and the experience of Yugoslav workers' self-management as an example of divergence from the capitalist world system. However, without fluency in
an Eastern European language I soon reached the conclusion that I
could only go so far in this area. So despite the admonitions of my
supervisor, Eric Dunning, I decided to turn down the chance to
switch to a PhD track and instead worked up my findings for the
M.Phil degree which I was awarded in 1979. Had I known then that
the election of the first Thatcher government in June of 1979 would
result in a virtual moratorium on academic appointments in British
sociology I would probably have opted for the Leicester PhD track.
As it turned out I had over two years of 'reserve labour' experience
to contemplate my next, or in truth, my first career move. During
this time – 1979–81 – it was clear that the leisure industry was
growing. While British manufacturing was rolling over with four
paws in the air, British heritage centres and literary landscapes appeared to be expanding by leaps and bounds. I was struck by the
contrast between a buoyant leisure industry and the reality of
mass unemployment. But it was not until I arrived at the College of
St Mark and St John that I started to investigate what academics
had been writing about leisure. I found an area becalmed in the
functionalist preoccupations of the 1960s. Nobody had seriously
tried to situate leisure in the context of classical social theory. Marx,
Durkheim, Weber, Freud and Veblen seemed to count for nothing in
the academic study of leisure. True, I found references to a student

of the cultural studies approach and one of the old gallants of functionalism crossing swords in the early 1980s. One refused to speak to the other on the punkish grounds that discussion was pointless between minds set so far apart. But this seemed to be the outer limit of critical exchange. As for feminism and leisure, I heard rumours of research projects in the North of England and Scotland. However, next to nothing was published until the mid 1980s. All in all, I decided, leisure looked like a fair bet for making an impact. If this sounds unduly Machiavellian, it had less to do with my nature than with a sober assessment of the academic career options open for a young sociologist in Thatcherite Britain. During my spell in the reserve army of labour I had worked as a dishwasher in a Hyde Park hotel, a warehouseman for a department store in Piccadilly, and a census collector in Caversham. Much of it was more congenial than I had imagined, but in all conscience I decided that none of it was my scene.

So it was that I came to submit a proposal for a book on leisure theory and capitalism to Gill Davies of Tavistock. In the early 1980s capitalism seemed to be the obvious context for exploring leisure theory. As a student in the seventies I had been caught up in the various neo-Marxist and feminist attempts to unravel capitalism. The feminist argument that capitalism supported the systematic oppression of women seemed to me to be incontrovertible. I was less convinced by the radical feminist argument that women should organize and act independently of men to combat capitalism. This sexual politics, I felt, smacked of the recrudescence of determinism by implying that men were incapable of trying to build equal relationships with women. As for neo-Marxism, the marriage between Althusserianism and Gramscianism which was ascendant in my teens and twenties seemed to me to be over-abstract and to have more to do with office politics in polytechnics and universities than the experience of the much invoked 'ordinary people'. I preferred the writings of the young Marx, especially the *Economic and Philosophic Manuscripts of 1844*, *The German Ideology* and that marvel of compression and acumen, *The Communist Manifesto*. In any case, at Leicester it was difficult to avoid the impression that the greatest critical sociologist of the twentieth century was someone who virtually nobody had heard of: namely Norbert Elias. *Capitalism and Leisure Theory* was widely seen as being sympathetic to figurational sociology. Certainly it shared Elias's hostility to false conceptual dichotomies (individual and society, work and leisure, private and public) and it recognized Elias's unquestionable achievement in pinpointing 'the civilizing process'. All the same, those who criticized me for being a 'figurationalist' ignored my (1985: 169–72) criticisms of the figurational approach and my (1986) article which attacked many aspects of Elias's methodology. Today I would say that figurational sociology is enormously stimulating and crucially important in my own journey in leisure studies. But I have long since ceased to imagine that it could act as a rallying point for sociologists. Now it just seems to me to be one interesting approach among many.

If *Capitalism and Leisure Theory* were to be rewritten today the focus would change. This time it would be on 'Modernity' rather than capitalism. 'Modernity' brings to mind the restless, contradictory, unfinished relations which, I think, characterize leisure relations and social relations most accurately. I attribute my interest in Modernity and its classical exponents – Simmel, Kracauer and Benjamin – to my doctoral research experience at Glasgow University. In particular, Harvie Ferguson introduced me to a range of literature and ideas that I would never have encountered otherwise. And David Frisby reinforced my interest in 'the ephemeral', 'the fugitive' and 'the contingent'. Anyone who is familiar with his book *Fragments of Modernity* (1985) will be aware of how much the present book owes to his important study.

One year after starting with RKP a market collapsed, a cash limit held and I found myself in charge of the biggest sociology list in Britain, comprising the titles of the old RKP, Tavistock and Croom Helm imprints. In 1991 the Unwin Hyman list was merged into Routledge. In the course of all this I have made friends with many sociologists and exploited my position with single-minded ruthlessness to get them to comment on the ideas in *Ways of Escape* as they unfolded. John Urry, David Frisby, Stjepan Mestrovic, Eric Dunning, Harvie Ferguson and Soile Veijola have all read the manuscript and provided me with well-considered and helpful criticism. I have also benefited more indirectly from conversations and correspondence with Zygmunt Bauman, Jay Bernstein, Lauren Langman, Dean and Juliet MacCannell, Barry Smart and Bryan Turner.

All of this professional life has been conducted in tandem with a busy and complicated private life – and what busy and complicated private lives we lead under Modernity! Undoubtedly, there are connections between my private life and what I have written here. There may be influences that I am only dimly aware of and conjunctions that I would find startling. But, in the immortal words of Karl Kraus, 'I don't like to meddle in my private affairs'.

London, 3 December 1991

Consider, then, for an instant, my increasing delight and astonishment as I discover myself a thousand leagues from my homeland and let my senses slowly absorb the confused impressions of a world which is the perfect antithesis of ours.

Gerard de Nerval
Voyage en orient (1844)

Everything declines, with the exception of the West.
Ernst Bloch
The Principle of Hope, vol. 1 (1938–47)

Introduction: Welcome to Greenfield Village

Greenfield Village. Yes, Mister, Madam: *Green Field Village*. What a beautiful idea for the heritage merchants, the purveyors of escape, the dream-dealers in leisure and travel experience. The green field, like the legendary greenwood, is a place beyond the reach of the mundane world. It is 'natural', whereas so much that surrounds us in the metropolis is obviously fake. It is also a village – a cosy concept which immediately suggests images of community, warmth and safety. We are in an immaculate escape centre: a place where we can shrug off the chained obligations of daily life and take a leap into 'freedom'.

Greenfield Village is in fact the home of the Henry Ford Museum, an outdoor collection of American heritage situated in Dearborn, Michigan. Ford devised it as 'a true picture of the development of the country' (Ford quoted in Flink 1975: 74). But what, after all, is a picture? A true reflection of 'reality', or an impossible representation of what has never been and never can be? This is the Henry Ford Museum: a jangling collection of illustrious and fêted artefacts in 'the American story'. Here you can see Edison's 'Menlo Park' laboratories reassembled joist-by-joist, brick-by-brick, from the dismantled buildings hundreds of miles from the Greenfield site. Here too, you will find the workshop of the Wright Brothers, the Courthouse where Abraham Lincoln practised, the house of Stephen Collins Foster (composer of 'Way Down Upon The Swanee River' and 'My Old Kentucky Home'), the birthplace of tyre magnate Harvey Firestone, the schoolhouse where Mary was allegedly followed by her little lamb, the home of Noah Webster (of *Webster's Dictionary* fame) and the home of plant technologist Luther Burbank. The village also boasts a duplicate of Philadelphia's 'Independence Hall', reconstructions of the Sarah Jordan Boarding House, the nineteenth-century river steamer 'The Suwanee' on which Thomas Edison often travelled in Florida (Henry Ford Museum and Greenfield Village Tourist Brochure 1987). All co-exist in startling equivalence.

1

Greenfield Village is, of course, an entirely artificial construction. It was devised to tell a heroic story of matchless progress. Thus its constituent attractions are contrived to evoke reassuring feelings about the direction in which society is moving. Nonetheless, doubts of a specific and general kind must be cast at the Greenfield story. The specific doubts pertain to the authenticity of some of the Greenfield exhibits. For example, Lacey (1986: 240–6) contends that the story of Mary and her little lamb was invented by the Boston poet, Sarah J. Hale. Ford's painstaking and expensive reassembly of the old schoolhouse from the village of Sterling, Massachusetts where Mary was supposed to have been *really* followed by her little lamb is therefore dismissed as a folly. Similarly, Lacey (1986: 246) asserts that the purchase and reassembly of the old Collins Foster home in Greenfield Village is disabled by one blunt fact: Stephen Collins Foster almost certainly never lived there! The more general doubts centre upon the status of the Village as a reflection of history. It is surely wrong to see the Greenfield exhibits as elements in a coherent story. Divorced from their historical and geographical contexts they are deprived of any determinate meaning. They become a collection of displaced curios. Far from being 'a true picture' of history, the Village is a phantasmagoria of the past.

Greenfield Village is one of a number of heritage sites which have been developed in recent years as centres of recreation. Other examples include the 'Way We Were' centre at Wigan Pier; 'The Canterbury Pilgrim's Way', the Jorvik settlement in York; the 'Into the Thick' simulation of a coal-mine in the Midlands; the Plymouth plantation in New England which attempts to reproduce the life and times of the original British settlers from the *Mayflower*; the Old Tucson Wild West town which employs actors attired in period costume imitating cowboy townsfolk; and the 'Seaport Experience' in New York which claims to return you to the 'world of New York's South Street Southport', where you can 'take a white-knuckled trip around Cape Horn, the sea spray is real' ('The Seaport Experience' Tourist Flyer 1990). Heritage culture has also been used to spearhead urban regeneration programme in towns such as Pittsburgh and Glasgow suffering industrial decline.

At the same time the development of new technologies have encouraged greater flexibility in work patterns. Personal computers enable people to reproduce essential office facilities in the home. In addition office landscaping has introduced many characteristics of domestic space into the office. More relaxed styles of interior decoration and personal features such as pot plants, pictures of the family, posters, tea and coffee making facilities and so forth, routinely occupy office space. Work advertisements, which used to focus on details of the job and the company, now regularly refer to the leisure amenities with the job package and the recreational resources of the surrounding countryside. Doubtless these developments did not originate in the 1970s and '80s. But they did proliferate, causing some commentators to observe that Britain is being turned into a gigantic theme park and that new orientations to work are emerging (Hewison 1987; Gorz 1983, 1985). It is true that some of these arguments had been anticipated in the 1960s and early '70s in the debate around 'post-industrial society'. However, the decline of the primary and secondary sectors coupled with the rise of the service sector in the core economies during the late 1970s and the '80s gave them renewed force. In addition, the rapid rise of micro-chip technology in a variety of domestic and work settings heightened the sense of epochal change in daily life.

POSTMODERNISM AND DE-DIFFERENTIATION

The debate on postmodernism brings many of these themes together. Postmodernism proposes that society has left the conditions of Modernity behind (Lyotard 1984; Kroker and Cook 1986; Harvey 1989). For example, as schoolchildren we were taught that the past and the present, work and leisure are separate categories (see Figure 1).

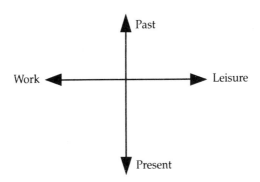

Figure 1: Some Modernist categories

Of course, relations between the categories were recognized. Thus it was generally accepted that the events of the past shape the world in which we live; similarly, students of leisure recognized a 'spillover' of work experience into leisure and that some patterns of leisure 'compensate' for the demands of work. With the twin categories of past and present, work and leisure, therefore, partial convergence between the categories was recognized. All the same, most people maintained that in the final analysis clear distinctions between each side obtained and could be demarcated. That is, past and present, work and leisure were ultimately seen as separate states.

For postmodernists these commonsense distinctions have evaporated. For example, from a postmodernist standpoint the past bursts into the present through stage representations like Greenfield Village or the 'Way We Were' centre at Wigan Pier where actors wear the costume of turn-of-the-century schoolteachers and keep classes of day trippers in order. In addition, and more generally, branches of the mass media keep the past constantly 'alive' in the present. Nostalgia industries continuously recycle products which signify simultaneity between the past and the present. For example, hit television shows from the sixties are retransmitted in the 1980s and '90s and reproduce or beat their original success; top pop songs from the fifties, sixties and seventies are re-released and become number one hits all over again; and fashions that were discarded as infra dig in our twenties are triumphantly championed by our children thirty years later. Increasingly, popular culture is dominated by images of recurrence rather than originality.

And what of leisure – that arena of 'freedom', 'choice' and 'self-development' beloved by liberal authors – can it really be described as a separate sphere of experience? Many forms of contemporary leisure involve aspects which remind us of work. For example, participating in competitive amateur sports involves training, drill and timing-practice. Keep-fit programmes in the home are based in routine physical exercise. Amateur photographers in trade publishing are encouraged to aim for 'professional standards'. And underlying nearly all leisure forms is a characteristic which most liberal and radical writers tend to pass over in silence: self consciousness. If we are aware of the significance of our leisure activity – whether it can be said to be good or bad, whether it has high or low status – can we really be said to be 'free'?

Postmodernists speak of the generalized 'de-differentiation' of Modernist categories (Lyotard 1984; Harvey 1989; Lash 1990). De-differentiation may be formally defined as a condition in which former social, economic and political distinctions cease to obtain. For example, the private sphere can no longer be analytically or symbolically separated from the public sphere; the Cartesian separation of body and mind ceases to hold good; the categoric distinctions between male and female roles seem unsupportable; the division between work and leisure is no longer clear-cut; in short, the divisions which gave stability to the Modernist order of things seem to be untenable – they do not correspond with people's actual experience of things.

This book undoubtedly springs from the intense debate around postmodernism and de-differentiation which dominated the 1980s. However, it is also inevitably marked by the preoccupations of more localized debates in leisure studies during the postwar period. In particular, it seeks to oppose the traditional idea that leisure affords us real freedom and choice. Instead in Chapter 1 I use the neo-Durkheimian concept of 'moral regulation' to show that forms of identity, practice and association in leisure and travel are highly organized. The issues raised by postmodernism may point to important changes in society which mean that class, elite, statist or corporatist types of moral regulation are no longer viable. Nonetheless the burden of this chapter is that from at least the Middle Ages to the middle of the twentieth century we have been taught to see leisure and travel experience as parts of an encompassing moral order of things. The theme is continued in the next two chapters of the book. The second chapter starts from the proposition that the feminist contribution to leisure studies has been one of the most significant developments of the 1970s and '80s. However, certain political characteristics of feminism have produced a misleading view of the history of some aspects of women's leisure. In particular, the chapter concentrates on the nineteenth and early twentieth century history of bourgeois women's leisure. The aim is to show that, especially after the 1860s, inequality between the sexes was successfully challenged by many bourgeois women. To illustrate the point the chapter examines the influence of bourgeois women in 'the aestheticization of everyday life' and in shaping patterns of consumption and public awareness of poverty and unrestrained masculine values. I argue that it is wrong to see women simply as passive recipients of donatory male culture. Many women, especially the 'leisured' women of the bourgeois class, played an important active role in influencing the patterns of moral regulation to which leisure and travel were subsumed. The third chapter adopts a more general analytical approach by asking what we mean by 'Modernity' and 'Postmodernity' and how these categories relate to the experience of leisure and travel. I argue that Modernity identified leisure and travel experience with the business of 'self making'. Leisure and travel were seen as spheres of activity in which self-realization could be pursued in a more authentic way than in work and family life. The chapter moves on to discuss the decomposition of this worldview. It explores the relevant processes which precipitated decomposition. It closes with an analysis of the meaning of Postmodernity and an attempt to show the general relevance of postmodern arguments in contemporary culture. The next two chapters are more empirical in tone. Both seek to pinpoint specific forms of contemporary leisure and travel experience. Chapter four examines four commercial types of leisure which became prominent after 1970: Black Spots; Heritage Sites; Literary Landscapes; and Theme parks. The object is to describe concrete examples of these forms and to consider the ways in which they may be said to exemplify modern or postmodern conditions. The fifth chapter pursues the same object, but this time with reference to travel experience. The chapter asks, 'What is a tourist?' It distinguishes between 'travel' and 'tourism', 'tourist' and 'post tourist'. It discusses how tourist sites are constructed by the travel industry and considers the depthless and eclectic qualities of these 'areas of escape'. The chapter ends with a discussion of the de-differentiation of travel experience and the reproduction or simulation of 'exotic' features from remote lands in the home and in the Main Street shopping mall. The Conclusion returns to the association of leisure and travel with escape. It considers the roots of this association in contemporary culture and asks 'Is escape still possible?' Again, aspects of the de-differentiation of leisure and travel are considered. The diffusion of 'leisurely' values and 'exotic' features to domestic, work and public space settings has been one of the most notable social and architectural characteristics of the last fifty years. The Conclusion asks if de-differentiation has weakened the allure of leisure and travel.

Finally I want to say a few words about the audience for the book and the line of enquiry that I have pursued. I see the book as a contribution to the critical sociology of leisure and culture. Anyone under 35 who enters this field will surely be depressed by what he or she encounters. The place resembles a battlefield of hopelessly entrenched positions. The main academic battalions represent liberal pluralism, cultural studies, figurational sociology and a variant of radical feminism. My experience is that, far from encouraging open debate, these battalions actually work to close it down. Critical discussion never rises very much above hurling slogans at each other. Such is the condition of palpable belligerence and scapegoating that paranoia is never far behind. I have myself been a victim. My last book was reviewed by a representative of the cultural studies position who was clearly determined to reject the book *tout court*. That, I admit, was painful. To my mind rejecting anything *tout court* reflects the values of the bar-room rather than the academy. It is not a practice that I have followed or encouraged in my own work. But what really irked me was the suggestion made by the same reviewer that I was instrumental in forming a 'Leicester/Glasgow axis'. This is lamentable stuff. Anyone with any knowledge of the departments of sociology in either Leicester or Glasgow will recognize that the notion of an 'axis' is fanciful in the extreme.

What accounts for the belligerence between the four camps? One is reminded of Marx's (1847) shimmering analysis of Proudhon's 'philosophie de la misère'. In the 'Prologue' he notes that M. Proudhon's work 'is not just a treatise on political economy, an ordinary book: it is a bible. "Mysteries", "Secrets wrested from the bosom of God", "Revelations" – it lacks nothing'. Now consider some methodological and strategic advice from one of the most vociferous students of the cultural studies approach:

> Always be ready to see the familiar as strange, the at-first-sight innocent as redolent with significant meaning . . . Cultural Studies has been concerned with struggle and intervention, in which the analytical itself is a form of practice, or more accurately, praxis. (Tomlinson 1989: 105)

'Be ready to see the familiar as strange', examine 'the innocent as redolent with significant meaning', aim for 'struggle and intervention' – Marx's *bêtes noires* remain evident in the politically committed academic analysis of leisure.

And yet I hope that my book will be seen as being motivated by more than a reaction to highly 'involved', political forms of academic analysis. Quite deliberately, the book focuses upon imposed moral values and dominant ideologies of leisure and travel. I do not concern myself much with the story of the worker's struggle to wrest time from the master's'. Contrary to what might be automatically assumed in some quarters this decision is not occasioned by the feeling that the processes of worker's resistance and subcultural struggle are of negligible importance. Who can read E.P. Thompson's monumental and path-breaking work, *The Making of the English Working Class* and fail to be convinced by his contention that something rotten was at the heart of historical sociology up to that point: namely the relative neglect of working-class experience, struggles and ideals? However, Thompson's book was originally published in 1963. Surely it is time to say that the balance has now gone too far towards telling the story from the standpoint and perspective of the oppressed. Surely it is time to examine more openly the changing order of things in which these standpoints and perspectives emerged and developed. This is very different from aligning oneself with the values of the oppressor. Rather one is trying to consider the network of relations in which both oppressor and oppressed are caught up and which predisposed actors to pursue certain courses of action. And here it will simply not do to assert that nothing in leisure or culture will be understood unless one starts from the situation of workers or women: masters and men were also enmeshed in an immense cosmos of 'order' which gave meaning to the particularity of their actions.

Admittedly, critical contributions to the sociology of leisure and culture have recognized the existence of encompassing networks of power which support some willed actions and make others impossible. However, their attempts to make sense of them seem to me to be vulnerable to the charge of essentialism. To illustrate the point, the cultural studies approach seems to account ultimately for leisure identities, practices and associations in terms of *production*; radical feminist contributions emphasize *reproduction* and itemize a whole machinery of sexual oppression; and figurational sociologists can never seem to encounter leisure and culture without seeing the hand of *the civilizing process* far behind. What seems to have been ignored is the rich heritage left by Georg Simmel, Walter Benjamin, Siegfried Kracauer, and the contemporary historian Wolfgang Schivelbusch. These writers emphasize the centrality of *circulation* and *consumption* in the constitution of Modernity. Moreover, they treat these processes as irreducible to processes of production, reproduction or the civilizing process. I have claimed this heritage as a legacy in planning and executing this study. I have tried to follow processes of circulation and consumption with a view to discovering what bearing they have upon the experience of leisure and travel.

Notions of escape abound in modern social life. Not surprisingly they constantly recur throughout modern social theory. With Weber we stare out from the bars of our iron cage at a world teeming with possibility but which is always just out of reach. Studying leisure and travel entails considering how people have tried to capture this elusive and exciting world. It means entering their hopes, fears, desires and ideals. Leisure and travel open the door to the dream-life of Modernity. But the study of these forms also involves discovering how people reconcile this dream-life with the monotonous obligations of daily life. Most of us combine our escape experience with holding down a job and performing the ordinary duties of family life. Our dreams of escape are filled with what Benjamin (1983: 153) called 'the magic of distance'. This fantasy element is a common denominator in leisure and travel activity. It probably explains why many of us find the actual experience of 'free time' or visiting a tourist sight is often anti-climactic. The magic of distance is pierced when the spectator steps too close to the dream-scene. But if we are disappointed it hardly seems to diminish the energy of the dream-life. We return again and again to leisure and travel as ways of escape.

1

The Management of Pleasure

Classical political economy never produced a theory of leisure and travel. However, it never tired of gnawing away at the question of pleasure. Both Hobbes (1651) in the *Leviathan* and Locke (1689) in the *Essay on Human Understanding* operated with a *homo duplex* model of desire. Man was presented as riven between the desire to gain pleasure and to avoid pain. In positing this as the State of Nature, both writers recognized that conflict is inevitable in human affairs. Both appealed to Reason to raise Man up from this low state of affairs. Hobbes argued that Reason should be used to check and oppose Nature by creating a sovereign state vested with powers of regulation and punishment. Locke, in a seminal contribution to English individualism, held that Reason must be employed to hammer out social contracts to obey the word of God and defend private property.[1]

The argument for restraining Nature by Reason has a rich pedigree in modern social thought. In a variety of forms it can be identified in the writings of Kant, Diderot, Smith, Hume, Rousseau, Bentham, J.S. Mill and Spencer. Freud (1979), of course, elevated it to the central psychological principle in modern civilization. However, history is wrenched by disputes regarding the capacity of Reason to subdue what Hume called 'the passions'.

Mention of the passions deserves pause for reflection. At least one major contribution to the sociology of leisure proposes that a general 'dampening' of the passions has occurred in modern society. It goes on to identify leisure and sport as a release route enabling the passions to be liberated in a relatively controlled way (Elias and Dunning 1986: 63–90). There is no real parallel to the argument that society has been marked by a general dampening of the passions in traditional thought.[2] If anything, the traditional position sided with the view that the passions are violent and dangerous forces which are liable to engulf the individual in tribulation without warning.

However, traditional thought does contain the theme of the rehabilitative effect of leisure and travel. Consider Robert Burton's *The Anatomy of Melancholy*. Burton identified six passions 'drowned in corporeal organs of sense' (1924: 169): love, joy, desire, hatred, sorrow and fear. He associated them with affliction, disturbance and catastrophe. The passions, he claimed, 'macerate the minds of men,' 'plunge them into a labyrinth of cares' and 'cause them to crucify their own souls' (170). Although Burton understood the passions to be God-given and bred in the bone, he nevertheless accepted that social conditions played a major role in exacerbating or containing them. In particular, he connected excessive wealth and leisure with the melancholy passions. 'Idleness,' he wrote (158), 'is the badge of gentry'. Moreover, idleness, he continued (158), is 'the bane of body and mind, the nurse of naughtiness . . . the chief author of all mischief'. The remedies which he proposed were work and, interestingly, recreation and travel. Recreation, he observed (338), 'is nature's physician'; and on travel he remarked (335) that there is 'no better physic for a melancholy man than change of air, and variety of places, to travel abroad and see fashions'.

Burton died in 1640. He can hardly be allowed to have had the last word on the subject of the passions. For example, Hume's understanding of the passions may not have been more learned than Burton's,[3] but it was unquestionably more refined. He distinguished (1739: 413–18) between 'the direct passions', of joy, grief, hope and fear which arise from our natural desire to acquire pleasure and avoid pain, and 'the indirect passions', such as pride, humility, love or hatred which spring from cultural circumstances. Hume was hardly more sanguine than Burton on the issue of commanding the passions. 'Reason,' he wrote (415) in a famous conclusion, 'is and ought only to be the slave of the passions, and can never pretend to any other office than to serve and obey them.' However, it does not follow that Hume rejected Reason as worthless in the management of the passions. Rather, he argued that Reason was capable of distinguishing between truth and falsehood. While Reason cannot tell us how to live, it can act as the pivot for basic agreements regarding need, virtue and freedom.

Hume's delineation of the direct and indirect passions reflected the central Enlightenment concern with man's nature and history. The development of classification and natural history in the eighteenth century made the question of separating 'Man' from the rest of nature crucial (Hirst and Woolley 1982). A fascination with the savage was the corollary of this burgeoning 'human science'. For the savage represented origins, naturalness, the clean slate of human existence. Comparisons of the savage and the civilized man, usually came down in favour of the latter. The ideology of the Enlightenment demanded that 'science' and 'progress' should be adduced as universal benefits to Man. However, contained within this ideology was the counter-argument, 'the dialectic of the Enlightenment' in Adorno and Horkheimer's (1944) memorable phrase. According to this argument, civilization produces unique forms of misery and discontent. It multiplies idleness, lassitude and anxiety, and tears apart the balance between Man's passions and Nature. Rousseau (1974: 52–70) contributes to the argument in the form of a comparison between Man in the civilized state and Man in the state of Nature. For Rousseau, civilized man enjoys the comforts of Reason, but is also made frantic by the labours of Reason to devise new things and experiences to enjoy. His desires constantly race beyond his natural wants. The difference either breeds lassitude and idleness as man finds that he cannot satisfy his desire, or it produces agitated, frenzied passions such as greed, pride, envy and anger. The condition of man in the natural state is very different. 'Who', asks Rousseau (1974: 70–1), 'has heard of a savage who took it into his own head, when he was free, to complain of life and to kill himself?' The desires of the savage never go beyond his immediate wants. Deprived of the comforts of Reason he nonetheless is immune to its terrors.[4] 'The only evils he fears are pain and hunger,' declares Rousseau (1974: 61). 'I say pain, and not death: for no animal can know what it is to die; the knowledge of death and its terrors being one of the first acquisitions made by man in departing from the animal stage.'

Rousseau's vindication of the savage is often criticized as a romantic position. However, his remedies for the ills of civilization are notably hard-headed. He held that the destructive passions in civilized life, especially hatred, pride, fear and envy, could be held at bay by the use of Reason to produce a society based upon justice and equality. He argued for the egalitarian redistribution of wealth and the promotion of a progressive system of education.[5]

Rousseau's work anticipates the modern view that pleasure must be considered as a social force and not a mere force of Nature. Reason and association are the authors of ceaseless novelty and deviation. Through foresight and control, that is *social* relations, Man has the means to regulate his desires in sensible and even pleasurable ways. He is not locked in the eternal struggle with Nature forever. He can break out of his chains and create a secure, orderly world fit for his passions to abide.

THE GROWTH OF MARKET SOCIETY

Rousseau's preoccupation with finding a just and enduring order in society was a response to the deep changes in the conditions of life wrought by industrialization and the growth of market society. The late seventeenth and eighteenth centuries witnessed an accelerating course of expansion in which society exceeded its boundaries in at least four directions: demographically, economically, territorially and politically. These changes were simultaneous, interconnected and mutually reinforcing.

Demographic change was perhaps the most dramatic. In 1700 the population of England stood at 5 million. By 1750 it had climbed to 5.7 million, and in 1800 it stood at 8.6 million.[6] Moreover, during the same period the distribution shifted dramatically from rural locations (with the exception of London, Bristol and Norwich – all big towns in 1700) to urban concentrations (Porter 1982: 25, 333, 356). The demographic mass was more dense and mobile by the end of the century than the start, and this had clear results in expanding production, distribution and exchange.

To come to economic change, industrial production expanded slowly between 1700 and 1780, then grew spectacularly thereafter. New machines, new occupations, the factory system, vast improvements in communications (principally road, canal and maritime transport), transformed time-honoured lifestyles. Commodity production increased and international trade grew in importance. Between 1700 and 1750, home industries increased their output by 7 per cent, export industries by 76 per cent; between 1750 and 1770, the respective figures were 7 per cent and 80 per cent. Relations of production became more specialized and diverse, and economies of scale became more important as an element in determining margins (Hobsbawm 1969: 48).

Turning to the question of territory, the late seventeenth and eighteenth centuries saw the discovery of new lands and the expansion of knowledge of remote climates, topographies, vegetations and peoples. British colonial rule expanded in India, Africa, Canada, Australia and the Caribbean islands. Classical sociological theory was divided on the economic significance of the colonies for the development of modern capitalism. Marx (1887: 703–5) held that colonial exploitation produced a gigantic accumulation of wealth in Europe and boosted economic activity. Weber (1923: 223) agreed but argued that the colonies were not crucial to the progress of modern capitalism. The reason for this, he maintained, was that colonial administration depended upon ancient militaristic methods of seizure and force. What was unique and irresistible about modern capitalism was the specific form of the organization of labour which it perfected. For Weber, it was this which was the secret of the remarkable accumulation which was sustained after 1770. He also cited the cost of maintaining colonial garrisons as a drain on European resources.[7] Be that as it may, there is little doubt that the new colonies figured as an important source of trade and the exchange of people. For example, in 1700 colonial trade accounted for 15 per cent of British commerce, by 1775 it has risen to 33 per cent. As for the exchange of people, emigration, especially of dispossessed Irish and Scots, swelled the ranks of colonial settlers. In 1701 the population of the Thirteen Colonies of North America was less than 300 000; by 1760 it had soared to 1 200 000; similarly the population of Canada rose from 14 000 in 1695 to almost 500 000 in 1800 (Hobsbawm 1969: 53; Porter 1982: 50).

The effect of the colonies on travel-consciousness was just as striking, if harder to measure. For the first time, Europeans could fix their dreams of Arcadia upon distant lands beyond navigable seas which offered the virtues of an idealized home, but contained none of its defects. For example, the Thirteen Colonies of North America were lauded as a land of abundance, disfigured by no monarchy, peerage or pauperism. Among European radicals the American War of Independence simply polished this image. Paine (1792) wrote of the war as the triumph of Reason over Privilege, and celebrated the American constitution as its embodiment.[8] Arcadia was not a one-dimensional concept. For Europeans half in love with the idea of ancient society, the British Raj was a living attraction. It combined an exotic appeal with the promise of riches beyond the dreams of average men. 'British India,' commented Porter (1982: 51), 'offered a *pukka* England where nabobs – officials of the East India Company –

could enact their plundering fantasies before a captive audience of natives.' Elsewhere Africa and the Caribbean offered similar opportunities. By the early nineteenth century, the romantic and military colonial traditions were joined by the Evangelical mission to internationalize Christianity: the so-called "white man's burden".

Politically, the eighteenth century divides into two halves. Up until 1750, the ruling oligarchy strengthened their position. The snuffing out of the Jacobite rebellions of 1715 and 1745 symbolized the resilience of the old order. However, after 1750 this order was dented by a volley of challenges. The French and American Revolutions rejected the hereditary system of government and sought to replace it with representative government based on a bill of rights. In England, the Gordon Riots of 1780 were a major civil disturbance. Although inflamed by the fear of popery, they spread out to attack privilege and wealth. The development of radical bodies such as the Friends of the People (1791) and the London Corresponding Society (1792) challenged the old order through the weapon of Reason – by education, pamphlets and petitioning. The religious movement of Dissenters and Nonconformists acted as an important catalyst for the development of bourgeois conscience. They protested against the brutality, injustice and inveterate privilege of the old order and they lent their energies and finances to an array of 'deserving causes'.

Finally, the extension of industry in the closing decades of the century provided the stimulus for working-class protests movements. The factory and the workers' houses constituted the immediate and concrete base for collective consciousness raising, organization and action. Workers' organizations which aimed to improve the terms and conditions of work were fiercely resisted by employers. The notorious Combination Acts of 1799 and 1800 gave summary powers to justices of the peace to convict workers who banded together in pursuit of their collective interests.[9]

The demographic, economic, territorial and political changes described above worked through society unevenly and at different tempos. Their effect was to dislocate existing social and economic conditions, but from this dislocation new connections were formed, new rules of life determined. Market society separated labour from other activities of life, notably play and recreation, and destroyed traditional forms of existence. It moved 'to replace them', remarked Polyani (1944: 163) 'by a different type of organization, an atomistic and individualistic one'.

PLEASURE, REASON AND THE MARKET

Pleasure could not be ignored in market society. For one thing it inherited the *homo duplex* model of man which recognized bodily pleasures as essential to the state of being human. Furthermore, as market society developed it became more and more dependent upon the principle that the experience of consumption must be pleasurable. On the other hand, it was apparent that a system of consumption in which consumers are solely required to fulfil their personal needs and wants regardless of the rights of others would quickly collapse. The desire to consume would replace the desire to work. Idleness and the love of excess, the greatest of human maladies according to Puritan philosophy, would reign supreme. The solution was not to use Reason as a truncheon to batter the passions into submission. That would be contrary to both Nature and Culture, for Nature equipped man with passionate dispositions at birth, and Culture refined them through human association and company. Rather, the solution was to devise an objective system to distinguish good passions from bad passions, useful pleasures from dangerous ones and real wants from false wants.

Malthus's doctrine of 'moral restraint', outlined in his *Essay on the Principle of Population* (1803) is one of the clearest and most influential arguments in favour of the use of Reason to subdue 'bad' and 'dangerous' passions. The force of the doctrine stemmed from its directness. Malthus held that mankind is animated by two universal 'urges': to eat and to satisfy the sexual passions. These urges conflict, since human fertility far outweighs the fertility of the soil to produce food. For Malthus, the 'melancholy' conclusion was obvious: the unchecked satisfaction of the sexual passions would inevitably propel man into a state of catastrophe through overpopulation and starvation. The remedy was not to rely on the 'positive checks' of famine, sickness, war and infanticide to reduce populations. Rather it lay in the cultivation of Reason and the practice of 'preventive checks', such as the delay of marriage and the strict regulation of the sexual passions.

Although Malthus wrote of 'human nature', 'universal urges' and 'common laws', he nevertheless identified a 'part of mankind where the retrograde and progressive movements (of populations) chiefly take place' (1803). The poor possessed a glimmer of Reason, but lacked the cultivation to practice moral restraint. Their habits of life and wants expressed imprudent and careless attitudes. Malthus found proof positive of this, at least to his satisfaction, in the leisure practices of the lower classes. He asserted (34) that they squandered money on 'drunkenness and dissipation', and he contrasted this with the behaviour of tradesmen and farmers who practised delayed gratification through saving. Malthus used 'evidence' like this to support a functionalist theory of inequality which argued in favour of the necessity of poverty and pointed to the folly of excessive private charity and public welfare. In his view, to abolish poverty would be to abolish the main spur to human striving. The fear of poverty stimulated the middle orders to exert themselves, and the experience of poverty encouraged the lower orders to scramble from their meagre station in life. Poverty was therefore valued as a social good. Without it, the 'bad' passions in human nature, which led man to be 'inert, sluggish and averse to labour' (131), would come to the fore.

Malthusianism was a prototypical attempt at formulating an 'objective' system for managing pleasure in bourgeois society. This can be illustrated in three ways. Firstly, it offered a 'scientific' analysis of the passions and pointed to the dire consequences of their unrestricted growth. Secondly, it adduced the living conditions of the poor as 'proof' of the effects of the absence of cultivation and the inhibition of Reason. Thirdly, it identified the remedy of 'moral restraint' for cultivated sections of society to put into practice. Although Malthus was right to identify population growth as a pressure on natural resources, his great weakness was to fail to predict the changes in agricultural technology which would permit intensified cultivation and produce sufficient food to meet the increased demand. Marx (1887: 495n) criticized Malthusianism for confusing a law of Nature with an historical law of capitalist production. In his view, famine was not the result of overpopulation, it was the consequence of the unequal class system of production, distribution and exchange.

Malthusianism, however, was far from being the last or even the most influential system for managing pleasure devised in bourgeois society. Of greater historical significance was the philosophy of utilitarianism cast off by Bentham and developed by J.S. Mill. Bentham's utilitarian ethics was founded on the classical position that mankind is motivated to acquire pleasure and avoid pain. He also held that the object of intervention was to place the passions in the hands of Reason and the law. What was different about his system was that it proposed a rational basis for judging the quality of acts and there-

fore managing the passions practically. Bentham's 'principle of utility' states that human actions can be judged praiseworthy or negative to the extent that they increase or decrease the sum of human
happiness. By the term 'human action' Bentham meant the actions of
individuals. His philosophy found no place for 'abstractions' such as
'society' or 'community'. As he explained:

> The community is a fictitious *body* composed of the individual
> persons who are considered as constituting as it were its *members*.
> The interest of the community then is, what? – the sum of the
> interests of the several members who compose it. It is in vain to
> talk of the interest of the community, without understanding
> what is the interest of the individual. (1981: 3; emphasis his)

Bentham's (1988: 33–42) taxonomy was designed to codify pleasure
and pain with sufficient detail to serve as a comprehensive and
infallible guide to judging the value of human actions. He distinguished fourteen varieties of pleasure: (1) The pleasures of sense.
(2) The pleasures of wealth. (3) The pleasures of skill. (4) The pleasures of amity. (5) The pleasures of a good name. (6) The pleasures
of power. (7) The pleasures of piety. (8) The pleasures of benevolence. (9) The pleasures of malevolence. (10) The pleasures of memory.
(11) The pleasures of imagination. (12) The pleasures of expectation.
(13) The pleasures dependent upon association. (14) The pleasures
of relief. Of pains, Bentham was only a little less precise: (1) The
pains of privation. (2) The pains of the senses. (3) The pains of
awkwardness. (4) The pains of enmity. (5) The pains of an ill name.
(6) The pains of piety. (7) The pains of benevolence. (8) The pains of
malevolence. (9) The pains of the memory. (10) The pains of the
imagination. (11) The pains of expectation. (12) The pains dependent
on association.

In addition to number Bentham recognized that pleasures and
pains vary in intensity, duration, certainty, uncertainty, nearness or
remoteness, purity and extent. Bentham believed that by referring
human action to this taxonomy it would be possible at any moment,
and for any given action or policy, to select the appropriate alternative which will produce the greatest happiness of the greatest
number.

Bentham hoped that his utilitarian system would be as exact in
human ethics as mathematical methods in natural science. J.S. Mill
took over Bentham's system and introduced important amendments
to the received ideas of pleasure and pain. Bentham had insisted that

the varieties of pleasure and pain which he identified were common, undifferentiated properties in mankind. Within each category of his taxonomy the only variations which he allowed for were variations of quantity, not quality. Mill (1863: 258–9) on the other hand, insisted that 'some kinds of pleasure are more desirable and valuable than others'. He rejected the idea that the evaluation of the pleasures and pains should be confined to quantity alone. Mill introduced (259–61) the distinction between 'higher' and 'lower' pleasures. The former he associated with creativity and the cultivation of the mind; the latter he held to refer to the body.

The main criticisms of utilitarianism are so firmly established that I can afford to be brief in recounting them. It is necessary to make three points. In the first place, Mill's concession that the pleasures and pains are variable in their qualities drove a stake through the heart of Bentham's claim that utilitarianism is an 'exact' and 'scientific' system. For as soon as pleasure and happiness are understood to have a polymorphous character the argument that they should be subjected to an unbending, unitary value system becomes intolerable as well as insupportable (MacIntyre 1981: 63–4). The 'scientific' claim of utilitarianism can be attacked from another angle. This brings me to my second point. Utilitarianism was woefully empiricist in its main assumption. 'The utilitarian conviction that all values are measurable', wrote Kolakowski (1972: 108) was 'merely the resolve to recognize as value only that which is measurable'. The assumption that the observer can confront a fact or a value directly without any discursive influence interposing itself, is simply not tenable on both logical and historical grounds. The third and final point centres on the mechanical and unsatisfactory view of history which underpins the utilitarian system. It is too gross to accuse utilitarianism of being ahistorical. Bentham certainly acknowledged that social and economic conditions change. 'Nevertheless,' remarks Ryan (1984: 111), 'there is a sense in which history for him has only two epochs. In one of them men are rational, well-informed and benevolent; the other epoch embraces all ages in which they are not. The enlightened legislator sees his task as getting his subjects from the second stage to the first as painlessly as possible.' This nononsense view of history inevitably sacrificed complexity and subtlety for the sake of directness and expedience. The result was a staged view of history, with all of the anomalies and contradictions shorn. The past, in brief, was 'deduced' from the requirements of Reason and Benevolence in the present.

PLEASURE, REASON AND THE STATE

Classical political economy deduced pleasure from the market struggle between Nature and Reason. It equated the invisible hand of the market with the advance of the general interest. Thus, each was seen as pursuing his private interest and thereby, without knowing or willing it, serving the public interests of all (Marx 1973: 156). The argument recognized that bad pleasures such as laziness, cruelty and sexual abuse and aggression are bound to rear their heads from time to time. For, in the real world, Reason and the passions are seen as fixed in eternal combat. Because of this 'fact', only a reckless gambler would bet on the total submission of the passions to Reason forever. On the other hand, since the market was celebrated as the embodiment of Reason, it was held that the invisible hand of the market could be relied upon to intervene and despatch bad passions. This 'guarantee' was advocated as sufficient grounds for limiting the regulatory power of the state to a minimum.

However, this whole argument is overturned if it can be shown that the state is a *seminal* influence in the formation and constitution of market society. For, in that case, the thesis that the market is nothing but the sum of transactions involving the private interests of free individuals becomes untenable. For by presenting the state as a necessary condition for the emergence of market society, private interest is revealed as a socially determined interest. It follows that while the wants of individuals certainly belong to the individuals concerned, they spring from social conditions which cannot be reduced to the expressions of individual will.

This was, of course, the first lesson taught by critical political economy in the nineteenth century. From Marx to the sociology of Durkheim, intellectual life was distinguished by a growing awareness of the structural dimensions of personal behaviour. One of the most important consequences of this was a reappraisal of what is meant by the term 'human agency'. Classical liberal and utilitarian thought was built upon the distinction between the state and private interest. Action was thought to be the preserve of the individual, while the state and other corporate institutions, like the church and business enterprise, were presented as simply the mechanisms through which individuals realized their interests. By treating cultural forms as aspects of state formation, critics of this received view rejected the distinction between the state and private interest. The structure of the individual personality, with its desire to accumulate pleasure and avoid pain, was presented as a corollary of the social structure. Pleasure ceased to be defined essentially in terms of the fixed struggle between Reason and Nature. Instead it tended to be defined structurally in terms of the possibilities of identity, practice and organization given by the social structure and the conditions of history. None of this could be sustained without allowing that corporate institutions are meaningful human actors holding interests which are independent of the sum of individuals who compose them. Although critical thought varies as to the significance of class and organic bonds in the formation and constitution of modern society, it acknowledged the fundamental importance of the state.[10] This assent continues to be a feature of social thought in the present day.

Historians and sociologists of leisure have certainly recognized the direct managerial role of the state in the provision and conduct of leisure (see Cunningham 1980; Henry and Bramham 1986). A variety of studies trace the elaboration of state powers of licensing, taxation and policing in regulating pleasures and amusements relating to drug use, liquor consumption, the use of public space, sexual practice, print, film and the performing arts.[11] However, what has not been emphasized so much is the first lesson of critical political economy, which described the rooted and ubiquitous character of state involvement in the regulation of personal conduct. The state, as Durkheim (1904: 72) put it, 'is above all, supremely, the organ of moral discipline'. It is this supreme, final and pervasive quality of the state in organizing the subjects of work, leisure, family life, crime, legality and so on, which writers like Foucault, Elias, and Corrigan and Sayer have commented upon in their work.[12] Thus, at the heart of Foucault's explanation (1967, 1973, 1975, 1981) of the construction of madness, illness, deviance and sexuality is the recognition of the penetrating power of state networks of training, discipline and moral force. Similarly, Elias (1978, 1982), who comes to the matter from a rather different intellectual tradition, nonetheless regards state formation as the key to the organization of the personality in modern society. Before these formidable contributions, to say nothing of the legacy of classical critical political economy and sociology (especially the work of Marx and Durkheim), Corrigan and Sayer (1985) claim neither originality nor privilege. However, such is the remarkable synthetic power of their historical sociology, that their work on the emergence and reproduction of state power amounts to one of the most convincing of all recent contributions to the field. Their book indeed succeeds in conveying the rooted and ubiquitous character of state involvement in the organization of culture and subjectivity. They see state formation as a process of cultural revolution based in moral regulation. By the term 'moral regulation' they mean 'a project of normalizing, rendering natural, taken for granted, in a word 'obvious' what are in fact ontological and epistemological premises of a particular form of social order' (1985: 4). Nationalism is perhaps the crucial symbol of state formation. Indeed, Corrigan and Sayer (195) define the state as 'the nation made manifest'. The reason for this is that the nation expresses 'naturally' and 'obviously' distinctions which are vital to moral regulation. One thinks of the distinctions relating to private and public affairs, domestic and foreign things, self interest and national duty. Such forms of regulation are deeply imperious. They seek to annihilate forms of identity, practice and organization which are contrary to their interests and vision. It is not for nothing that Corrigan and Sayer (1985) remark:

> To define 'us' in national terms (as against class, or locality, or ethnic group, or religion, or any other terms in which social identity might be constructed and historical experience comprehended) has consequences. Such classifications are means for a project of social integration which is also, inescapably, an active disintegration of other focuses of identity and conceptions of subjectivity (195; emphasis theirs).

When did this 'project' begin? Nairn (1988) defines nationalism quite formally as:

> The systematic prominence of factors of nationality in modern development – where 'modern' has as one of its key connotations the political idea of popular sovereignty. Only when the latter broke through with the American and French Revolutions did 'nations' acquire their decisive importance as vectors of both political and economic development (134).

This dates nationalism quite precisely as an invention of the late eighteenth century. It also ties the concept to the administrative nucleus of the modern state, notably the establishment of monopoly mechanisms of taxation and the legitimate use of physical force (see also Elias 1982: 99–100; 104–17); the imposition of an officially approved language; a uniform legal system; a co-ordinated education system; and an efficient and comprehensive transport and communications system.

Although many of the moral campaigns and training initiatives to regulate leisure practice were conceived during the rise of nationalism, it would be short-sighted to date the management of pleasure from this period. Again, following Corrigan and Sayer, it is necessary to stress the rooted and ubiquitous character of state formation, especially with regard to the experience and modalities of pleasure. Corrigan and Sayer argue for three 'moments' in English state formation: the twelfth to fourteenth centuries, the sixteenth and seventeenth centuries and the 1830s.[13] At each juncture the agencies of state regulation did not simply change their spots, they devised new powers of getting at the individual, of defining acceptable behaviour and driving unacceptable behaviour underground or eliminating it altogether. While this is not an historical study, it might be helpful to sketch in some of the main features of the management of pleasure in each of these periods. Let me begin with the twelfth-fourteenth centuries.

Twelfth–Fourteenth Centuries: 'Fettered Individual Activity'

Superficially, the case for the management of pleasure looks weakest for the feudal period. A long and rich tradition of European historiography has emphasized the monumentality of feudal society.[14] The stubborn superstructure of tradition fixed one's position at birth and presented an implacable face to change and resistance. 'Its business was to work over traditional material, whether Christian or classical, and assimilate it afresh' (Huizinga 1944: 179). This was evident in Carnival, the most developed of all 'leisure' events in feudal culture. The people participated in jesting, foolery and savage parodies of the official system of rule (Bakhtin 1968: 5–36; Stallybrass and White 1986: 6–20; 171–90). Most of the leading authorities agree that the passions were certainly aroused at these events. Popular culture could easily pass the limits of acceptable behaviour and result in armed conflict (Davis 1975; Burke 1978; Le Roy Ladurie 1981). However, what was ultimately revealing about carnival is not so much that it overturned the official hierarchy temporarily, or that it sometimes escalated into violence, but that after its inevitable climax everything was as before.

Regulation in feudal society had a decentralized character. The legal definition of serfdom was *glebae adscripti*, meaning 'bound to the earth' (Bloch 1962: 89–90). The definition reflected not merely the lack of mobility in feudal society, it also pointed to the significance of local conditions in defining permissible behaviour. The manorial system gave the lord power of jurisdiction over his serfs (Weber 1923: 63–5). The character of this jurisdiction varied locally, but everywhere 'the rights of the lord fettered individual activity' (Pirenne 1936: 66). These rights constituted the backcloth for labour, exchange and association in the manor. They advanced the lord and his family the power of immunity to condition all that was said and done (Weber 1923: 63). Le Roy Ladurie (1980: 330) recounts the story of the ruling family of Montaillou who had the tongue of a peasent cut out for insulting them. We can be sure that the relation of inequality in manorial life allowed for all manner of hideous acts and abuses of power. Moreover, the fact of territorial lordship was itself part of a wider backcloth of Christian belief and ritual which backed the conservation of private property and the rule of obedience (Abercombie *et al* 1980: 70–1). However, it is necessary to resist the temptation of presenting the peasentry as powerless. The fact that the peasents of Montaillou neither forgot nor condoned the punishment exacted upon one of their number, shows that peasent life could be conditioned but it could not be determined. Abercombie *et al* (1980: 72) argue that the peace of feudal society was regularly punctured by 'popular revolts'. Furthermore, in the century after the Black Death the labour shortage increased the bargaining power of the serfs to win concessions from the lords.

Somewhere a shift in the balance of power occurred (Elias 1982: 15–65; 91–5; 104–15). Competition between the lords eliminated some of the competitors and amalgamated manors and their tenants in larger territorial units. Gradually regulation of the actions and opportunities of more and more people became concentrated in fewer and fewer hands. Monopoly mechanisms, based in the centralization of taxation and the legitimate use of physical force, grew and cohered (Elias 1982: 104–12). In the case of England the symbols of centralized power were official surveys, the inventories of the nation, which continue to be an essential feature of administration in the present day. The Domesday survey of 1086, the 1274 survey that began the Hundred Rolls records, the Quo Warranto survey of 1279, the 1291 valuation of church funds, Edward III's ministerial inquiries of 1340–1 – these great official enterprises in accounting and information-gathering oiled and developed the state machines of regulation and surveillance 'in which individuals [became] caught up' (Foucault 1975: 202). Examples of such state machinery include the shire courts; the Exchequer; the sheriffs who were 'directly appointed by royal officials' (Corrigan and Sayer 1985: 20); Parliament; the law and legal institutions. The state machines were agencies of moral regulation and they operated, directly, to manage association, organization and practice geared to pleasure. For example, Burke (1978) draws attention to the early role of state interference in popular culture – printing, publishing, dramatic performances, preaching, singing, speaking and so on. The state regulated forms of association, organization and practice in three ways. First, by *licensing*, the state labelled some activities as acceptable and others as not. Second, by *policing* and *punishing*, the state enforced its values upon popular culture. Third, by *stereotyping* certain forms of association, organization and practice in pejorative terms as 'vulgar', 'unseemly' or 'riotous', the state established and reinforced a moral and aesthetic hierarchy which devalued and marginalized certain forms of being human.

The question of regulation can be examined from another angle: the angle of identity, and specifically feminine identity. Feudal society debarred a married woman from the right of property ownership and the right of making contract. At marriage, she bound over her personal property to her spouse. She had no right to sue or be sued in common law under her own name. Daughters were required to be chaste and virtuous. An unwanted pregnancy would be punished by depriving the daughter of part of her dowry. The chivalry displayed towards women in the romantic tradition of courtly love was just that: *display*, which concealed a gnomic vision of female capacities, achievements and value (Corrigan and Sayer 1985: 36–7; Abercrombie *et al* 1980: 90–1).

What emerges most unequivocally from the discussion is the seminal influence of moral regulation in feudal life. Force was used to open up some human capacities and possibilities, and to repress others. If this was done at the beginning of the period in the name of the individual lord, his bailiff or his priest, it subsequently and gradually became the business of the state. The rights of policing, punishing, judging and stereotyping were gradually appropriated by the agents of the state and conducted in the name of 'the nation'. This was not a monolithic process. Both Weber (1923) and Elias (1982) note the resistance from the nobility to the usurpation of powers by the monarch and his state officials. Furthermore, resistance did achieve some notable successes. For example, in England the Magna Carta 'placed' a definite limit on the growth of state absolutism' Abercrombie *et al* (1980: 79). Nevertheless the trend is unmistakable. The centre slowly increased the power to regulate conduct and morals throughout the periphery. The management of pleasure gradually began to lose its uneven, localized character. The state, meaning a coherent administrative unit with legitimate powers of jurisdiction, interference and judgement, became the established means of moral regulation.

Sixteenth and Seventeenth Centuries: 'Moral Cleansing'

The use of Christianity as a vehicle for nationalism is well understood and well documented by historians. In the Middle Ages the idea of national difference may have been inchoate, but the idea of religious difference was clear enough. The Christian Crusades stigmatized Islam and, through this, planted the prejudice that the Orient was the haunt of perversity (Said 1978: 58, 75, 170–2, 192; Kabbani 1986: 5, 24). These constructs, although hardly unmodified, still influence travel consciousness and East–West relations in the present day. Christian distinctions have been assimilated into national self-images and confrontative racial stereotypes.

However, the processes here are very subtle and the history extraordinarily complex. A clearer example of the teaming of Christianity with nationalism in the management of pleasure is to be found in sixteenth- and seventeenth-century England: the second 'moment' or 'wave' in Corrigan and Sayer's theory of state formation. Hill (1975), Larner (1981: 161) and Corrigan and Sayer (1985: 47) have argued that 'the Tudor revolution' defined the good society in terms of that which was closest to God. Of necessity, this involved an interventionist stance in ideology and moral regulation. 'It was the acknowledged duty of the secular arm,' wrote Larner (1981: 58) 'to ensure that "the crown rights of the Redeemer" were demonstrated in the everyday behaviour of his subjects.' This led to unparalleled state intrusion into civic and rural culture. Crown and clergy combined in a mission to eradicate indulgence, idleness and excess in everyday life. A number of texts bemoaning the low state of affairs were published, e.g. John Northbrooke's (1579) *A Treatise Wherein Dicing, Dancing, Vaine plaies . . . are reprooved*; Philip Stubbes's (1583)

The Anatomie of Abuses. They were matched by more intrusive and coercive forms of state regulation. 'The Reformers', observed Burke (1978: 208) 'burned – or buried – books, smashed images, closed theatres, chopped·down maypoles, disbanded abbeys of misrule'. Puritans had a horror of excess and waste, nowhere more profoundly expressed than in the matter of time. Sport and recreation was accepted as fulfilling rational ends, notably recuperation for physical efficiency. However, as means of impulsive enjoyment and undisciplined activity they were condemned (Weber 1930: 157, 167). Specific recreations were not only subject to moral condemnation, but debarred by royal prohibition. A long succession of statutes, reaching back to the time of Edward III, outlawed sports including tennis, bowls and football, and various games of hazard, like dice and cards (Vale 1977: 4–5). The programmes of moral reform initiated by the Puritan revolution tightened up and extended such restrictions. In part this was dictated by the necessities of state formation which required a male population well versed in 'the manly pursuits' of archery, shooting, darting, running and wrestling. Such skills could be transferred to the arena of war and the service of the nation, when circumstances required.

Nationalism demandéd ideological conformity. The Puritan revolution played an important role in providing this. By opposing earthly matters with a spiritualized God and an equally spiritualized Devil, it provided a coherent ideology to justify programmes of 'moral cleansing' (Larner 1981: 58, 161, 194–5). 'The good society' depended for its moral gravity not only upon spiritual images of degradation and evil. The ruthless Protestant persecution of ethnic minorities (the 'tribal' Welsh, the highland Scots and, above all, the Irish), the horror and suspicion of 'popery' and the infamous witch-hunts of the seventeenth century must be understood as weaving an imagery which helped to bind 'Englishmen' together in national unity.

One aspect of rising nationalism was colonialism. The Tudor and Elizabethan periods witnessed the rapid growth of maritime exploration and the proportionate acquisition of foreign territories. Christianity was again used instrumentally to legitimate this process of 'primitive accumulation' (Marx 1887: 703–6; 706–9). For example, Elizabeth I's letter of patent for Sir Walter Raleigh in 1584, applied a firm distinction between the Christian and non-Christian world, and regarded it to be the duty of the former to possess the latter:

Elizabeth by the grace of God of England, France and Ireland Queen, defender of the faith, &c. To all people to whom these presents shall come, greeting. Know ye that of our especial grace, certain science and mere motion, we have given and granted to our trusty and well-beloved servant, Walter Raleigh Esquire, free liberty and licence, from time to time to discover, search, find out and view such remote and heathen lands, countries and territories, not actually possessed by Christian people. The same to have, hold, occupy and enjoy to him, his heirs and assigns for ever, with all prerogatives, franchises and preeminences, thereto and thereabouts, both by sea and land, whatsoever we by our letters of patent may grant.[15]

Elizabeth's monarchy was an 'Imperiall Monarchy' which gloried in the aim of making her pilot of the 'Imperiall Ship' of Christendom (Yates 1975: 50). Remote peoples were to be seized, tempered and the values of 'the celestial body' of Queen, Christian God and country, printed upon their faces and their lands. This was granted by the necessities of 'certain science' and 'mere motion'.

The sixteenth and seventeenth centuries, then, witnessed the accretion of state powers within 'the nation', and the partial transfer of moral regulation to a world stage. Christianity, with its appeal to universal brotherhood, played a leading role in cementing domestic and international programmes of moral cleansing. Indeed nationalism affected to suggest that what was done in the name of the nation and the name of God.

The crucial metaphor of moral regulation in the sixteenth and seventeenth centuries was the Fall of Man. The Parliamentary gentry looked back to the reigns of strong monarchs like Henry II and Edward I, when the interests of the Crown, nation, God and the landed elite were thought to be in harmony. The Puritans invoked what they imagined to be the state of the primitive Christian Church of the early Fathers, unsullied by the anomalies and aberrations of history (Stone 1972: 50–1). This climate of thought influenced attitudes to recreation and pleasure. Gosson (1579) in his *The Schoole of Abuse* complained of the dismal morality of the times in which the passions were agitated by 'banqueting, playing, pipying and dauncing', and he contrasted this with the olden days when the recreation of an Englishman consisted of 'shootying and darting, running and wrestling'. Similarly, Northbrooke (1579), in a dialogue which ferociously condemns the popular pastimes of the day, has

Youth ask what exercises and recreation are lawful, and Age reply: 'That which was used in olden time'.[16]

The examples suggest degeneration, the building-up of fatty and morbid substances in the social body. The remedy was to cut out the diseased particles and restore the organism to health. Organic comparisons are, of course, part of the paraphernalia of conservative thought. For they suggest a condition of normality which is 'obvious' and 'natural', and from which 'deviations' can be calibrated and surgically removed. However, it would be wrong to infer that the metaphor of the Fall of Man wanted for radical exponents in the sixteenth and seventeenth centuries. On the contrary, there were a number of social movements which contested the assumption that the ruling order was the natural and inevitable order of things. They pointed to social factors including oppression, exploitation and the manipulation of 'facts' to support ruling interests. Chief among these were the Levellers. Winstanley (1983), the true Leveller, made a distinction between 'kingly government' and 'commonwealth's government' in his *Law of Freedom*. 'Kingly government,' he wrote (1983: 306), 'governs the earth by that cheating art of buying and selling, and thereby becomes a man of contention, his hand against every man, and every man's hand against him . . . And if it had not a club law to support it, there would be no order in it'. Winstanley saw the Cromwellian revolution as an opportunity to sweep away the props and splints of the old order. 'Commonwealth's government,' he wrote (1983: 311), 'governs the earth without buying and selling; and thereby becomes a man of peace . . . he makes provision for the oppressed, the weak and the simple, as well as for the rich, the wise and the strong. He beats swords into pruning hooks and ploughs; he makes both elder and younger brother freeman in the earth.'

The variety of models of the past and the contradictions among them indicate three important changes in the character of moral regulation. In the first place, the widespread recourse to the symbol of 'the nation' was itself evidence of the growth of the centralization of power and the standardization of conduct through state formation. Conservatives and radicals jockeyed for national programmes of moral cleansing with expectations regarding the penetration and uniformity of their initiatives which were simply absent in feudal times. In the second place, the fact that the state, 'the very organ of social thought' (Durkheim 1904: 50), and its critics, glorified 'the nation' and its history in quite naked and contradictory ways is revealing. In feudal times the past and the symbols of moral regulation were *received*, intact and unalterable, in the form of myth and the output of the Christian 'culture industry'. The sixteenth and seventeenth centuries witnessed the consolidation of a change which had its origins in the Renaissance. The past beings to be *chosen* (Heller 1978: 90–4). It is sentimentalized, idealized, tidied-up, and used to suggest that the difficulties of the present can be solved by turning back the clock. Dissent and contradiction are basic to this development. Ideas of appropriate ways of living and standards of conduct for 'the nation', became pluralized. The symbols of 'the nation' and 'heritage' begin to be contested. This brings me to my third point. The period displayed an increasing reliance upon the economic sign system to regulate moral behaviour. This is not to say that the use of physical force, direct threats, personal entreaties and campaigns of scapegoating were not used. On the contrary, we know only too well that they were practised, often with deadly results (Larner 1981: 58; 156–89). However, the sixteenth and seventeenth centuries also experienced the rise of mercantile capitalism and the spread of primitive accumulation and market society. As several authors have argued, the development of a universal market in commodities restructured the subjective inner world of sentiments.[17] Money and labour power began to be regarded 'naturally' and 'obviously' as general commodities. The value of labour and the fruits of labour ceased to be expressed in multidimensional terms and were calculated narrowly in terms of exchange value. As Marx (1964: 147) put it, 'money reduces everything to its abstract form'.[18] The distribution of the passions became more closely tied to the rhythms of the market. This was expressed institutionally in the gradual development of an entertainment industry in which players were divorced from their folk origins and performed only for a fee; and in which spectators were inured to the idea that the act of spectating involved prior payment. It was expressed more generally, in the organization of the sentiments around the principle of self-renunciation. Self-renunciation began to be practised both as a method of moral improvement and as a means of wealth accumulation. 'The less you eat, drink, and buy books', wrote Marx (1964: 150) ironically, 'the less you go to the theatre, the dance hall, the public house; the less you think, love, theorize, sing, paint, fence, etc., the more you *save* – the greater becomes your treasure which neither moths nor dust will devour – your *capital*' (emphasis in the original). Now Marx is obviously writing from a nineteenth-century standpoint, with a consciousness formed by the shock-waves of full-scale industrialization and generalized commodity production. However, the point is that sixteenth- and seventeenth-century mercantile capitalism already carried, albeit in embryonic form, the principle of self-renunciation and the notion of accumulation as a means of personal improvement.

1830s: 'The Eye of Power'

With industrialization and the creation of the modern state, the art of moral regulation rested increasingly upon an enveloping technology of representation. If we follow Foucault in taking the anatomy of power as our presiding metaphor, in the nineteenth century the management of pleasure became increasingly dominated by 'the eye of power' (Foucault 1980: 146; 1975: 104). The use of physical force was never entirely eliminated. Historians of leisure have pointed to the physical repression of worker's traditional leisure rights (the attack on 'Saint Monday'), animal sports (which were held to increase the worker's propensity to self-subsistence and therefore decrease the worker's reliance upon the market), and fairs and wakes (which were criticized for contributing to the immoderate arousal of the passions) (see Thompson 1963: 443–7, 1967; Cunningham 1980: 22–3; Poole 1983: 71–98). However, only with regard to the first thirty blood-spattered years of the century, 'the English terror' as Corrigan and Sayer (1985: 115) characterize it, is it plausible to argue that physical force was the method of first resort in the regulation of leisure. As the century developed, physical force was crowded out and pushed back to the method of last resort, by other 'psychological' practices of regulation: parable, training, drill, the rote inculcation of respect for the rule of law, devotion to private property and family life, automatic love of Nation and Empire and always – the bottom line of moral regulation in industrial capitalism – fear of unemployment, abandonment and destitution.

The nineteenth century has been called 'the bourgeois century' (Hobsbawm 1969; Gay 1984, 1986). While this overstates the case in respect of the solidarity of the bourgeois class (Siegel 1986) and the capitulation of the working class (Stedman Jones 1971), it does succeed in conveying the aggressive buoyancy of industrial and commercial bourgeois values in moral regulation between the 1830s and 1900. A rich tradition of postwar historiography has documented the imposition of these values on a number of wide fronts: health (Foucault 1974); childcare (Walvin 1982); education (Lawson and

Silver 1973); welfare (Stedman Jones 1991); poverty (Himmelfarb 1984); juvenile delinquency (Pearson 1983); the penitentiary system (Foucault 1975, Melossi and Pavarini 1981); animal rights (Ritvo 1987); the care of the mentally ill (Scull 1979, Skultans 1979). Rational recreation must be considered as another front of regulation. Through it the bourgeoisie sought to bring about moral improvement, not by physical repression, but by example and persuasion (Bailey 1987: 177). This was 'the gentle way' of moral regulation (Foucault 1975: 104–31).

The central metaphors of moral degeneration in bourgeois society were idleness and pollution. Rational recreation aimed to exert 'a civilizing influence' upon the twin carriers of these aggravations which were thought to be the working class and licentious women. The next chapter examines the neglected question of the moral regulation of women and leisure, I will restrict myself here to the subject of the working class.

The main vehicles of rational recreation in the nineteenth century were based in the voluntary sector. Associations like the Society for the Prevention of Cruelty to Animals (1824), the Lord's Day Observance Society (1831), the United Kingdom Alliance for the Suppression of the Traffic in Intoxicating Liquors (1853) and the Society for the Suppression of the Opium Trade (1874), were basically middle-class organizations which sought to regulate leisure time, space and practice to reflect middle-class values (for historical accounts of the Associations listed, see Ritvo 1987: 127–29, 174; Wigley 1980: 44–53; Dingle 1980; Berridge and Edwards 1987: 176–87). The policies of the rational recreation movement were often couched in the religious language of redemption. The working class was to be 'saved' from the 'temptations of the flesh', 'the evils of drink' and 'the vanity of idleness'. However, it would be a mistake to see rational recreation as a rerun of the sixteenth- and seventeenth-century movements which aimed to restore 'Man' after 'the Fall'. Construction rather than redemption was the real object of rational recreation. It was part of the phalanx of nineteenth-century regulative mechanisms formed to create an obedient, able-bodied, law-abiding and docile class of 'working people'.

What was the relationship between the voluntary sector and the state in the management of leisure and recreation? The state provided the essential legal and political framework for moral reform. Most authorities agree that by the beginning of the 1840s the bourgeois state had assigned negative capability to the working class.

'Politically', remarked Polyani (1944: 166), 'the British working class was defined by the Parliamentary Reform Act of 1832, which refused them the vote; economically, by the Poor Law Reform Act of 1834, which excluded them from relief and distinguished them from the pauper'. Negative capability was reflected in the stereotypes commonly used to describe the lifestyle of the poor. It was castigated as concupiscent, primitive, depraved and pestilential. Like all powerful stereotypes, these notions were founded upon very little practical knowledge and experience of working-class living conditions or culture. Apart from the workplace, the middle class had little incentive to mix with the class which had been legally defined as incapable of voting. As the factory system developed, even workplace relations were mediated through a hierarchy of supervisory staff. The migration of the middle class to the gentility of the suburbs, which occurred from the 1830s onwards, drove a wedge between working-class and middle-class domestic and leisure space which simply reinforced received stereotypes (Davidoff and Hall 1983: 336–41; Williams 1973: 190–1). Sutherland's visit to the working-class 'wynds and closes' of Glasgow recounts the conditions which he encountered, in the wide-eyed terms of a Victorian anthropologist discovering the haunt of a primitive, lost tribe:

> The interior of the homes is in perfect keeping with their exterior. The approaches are generally in a state of filthiness beyond belief. The common stairs and passages are often receptacles of the most disgusting nuisances. The houses themselves are dark, and without the means of ventilation. The walls dilapidated and filthy, are in many cases ruinous. There are no domestic conveniences even in the loftiest tenements, where they are most needed.[19]

Similar passages could be cited from Kay-Shuttleworth's (1832) *The Moral and Physical Conditions of the Working Classes Employed in the Cotton Manufacture in Manchester*, Robert Lamb's (1848) essay on the London poor,[20] and Chadwick's (1842) *Report on the Sanitary Conditions of the Labouring Population of Great Britain*.

There were significant regional variations in the relations between the classes and, as many historians have argued, this fact should be taken as a caution against making glib, global statements on the class question (Hobsbawm 1964: 272; Thompson 1978: 70). Nevertheless, the general picture between 1830 and 1860 is clear enough. Mort (1987) writes of 'a middle class logic' twinning poverty and immorality with contagion. This was unquestionably the dominant feature of class relations in the period. It influenced middle-class attitudes to the regime of working-class 'free' time activity, and it shaped the nascent attitudes of the 'respectable' working class. The logic pointed to a twofold strategy to the 'problem'; enhanced state activity in surveillance, policing and education in order to isolate and, if possible, alleviate pollution;[21] and, the example of the bourgeois class to show the benefits of self-help to the workers.

The strategy required increasing contact between the classes. It was first applied by the state in respect of health, welfare and housing, doubtless because these areas were judged to pose the most urgent and literal threat to middle-class life. The state constructed workhouses and introduced urban amenity schemes in the form of street lighting, paving, drainage and poor relief. Legal distinctions to define the rights of citizens in need and the obligations of the state were formulated. Of pivotal importance here was the Poor Law Amendment Act of 1834. The act introduced the distinction between 'the deserving poor' and 'the pauper'. The Act has been described as the embodiment of 'the doctrine of discipline and restraint' (Thompson 1963: 295). It gave the state legal powers to intern paupers forcibly in state administered workhouses. In these institutions of correction work tasks, exercises and diet obeyed the principle of 'less eligibility' i.e. conditions were designed to be 'less eligible' than those of the poorest 'free' labourers outside. The Act reflected and reinforced bourgeois distinctions between 'the deserving poor' and 'the residuum' – those who had the capacity to benefit from 'enlightened help' and those who were congenitally degenerate. The distinction ran through much middle-class activity in state policy and in the voluntary sector throughout the remainder of the century. Take the case of rational recreation. From the late 1860s the idea of 'civilizing a rough' through organised and edifying recreation became more popular in middle-class circles. Typical forms of rational recreation were physical exercise, educational instruction, craft, musical training, excursions and games. The aim was to instil habits of saving, perseverance, hygiene, temperance and self-control in the poor. Canon Barnett's scheme of bringing Art to the poor is a good example.[23] Barnett's cultural mission was stimulated by the problem of attracting parishioners to his church in the East End of London. He believed that by teaching the poor to appreciate beauty, their hearts would be opened to receive Christ. The first art exhibition was mounted in 1881 with pictures loaned by sympathetic patrons. Its success (10 000 visitors in 10 days at three pence a head), fixed the exhibition as a regular event in the East End scene until 1898.[24] Borzello's (1987: 32–78) account of the Whitechapel exhibitions leaves one in no doubt as to their regulative purpose. The paintings were monotonously academic and moralistic in style. Barnett insisted that each canvas should be accompanied by a written description explaining the meaning of the painting. He explained his rationale for this in a publication of 1888:

> It is impossible for the ignorant to even look at a picture with any interest unless they are acquainted with the subject; but when once the story is told to them their plain direct method of looking at things enables them to go straight to the point, and perhaps to reach the artist's meaning more clearly than some of those art critics whose vision is obscured by thought of tone, harmony and construction.[25]

There are stories and there are stories. Barnett, together with his wife Henrietta, was strongly attracted to subjects which afforded the opportunity for sermonizing or telling a parable. Christian themes, the virtues of family life, the vice of disobedience in women, lawlessness, the evils of drink, these figured prominently in Barnett's repertoire. Holman Hunt's *Strayed Sheep* and *The Light of the World* shown in Whitechapel in 1883, and A.W. Bayes's *The Return of the Wanderer* shown in 1887, provided him with ideal subjects for preaching. Yet this approach to art interpretation left considerable room for criticism. The essential point is well made by Borzello:

> What the Barnetts were imparting was not an aesthetic education, but their vision of a perfect world . . . as is shown by the 1883 entry for *Left in Charge:* 'The old grandfather is tired with watching and has fallen asleep, but the faithful dog is left in charge, and the baby will be safe.' The vision of a mutually caring society in which even animals play their part could be called the Seamless Society, and the Barnetts used the paintings to preach about it and prove its existence. (1987: 67)

The exhibitions presented a world without contradictions or anomalies. Essentialist concepts of good and evil were used to explain the

meaning of the paintings. Sociological interpretations which focused
on this-worldly inequality and power were eschewed.

A direct parallel can be found in Samuel Smiles's (1859) out-
rageously successful homily, *Self Help*. Smiles supplied his readers
with a platitude for every occasion:

> So far from poverty being a misfortune, it may, by vigorous self-
> help, be converted even into a blessing; rousing a man to that
> struggle with the world in which, though some may purchase
> ease by degradation, the right-minded and true-hearted find
> strength, confidence and triumph (33).

> Those who fail in life are very apt to assume a tone of injured
> innocence, and conclude too hastily that everyone excepting them-
> selves has had a hand in their personal misfortunes (171).

> All experience of life serves to prove that the impediments thrown
> in the way of human advancement may for the most part be
> overcome by steady good conduct, honest zeal, activity, persever-
> ance, and above all by a determined resolution to surmount diffi-
> culties, and stand up manfully against misfortune (209).

> Simple industry and thrift will go far towards making any person
> of ordinary working faculty comparatively independent in his
> means. Even a working man may be so, provided he will carefully
> husband his resources, and watch the little outlets of useless
> expenditure (189).

> A life well spent, a character uprightly sustained, is no slight
> legacy to leave to one's children, and to the world; for it is the
> most eloquent lesson of virtue and the severest reproof of vice
> (221).

> Morals and manners which give colour to life, are of much greater
> importance than laws, which are but their manifestations. The
> law touches us here and there, but manners are about us every-
> where, pervading society like the air we breathe. Good manners,
> as we call them, are neither more nor less than good behaviour;
> consisting of courtesy and kindness; benevolence being the pre-
> ponderating element in all kinds of mutually beneficial and
> pleasent intercourse among human beings (237).

These are rules to live by, but they are rules of a particular kind. They give priority to individual over collective achievement; they emphasize self-interest over-cooperation; they diagnose social ills as products of personal character faults, rather than the defects of the social system. They are the rules of bourgeois society, the bourgeois 'order of things'. Under them pleasure is pursued, but only as the reward for work and never to the detriment of wealth creation. 'Pleasure,' wrote Marx (1964: 157), 'is therefore subsumed under capital, and the pleasure-taking individual under the capital-accumulating individual.'[26]

The various activities that made up rational recreation, the games, sports, exercises, instructions and training schemes aimed to extend the rule of 'the capital-accumulating individual' over 'the pleasure-taking individual'. The desire to become 'respectable' insinuated itself into working-class culture. Bourgeois reformers may have seen themselves as shepherds in this respect, but working-class people were very far from being sheep. As Gray (1981: 39–40) observes, the working class of the 1870s was a very different kind of group as compared with the 1850s or 1830s. Crucially, it was generally richer, and the richest sections enjoyed appreciably more leisure time in the form of increased holidays, and leisure space in the form of improved housing. Several commentators have warned of the dangers involved in vulgar Marxist interpretations of rational recreation as simply a movement of class control (Stedman Jones 1977; Cunningham 1980: 91–2; Gray 1981: 39–40). For the most economically secure strata of the working class, saving, self-education, improved housing, craftwork, and so on, was an expression of class consciousness as opposed to the docile acceptance of middle-class values. Thus, Price (1971) shows that in the working-men's clubs there was a keen insistence on the need to maintain independence from the clergy and other middle class patrons.

'Respectability' is a relative term. The fact that class tensions existed between middle-class reformers and working-class artisans, must not obscure the equally important fact that both groups defined themselves in sharp opposition to 'the dangerous class' or 'the residuum'. This class consisted of unskilled, casual labourers and their dependents huddled in the slums of busy industrial and commercial cities. Legal distinctions inherited from programmes of public administration in poor relief and housing certainly influenced the attitudes of reformers here. 'The residuum' was seen as the lair of low things, a vile canker in the heart of the metropolis where drunkenness, improvidence, bad language, filthy habits, low amusements and ignorance reigned supreme.

Enthusiasts of rational recreation saw this territory as their greatest challenge. They endeavoured to make incursions upon it through the Sabbatarian and Temperance movements and, above all, through youth training campaigns. Smiles (1859: 205) had written gravely that 'nothing can be more hurtful to a youth than to have his soul sodden with pleasure'. The youth campaigns aimed to get young people from the breeding grounds of vice and hooliganism, the slum districts, and to husband 'smartness', 'good carriage' and 'proper moral standards'. For example, the Boys' Brigade founded by William Smith in Glasgow in 1883, aimed to teach working-class boys of 12 years and over, 'elementary drill, physical exercises, obedience to the word of command, punctuality and cleanliness' (Gibbon 1934: 36). There were also many more limited schemes of rational improvement for the young of 'the dangerous class', such as 'Pearson's Fresh Air Fund', introduced in 1896 by Arthur Pearson, founder of the *Daily Express*, to provide country holidays for city children (Pearson 1983: 69).

The mission to bring rational recreation to 'the residuum' after the 1880s reflected the faith in social engineering which underpinned the entire rational recreation movement. Poverty and immorality were defined in personal terms. They were diagnosed as spreading from bad habits, poor education and the lack of self-control. The remedy was instruction, discipline, developing moral conscience and prayer.

However, there was another side to 'rational' reform. It despaired of introducing 'civilization' to 'the residuum'. Philosophically, it aligned itself with Social Darwinism. Poverty and immorality were defined in biological terms. They were diagnosed as growing from the congenital inferiority of the indigent to adapt and survive. According to this view, planning for self improvement in 'the residuum' was tantamount to throwing away energy and money. Even Canon Barnett admitted that there were limits to rational reform and ventured:

> It is true that the extinction of the unemployed would add to the wealth of the country . . . The existence of the unemployed is a fact and this fact constitutes a danger to the wealth and well-being of the community. (1888: 753–4)

Stedman Jones (1981: 127–51) writes of a 'theory of urban degeneration' in the 1880s and 1890s which stigmatized 'the residuum' as
beyond help and beyond hope. Some very totalitarian policies to
deal with 'the feckless' and 'the work-shy' rode on the back of this
theory. For example, Whetman maintained:

> In dealing with men and women of this character where we
> cannot hope to accomplish individual radical cure, we must, as
> with the feeble-minded, organise the extinction of the tribe. In the
> old days the law attempted this extinction by hanging, a pre-
> ventative of the sternest and most efficient nature . . . For us, the
> old methods are impossible. We must attain the same result by
> the longer and gentler system of perpetual segregation in deten-
> tion colonies and with all the mitigations that are practicable.
> (1909: 214–15)

That Whetman judged 'the old methods' to be 'impossible', attested
to the power of the state as the pivotal moral and physical force in
advanced capitalist society. After the 1830s, its increasing moral
density in 'the life of the nation' made certain exercises in 'managing
the passions' illegitimate and illegal. On the other hand, the fact that
he could seriously advocate 'perpetual segregation' and the establishment of 'detention colonies' illustrated the elasticity of core concepts in state formation such as 'individual rights', 'the common
good' and 'natural justice'.[27]

Several sociologists in the twentieth century have pointed to the
inherent tensions and ambiguities in the concept of 'legal-rational'
authority (Weber 1968; Adorno and Horkheimer 1944; Marcuse 1964;
Foucault 1975, 1981). Legal-rational authority is held to engender a
reified world of impersonal standards and 'thing-like' relations which
become self-subsisting, and dominate the human subjects actively
involved in 'making their own conditions' (Lukacs 1923). Without
getting involved in the debate around 'the rationalization thesis'
here, it is worth noting the relevance of this argument to rational
recreation. The rational reform of working-class games and the organization of programmes of self improvement became increasingly
exploited by the consumer culture of capitalist society. Through the
closing decades of the nineteenth century the growth of poster and
press advertising contributed to the range and penetration of
consumer culture (Hamish-Fraser 1981: 134–46; Winstanley 1983:

58–61). In the twentieth century the new electronic technology of mass communications consolidated this process. The tendency was to intensify the commodification of leisure experience and strengthen the images of mass consumption. Desire in leisure became increasingly enmeshed with the representational system of capitalist consumer culture (Ewen 1976, 1988; Featherstone 1991). The travel poster and the fashion advertisement contributed to the dreamlike sensation which many observers claimed to experience as the overpowering feature of metropolitan life (Williams 1982). The consciousness of the emerging metropolitan 'dream-world' was an additional factor in motivating the rational recreationists to propel young men and women into 'real', 'manly' and 'womanly' pursuits.

One of the most powerful symbols used by the rational recreationists in their forays for self-improvement into the residuum was the Empire. Youth movements seized upon the spectacular qualities of Empire. They emphasized its might, its splendour, its heroism. They endorsed a 'one nation' view of patriotism which marginalized the importance of class distinctions. As Baden-Powell put it in *Scouting For Boys*:

> Remember, whether rich or poor, from castle or slum you are all Britons in the first place, and you've got to keep Britain up against outside enemies, you have to stand shoulder to shoulder to do it. If you are divided you are doing harm to your country.[28]

Other voluntary organizations like the Boys' Brigade (1883), the Jewish Lads' Brigade (1895), the Catholic Boys' Brigade (1896), the Boys' Life Brigade (1899) and the Girl Guides (1909), acted as switchboards for similar sentiments.

While voluntary organizations played an important role in disseminating the idea of Empire, it would be a mistake to imagine the institutionalized education systems was negligent in this respect. Schools were an important training ground for the inculcation of good habits and self-discipline in youth. Devotion to the ideal of Empire was ardently practised as part of the formal and informal curriculum. For example, generations of public-school boys after the 1850s were taught that the British gentleman was born with an innate and superior facility to rule. The Empire, 'the best thing that ever happened to mankind' in C.A. Vlieland's[29] opinion, provided the ultimate challenge. Several authorities have commented upon the importance of leisure activities, notably team games and national ceremonies, in solidifying devotion to Empire.[30] Through games like rugby and cricket, boys became physically fit and learned pluck, resolution, self-denial and cooperation, Mangan (1985) explicitly links the games ethic with the spread of imperialism. He argues (18) that the purpose of team games in the public schools was 'to create a universal Tom Brown: loyal, brave, truthful, a gentleman'. In contrast, working-class schools emphasized the values of cleanliness, obedience and respect for others.[31] Yet even here the ideal of Empire was cherished. Children were taught that civilization resided on the British mainland and that Empire was a great and noble enterprise in raising world standards. British history was presented as the forward march of progress, and instruction about the purpose and sacredness of the imperial mission admitted no contradiction. Schools taught that the poor, be they ever so humble, were still Britons and therefore innately superior to other races (Walvin 1982: 176–9).

Rational recreation in youth campaigns and the education system worked through personal persuasion, parable, drill and the construction of group identity. Empire supplied a rich fund of symbols to consolidate and strengthen these activities. Working and playing hard were presented as the keys to imperial might and character. The state and voluntary sector combined to spread these values throughout the nation through play and recreation activities. Beyond the enthusiasms generated through education and rational recreation the growth of secular collective rites of recreation became an important instrument of regulation. Durkheim (1912: 475–6) has speculated on the potential of collective recreation ceremonies, holidays and national festivals as a means of 'moral remaking' to replace the decline of religion in advanced industrial societies. But in late Victorian and Edwardian societies the state invented a series of solemn spectacles in which the life of the nation was reaffirmed and in which recreation and merrymaking played a central part. In Britain the centrepiece of these spectacles was usually the monarch, the emblem of nation and the most sacred totem of Empire. Nairn (1988: 220) cites the case of the investiture of the Prince of Wales. In 1911 the Chancellor of the Exchequer, Lloyd George, decided to revive this 'ancient' ceremony after centuries of neglect. According to Nairn (220–3) this revival was defined in modern terms and with modern political objectives in mind. Lloyd George stage-managed the event as a spectacular display of Welsh pageantry. Its political purpose was to quell the flames of Welsh nationalism. But it also aimed to bring the nation together and to use free time to cement collective bonding.

Representative secular rites of recreation left an abiding mark upon popular culture in two main ways. In the first place, they established a national calendar of leisure spectacles, such as the Trooping the Colour, Royal Ascot, the Royal Regatta at Henley and the Lord Mayor's Show, which signified belonging and membership (see Figure 2). At the same time, royal patronage was used to sanctify the presence of other collective recreation events which developed from business initiatives, notably in the public schools. The Wimbledon All-England Tennis competition (which began in 1877), the Twickenham Rugby International (which began in 1910), the Last Night of the Proms and the Highland Games, were all given significance in the life of the nation through royal patronage and involvement. The second way in which the symbol of monarchy left its mark on collective recreation and popular culture was in conferring a timeless quality on the set pieces of moral remaking. The staged spectacles of the Garter Ceremony, the Trooping the Colour and the Edinburgh Tattoo created a sense of an immovable, eternal order of things which dictated the sublunary patterns of life on the British Isles. As *Debrett* puts it:

> somewhere in this mixture (of events), it is hoped can be found that elusive and indefinable element which can be appreciated not only by those who trace their origins from Great Britain or who share the language and a common heritage, but by everyone who can appreciate a way of life unique to these islands. (1985: 91):

The result was a paradox about working-class leisure with which many on the left have found it hard to come to terms. At the very moment when working-class history had achieved so much in the way of economic, political and civil reforms, at the same moment when Marx's revolutionary ideas began to filter out of Maitland Park Road and fined populist expression, the working class became more militant in its support for Queen and Country. For example, as Mackenzie (1984: 30) notes, in the late 1870s the popular song was transformed from a vehicle of dissent into an instrument of conformity. Music halls, funfares, magazines and comics such as *The Young Britons*, the *Sons of Britannia* and Henty's *The Union Jack* glowed with self-satisfied xenophohia and chauvinistic self-regard. Nor will it do

January	February	March	April
Twickenham Rugby Internationals	Cruft's Dog Show Foyle's Literary Luncheon	Cheltenham National Hunt Festival University Boat Race	Grand National Badminton Horse Trials Harrogate Spring Flower Show

May	June	July	August
Middlesex Sevens Royal Academy of Arts Summer Exhibition Chelsea Flower Show Chester and York Race Meetings Royal Windsor Horse Show Rose Ball Caledonian Ball Eight Weeks Cambridge Mays	Lords Test Match Epsom Derby Oxford and Cambridge Balls Trooping the Colour Bath Festival Garter Day Ceremony at Windsor Royal Ascot Royal Highland Show Aldeburgh Festival Wimbledon	Glyndebourne Festival Royal Show Henley Royal Regatta Lakeland Rose Show Bisley Summer Meeting Royal Garden Parties Royal International Horse Show Tall Ships Race Goodwood Swan-Upping	Game Fair The Eisteddford Cowes Week Three Choirs Festival Highland Games Edinburgh Festival and Military Tattoo British Jumping Derby at Hickstead

September	October	November	December
Ryder Cup Doncaster Cup Last Night of the Proms	Nottingham Goose Fair Horse of the Year Show State Opening of Parliament	Lord Mayor's Show Eton Wall Game RAC London to Brighton Car Rally	Tattersalls December Sales at Newmarket Royal Smithfield Show Varsity Match Olympia Christmas Show Boxing Day Shoot

Figure 2: 'The Social Calendar' (*Debrett* 1985: 5–6)

to view this as a simple matter of class manipulation. Studies of the genesis of working-class sport show nationalism to be an original and self-loading part of working-class culture.[32]

The steady and, in many ways lasting, achievement of moral regulation in the Victorian and Edwardian period was to create a system of moral control which worked not through denying pleasures, but by arousing and cultivating them. Through the staged spectacles organized around monarchy, an apolitical, genderless, classless and 'glorious' past was constructed and presented as the inalienable heritage of the Briton. Bourgeois moral regulation never lost its mystical faith in the sanctity of the law or its ultimate reliance upon the use of 'legitimate' physical force. However, after the 1830s and especially after the 1860s, 'a gentler way' (Foucault 1975: 104) of discipline and regulation was preferred: one which emphasized the rule of Reason over Nature, nation over community and self-help over collectivism. The new collective rites of recreation invented and applied by officials of the state, such as the Trooping the Colour, the Investiture and national days of remembrance, were one important way in which free-time practice was used to rouse and cultivate consent to the ruling order of things. They developed hand-in-hand with the activities of the rational recreationists and popularizers of sports like cricket, tennis, rugby and football to create new mass forms of pleasure. The moral force of these 'natural' and 'obvious' conditions has been challenged on a number of economic, cultural and political fronts in the twentieth century. One aspect of the group of turbulent ideas grouped around the debate on postmodernism is that the state is no longer, necessarily, accepted as the ultimate moral force in moral conditioning. Somewhere along the line a change in the moral density of capitalist society has occurred which, in some circumstances, tolerates the flaunting of the rule of Reason over Nature, nation over community and self-help over collectivism (Lyotard 1984; Kroker and Cook 1986; Harvey 1989). These arguments are examined in Chapter 3, but though I don't want to defeat my purpose by exploring them here, there is one aspect of these matters which should be commented upon now.

Postmodernists see the period after the 1960s as involving gross discontinuities in production, consumption, identity, practice and association. They hold that the distinctively modern forms of character and organization associated with modernity, with bourgeois society, have been supplanted. Against this, I want to claim that present conditions are a mixture of continuities and discontinuities.

Benjamin (1983: 176) uses the phrase 'the ruins of the bourgeois world' to describe present times. This seems to me to be more plausible than the idea of apocalyptic change in life-space and the conditions of practice. Be that as it may, with regard to the professionalization of leisure management a clear line of continuity between the ideas and values of the nineteenth-century rational recreationists and the self-image and ideology of twentieth-century leisure professionals can be traced. The penultimate section of this chapter aims to substantiate this assertion.

THE PROFESSIONALIZATION OF LEISURE MANAGEMENT

The state in bourgeois society managed the essential economic, legal and political framework which supported moral regulation. The legislation in Britain here can be traced back as far as the 1840s to the Museums Act (1845) and the Baths and Washhouses Act (1846). However, it was not until the last quarter of the century that the role and status of public provision was defined in a recognizably 'modern' form (Cunningham 1980: 183). Legislation like the Public Health Act (1875) which provided for public waterways and pleasure gardens was important. However, the crucial interventions were made at the municipal level through the initiatives of the local authorities. For example, between 1869 and 1898 Glasgow Corporation acquired 584 acres of land for use as public parks and open spaces. Between 1878 and 1901 the corporation opened nine swimming baths, and built the People's Palace and Kelvingrove Art Gallery for the edification and relaxation of the people (Heeley 1986: 63–4). Similarly, Manchester Corporation opened Alexandra Park (1870), Heaton Park (1902), Platt Fields (1908), Queen's Park Museum and Art Gallery (1884) and extended the Belle Vue Zoological Gardens from 36 acres to 116 acres (1904) (Manchester City Art Galleries 1987).

A parallel process of provision occurred in the USA. For example, in 1864 Congress allocated the Yosemite Valley as the first extensive area of wilderness for public recreation. It was followed by the McKinac Island National Park (1875). The first wildlife refuge was opened in 1903. The Antiquities Act of 1906 extended Federal powers to designate areas as national monuments and thus to protect them from commercial and urban-industrial blight. In 1916 the National Parks Service Act created the National Park Service vested with the power to manage and develop public recreation space. As was the case with Britain, many of the most significant initiatives occurred at the municipal level. In 1857 construction commenced on 843 acres in Manhattan to a design by Frederick Law Olmsted and Calvert Vaux on the first major US metropolitan park: Central Park. It was followed by Bushnell Park, Hartford (1863), Fairmount Park, Philadelphia (1867) and Franklin Park, Boston (1883). In 1885 the Boston authorities levied a public tax to support the development of sandy areas for recreation (Shivers 1987: 111–25; Fazio 1979: 205–32; Kraus 1979: 91–5).

The philosophy behind these interventions in the public sector reflected the preoccupations of the rational recreation campaigns. Rational recreationists, like the Barnetts, argued that the moral turpitude of the lower classes can be corrected by wise leadership and the inculcation of respectable values. The public expenditure raised to finance the expansion of the public parks in Manchester followed the principle that the parks would 'feed the mind and exercise the body' (Manchester City Art Gallery 1987: 33). Oxygen, it was thought, was close to virtue, and foul air close to vice. The parks, argued the rational recreationists, would free people from 'the corrupt atmosphere generated in hot and crowded streets' (Fazio 1979: 210). However, it was never envisaged that the parks would be absented from the paramount reality of bourgeois society. From the very start policing went hand in hand with provision. For example, Olmsted and Vaux (cited in Kraus 1979: 93–4), in a commentary on the uses of Central Park asserted that 'the people will need to be trained in the proper use of it, and to be restrained in the abuse of it'. Similarly, the authorities running Alexandra Park in Manchester provided play facilities for boys and girls but insisted on segregation between the sexes. In addition, the Church saw to it that the original by-laws provided for closure of the play areas on Sundays – most people's only day off. Band performances were not permitted on Sundays and refreshment houses were closed during the hours of 'divine worship'. Similar restrictions applied to the dress and deportment of users on parkland (Manchester City Art Galleries 1987: 8–10). Self-consciousness of what could and could not be done dominated these activities, and the authorities supplied public recreation space on the understanding that individuals would be self-regulating.

The inevitable result of public provision was the growth of a series of specialized discourses around the question of leisure and leisure services. By the 1920s a professional ideology and self-image of leisure providers and managers had emerged. It drew heavily on the received ideas inherited from the rational recreationists. Leisure management was seen as a means of social engineering and rolling back crime and disease. For example, Cutten (1926: 92) argued that leisure planning was necessary in modern society because 'most vice and crime take place in spare time'. Similarly, Jacks maintained that:

> The recreation movement as I understand it is a great work of preventative social medicine. The social evils it prevents are disease, crime, vice, folly and bad citizenship in general. Prevention is better than cure and vastly cheaper in the long run. (1932: 143–4)

The designation of leisure and recreation management as 'a great work of preventative social medicine' may strike us today as incongruous. Especially if we have been brought up in a tradition which is inured to associating leisure with 'freedom' and 'choice'. However, it is quite consistent with the standard position of professional literature in the area of leisure and recreation management in the 1930s, '40s and '50s. For example, Slavson took it for granted that:

> because recreation is a response to pleasure cravings, it must needs be regulated by society or become a menace . . . when pleasure becomes indulgence, one grows unable to organize his life; he loses hold on self and situation. (1948: 20)

Pleasure here is associated with the body and not the mind. The body, with its easy states of arousal and its nagging 'pleasure cravings' was seen as a menace which reason alone could subdue. The body in bourgeois culture, being 'naturally' associated with lowness, the earth which will ultimately reabsorb it, and the absence of consciousness, was 'obviously' diagnosed as a problem of the untamed working class: the residuum and its appurtenances. The self-appointed task of the leisure and recreation professional was to make this class self-aware of its own defects and, through this, to raise the stock of society. As Nash put it:

> Organized leisure should aim at the highest common denominator, and in varying degrees and ways bring the average human nature up towards the highest human nature. (1953: 61)

Similarly, as late as 1963, Miller and Robinson (1963: 269) could argue that professionalism in leisure and recreation management is 'a matter of helping a person to internalize certain basic aesthetic and ethical values that he will utilize when he makes his recreational choices'. A donatory view of leisure and recreation provision is affirmed here. Persons are not invited to select or contribute aesthetic and ethical values. Rather they are required to succumb to them. Choice is only allowed within the parameters of these received ideas handed down by the leisure professionals. If leisure and recreation behaviour seeks to transcend these parameters it is liable to be stigmatized as a menace or as a danger to society.

CONCLUSION

The professionalization of leisure management was part of the technology of self-improvement and self-realization invented by the bourgeois class to promote cultural revolution and to manage moral regulation. Self-knowledge, not physical force, was defined as the key to the healthy organization of character and society. The pathos of bourgeois culture resided in the fact that its economic, political and social dynamism activated critical consciousness so that the legitimacy of 'universal' rules of 'normality' and 'respectability' became, more or less continuously, an object of contention and dissent. The moral cohesion and political order which adherence to the bourgeois 'cult of the individual' and market organization was faithfully believed to deliver, was at odds with the overt and seemingly inexorable divisions wrought through capitalist expansion. Capitalist modernity did not simply compartmentalize practices, identities and spaces, it pursued an inherent tendency to obliterate the divisions which it had created.

Leisure providers and professional leisure managers have not escaped these tensions. The attempt to define absolute and universal criteria of supply and demand created a hiatus between the producer and consumer of the leisure experience. 'The objectives of many public park and recreation systems,' remarked Gold (1980: 126), 'better accommodate to the needs of the supplier than the user.' Indeed, some users maintain that the professional management of some leisure sites has contributed to the denigration of the site. For example, members of the hippy convoy who travel to Stonehenge to celebrate the summer solstice complain that the professional site managers have profaned the mystery of the monument by providing car park space, refreshment areas and arc lights for visitors (Rojek 1988: 26).

The creation and management of what Lefebvre (1976: 82–4) refers to as 'ludic space' never succeeded in becoming independent of the conditions and constraints of the governing capitalist culture. As a symbol of freedom and pleasure, ludic space necessarily commanded high exchange value. This was exaggerated in an urban-industrial commercial culture in which the demands on 'free' space were intense. Ludic space inevitably became the object of massive financial speculation. Capital, which set out to create islands of recreation and relaxation in the metropolis, ended up by colonizing and destroying them. In Lefebvre's words:

(Ludic) space is sold, at high prices, to citizens who have been harried out of town by boredom and the rat race. It is reduced to visual attributes, "holidays", "exile", "retreat", and soon loses even these . . . Thus leisure enters into *the division of social labour* – not simply because leisure permits labour power to recuperate, but also because there is a leisure industry, a large-scale commercialization of *specialized* spaces, a division of social labour which is projected "on the ground" and enters into global planning. In this way the country takes on a new profile, a new face and a new landscape (84).

One important implication of Lefebvre's words is that the annihilation of 'free' space and 'free' time through commodification, contributes to the sense of homelessness and uprootedness which many commentators have remarked is a general feature of experience in modern capitalism.[33] The search for escape through travel and leisure endows these activities with transcendent significance. However, because leisure and travel experience is enmeshed with the division of labour they can never deliver genuinely transcendent experience. Everything eventually returns to the flat reality of the everyday world.

I want to return to these points and take them up in detail in Chapters 3, 4 and 5 of the book. It may appear facetious to observe that the sole and indispensable disadvantage of using travel and leisure as ways of escape is that you take yourself with you. On the other hand there is a real and crucial sense in which self-consciousness is central to understanding the meaning of pleasure and escape in our culture. In the chapters listed above, I want to explore this connection, the contradictions which follow from it, and how these contradictions are manifested in contemporary leisure and travel identities, practices and associations. However, before reaching that point, it is important to go further into the historical question of the construction of leisure identities, practices and associations in bourgeois society and to show how consciousness of the restrictive effect of the bourgeois order of things on leisure experience was activated and radicalized. The next chapter takes up these themes by way of an exploration of the leisure of bourgeois women in the nineteenth and early twentieth centuries.

2

Thoroughly Modern Woman

Ramazanoglu (1989: 40) maintains that using the concept of male domination as a universal generalization has the effect of making basic features of women's experience, notably class, race, nationality and subculture, invisible. Her analysis emphasizes the contradictions of women's oppression. So will mine in this chapter. My discussions of women and the passions, women and the home, women's space and women and medicine are linked by the design of revealing the rooted and tenacious fact of male domination. On the other hand, I will break rather sharply with the feminist received idea that we still live in patriarchal societies. 'Patriarchy' refers to a system of domination based upon the principle that men's physical and intellectual powers are normally superior to those of women. This is reflected in the legal, economic and political subordination of women and the institutionalized closure of female life-chances. Following Turner (1984: 149–56), I want to argue that the term patriarchy is only relevant to conditions in early capitalism – the capitalism that advocated the medical practice of clitoridectomy as a 'cure' for female masturbation, and campaigned in favour of the overtly sexist Contagious Diseases Acts of 1864, 1866 and 1869.[1] After the 1860s these institutions of moral regulation came under heavy and sustained fire from feminist critics. Attacks were also mounted in respect of inequality in employment law, property ownership, political representation and entry into the professions.

It would, of course, be wincingly complacent to depict these measures as a triumphant march of female emancipation. Against this, Poovey (1988) emphasizes that feminist opposition continued (and continues), to be waged against institutions of moral regulation which produce and apply representations of male domination as 'normal' and 'natural'. By the same token it is invalid to assume that the struggles for female emancipation have been finally won. Even within the ranks of women there are powerful voices raised in support of

51

the position that, in some respects, emancipation has gone too far. For example, the Anti-Abortion League, pressure groups like the Viewers and Listeners Association, and the Women's Institute in the UK, and the Women Patriots in the US, have stressed the importance of 'family values' and the 'homemaking' nature of women.[2] Nevertheless, taking all of this into account, it remains clear that the character of women's moral regulation has been changed by the campaigns of opposition and reform since the 1870s. Turner (1984: 155–6) argues that under late capitalism patriarchy has been replaced by patrism. Patrism means a culture of discriminatory, prejudicial and patronizing beliefs about the inferiority of women. The crucial distinction with patriarchy, is that patrism may be legitimately challenged and legally changed by means which 'objectively' expose male prejudice. Turner does not deny that institutionalized inequalities between men and women persist in society, e.g. in the areas of taxation law, banking facilities, welfare rights, educational opportunities, access to the professions, the availability of credit arrangements, etc. Rather, he is being a consistent Weberian in arguing that the traditional forms of inequality are widely contested by women and men and, more to the point, that they are incapable of mounting a plausible defence against 'legal-rational' authority and criticism.

The question of patriarchy is not the only matter in which my discussion will break company with the feminist orthodoxy in the sociology of leisure. In two other respects my arguments will reflect reasoning which, I believe, is at odds with this orthodoxy. First, I reject the feminist assumption that the differences between women which stem from inequalities in property ownership, are secondary to the common interests which women share through the experience of domestic reproduction. Both Deem (1986: 134–56) and Talbot (1988: 172–5) use this assumption to advocate a reformist feminist politics geared-up to organize women's groups, raise women's consciousness about male power and campaign for more resources from the state and the private sector to contribute to the empowerment of women. My position is that this is to take a rather generous view of the unitary character of women's experience of domestic reproduction, and the malleability of the material and ideological divisions between women relating to property ownership, race, nationality and subculture. Dorothy Smith's (1983: 40) remark that proper recognition of these divisions mean that 'women's dream of unity is almost certainly illusory', is pertinent here. At the very least, treating them as epiphenomena of patriarchy, in the manner of Deem and Talbot, is surely no more than wishful thinking.[3]

Second, I do not accept that it is accurate, or even a useful metaphor, to consider rationalization, commodification, commodity fetishism, monetary calculation, monopolization, reification and the centralization of state power as adjuncts of male domination. Yet in examining estrangement, hierarchy, repression and alienation among women many feminists have reached precisely the opposite conclusion (Bialeschki and Henderson 1986; Green *et al* 1987; Talbot 1988: 172–5). Indeed, Deem (1986: 9–10) has rather gratuitously dismissed the relevance of what she calls 'heavy male theory' on the grounds that it is too abstract and that it automatically treats male values as the norm. I have no axe to grind on the question of abstraction. On the whole, Western sociology has handled the discussion of social processes in a notoriously demanding, not to say, impenetrable fashion. However, I feel more belligerent against the suggestion that these abstract processes must be seen as the expression of male values. For example, Weber's discussion of the rationalization process undoubtedly comments on the unintended consequences of the intentional uses of Reason. But unless we are prepared to allow that Reason is an inviolate property of maleness as opposed to femaleness, there is nothing to endorse the view that rationalization is the embodiment of the masculine.

DIFFERENCES IN METHOD

The differences between my standpoint and feminist orthodoxy will be applied in what follows. They will be apparent not only in the substantive arguments that I make, but also in the method which I use to support these arguments. A note on method is therefore perhaps appropriate at this juncture. My practice will be to draw upon the historical experience of bourgeois women in actively shaping the conditions of their own lives. Talbot (1988: 172) has warned of the dangers involved in conceptualizing women as the passive recipients of male discrimination. I also reject the donatory view of women's culture. Unfortunately, the bulk of feminist writing on women's leisure has not followed suit. This is because it has over-concentrated upon the experience of working-class women. The themes of powerlessness, repression and privation have emerged quite inescapably, and quite correctly, from the analysis of this material. By the same token, feminist authors have given proper recognition to the efforts and imagination of working-class women in alleviating their negative experiences of leisure and domestic reproduction through positive action (Chambers 1986; Deem 1986; Wimbush and Talbot 1988). Nevertheless the overwhelming impression one gets from reading this material is one of deeply rooted sexual domination.

On the other hand, consideration of the question of bourgeois women's experience develops a rather more complicated and subtle picture. One is heavily reliant upon the research of feminist historians in this matter. Here a central theme is the active role of bourgeois women in breaking down barriers between household space and public space, and the separation of the domestic economy from the political economy (Hayden 1981; Poovey 1988). At issue here is more than the activities of a few spirited stagers such as Octavia Hill in England and Mary Richmond in the US who demanded a culture of caring capitalism and the development of the welfare state; or Annie Besant and Josephine Butler in England, and Margaret Higgins and Margaret Sanger in the US who advocated that women should have control over their own bodies and destinies. What in fact happened after the 1860s was the clear and undeniable contraction of male authority in the bourgeois household. Others have documented this process and the reader may be referred to their accounts for the fine details of the argument (Foucault 1981; Donzelot 1979; Hayden 1981). In making the broad brushstrokes of the case it is helpful to employ Giddens' (1981: 4) distinction between allocative and authoritative resources. Allocative resources refer to material sources of dominion over human beings, such as income and capital; authoritative resources refer to social sources of dominion over human beings such as status, taste, education and other forms of 'cultural capital' (see also Bourdieu 1986: 53–4; 80–3; 114–15). In early capitalism, allocative and authoritative resources were concentrated in the hands of the male, the head of the household: provider, protector and judge. As the capitalist accumulation process matured two changes in the labour market occurred to fracture this concentration of power. First, the growth in the number of domestic servants freed greater numbers of bourgeois wives to become leisured women. Thompson (1988: 247) puts the number of female domestics in 1851 at one million; by 1901, it had climbed to 1.4 million. Second, the production of higher surplus in the economy multiplied the opportunities for the head of the household to abstain from labour and live off capital, rent and interest.

According to Veblen (1925: 75), one important effect of this was that leisured existence became a legitimate and imperative authoritative resource for the bourgeois class because it symbolized exemption from ignoble labour. Yet he also noted that the rise of the leisured woman challenged the domination of the head of the household over allocative and authoritative resources. In early capitalism, argues Veblen (229), men stood in a relationship of ownership over their wives. This was reflected not only in the informal culture of bourgeois marriage, but also in formal, legal categories such as the property laws, which transferred the property and earnings of the wife into the absolute power of the husband (Perkin 1989: 293–5). The growth of the leisured class provided leisured women with the surplus time to challenge forms of state regulation which were overtly prejudicial to women. The creation of organizations to pursue 'the woman question', such as the Ladies National Association to fight the Contagious Diseases Acts, and the Married Women's Property Committee to campaign for the repeal of the 1957 Divorce and Matrimonial Causes Act, to say nothing of the more generic organizations of reform such as the Women's Liberal Federation and the Suffragettes, all campaigned against sexual discrimination. They were organizations in which recognition and membership could be proclaimed.

Interestingly, feminist historians have emphasized that these organizations were not gender exclusive. Mort (1987: 54) refers to 'a gendered alliance' between feminist reformers and male experts in medicine, public administration and the new sciences of psychology, sociology and sexology. The alliance acted as a switchboard for the development of rational understanding of the context of women's personal and social conditions. Of course, since the alliance itself originated in the context of early capitalism it could not avoid tendencies to re-establish sexual domination on a new basis, i.e. with the male experts 'guiding' the feminists. Mort takes this into account in his discussion. He shows the alliance developing dialectically, with female reformers challenging the authority of male experts and criticizing their gendered power relations.

This example of partnership, critique and counter-critique illustrates the uneven character of bourgeois sexual domination. Even at the supposed high point of male domination in mid-Victorian society, it shows that mechanisms and representations of male domination were simultaneously produced, applied *and* contested (see Poovey 1988). It is evidence which is at odds with gross feminist accounts which emphasize the polarization of interests between the sexes, and define men's relation to women essentially in terms of exploitation and repression (Talbot 1988; Scraton and Talbot 1989).

Instead of presenting the development of capitalism as the summation of male power, my course in this chapter will be to argue that it led to the collapse of the legitimation of male claims to monopolize allocative and authoritative resources. Although I want to follow feminist orthodoxy in insisting that rising feminist consciousness was crucial in this process, I also want to claim that it is tendentious to present it as the only meaningful influence. Structural transformations in the constitution of capitalism played their part, and it was an indispensable part. Let me illustrate what I mean by offering some remarks on the question of why feminist protest tended to be molecular and dispersed before the 1860s and why the opposite was the case afterwards. Three points in particular need to be mentioned.

First, high birth rates contributed to the mutual isolation of women before our period because, as mothers, they were fully engaged in child-bearing and child-rearing. For example, the case of Isabella Beeton, the author of the famous cookbook, was not untypical of the times. She was the oldest of a family of 21 brothers and sister.[4] She married at 20 and died eight years later of puerperal fever after the birth of her fourth child.

Second, the exchange of information between women was impeded by the absence of a well developed communications system. In fact, the first women's magazine, *The Ladies Mercury*, was published in London as early as 1693. By the start of the nineteenth century several other publications were available. However, before the 1850s women's magazines were aimed at an upper-class readership. Only the wives and daughters of the aristocracy possessed the literacy and leisure to appreciate them. It was not until the last two decades of the century that women's magazines for the middle class became economically viable. Several factors accounted for this. On the demand side, changes in the provision of education for women increased the spread of literacy. In addition, the development of new methods of birth control contributed to the reduction in family size and the generation of more leisure time for bourgeois women (Soloway 1982). On the supply side, production was improved by the invention of mechanical typesetting, the rotary press and the mass production of cheap paper. Similarly, circulation was improved by changes in retail distribution and the development of the transport network (Mennell 1985: 234–5).

Third, unlike men, women could not look to the workplace of paid labour to act as a basis for collective organization and action. Employment opportunities in industry and the professions were scant. It was not until the structural changes in the economy and technology which occurred in the closing decades of the century that the situation altered appreciably. Of particular importance to women's employment was the growth of opportunities in central and local government, elementary education and retail distribution. Most new working women were occupied in low-paid, low-status labour. Hobsbawm (1987: 201) notes that the new opportunities benefited daughters of workers and peasants. However, the main beneficiaries were the daughters of the bourgeoise who were attracted to posts which offered a degree of social respectability and independence.

In general, the feminist sociology of leisure suggests that capitalism, in the last instance, subordinates and pacifies women (Griffin 1985; Deem 1986; Green *et al* 1987). What the last three points suggest is that it also radicalizes and activates them. Through changes in birth control, and the economics and technology of communications and the labour market, women gained more power and more freedom. This is hardly a justification for sexual inequality. On the contrary, male power clearly repressed women's leisure activities in a number of areas. Men were assumed to be active, energetic, independent and intellectually assured. Women, in contrast, were regarded to be weak, passive and equipped by nature to concentrate on the domestic sphere. Travel and the exploration of foreign countries was seen as a manly, not a womanly occupation. There is no doubt that women from all walks of life suffered a variety of disagreeable experiences because of this male prejudice. However, the point to emphasize is that the barriers to male power were gradually overcome. Women authors like Ida Pfeiffer (1851) in *A Lady's Voyage Round the World* and Isabella Bird (1880) in *Unbeaten Tracks in Japan*, richly documented women's travel experience.

The feminist concentration upon reproduction and production is necessary, but not a sufficient requirement for understanding women's leisure experience under capitalism. The neglected categories of feminist thought of *circulation* and *exchange* are also crucial. The rise of consumer society increased the velocity of circulation of consumer goods, services and revenues. By multiplying opportunities for exchange it helped to break down the bourgeois 'separation of the spheres' (home from work, private life from public life) (see Davidoff and Hall 1983: 326–45). Increased velocity, comments Harvey (1985: 265) provided 'abundant opportunities for different structures of distribution to assert themselves, for the creation of new centres of economic power (finance capital, property capital, etc.), and for the circulation of marks of distinction, status and even consumption classes and communities (perhaps opposed, perhaps integrated into the powers of money and capital)'. The result was twofold. First, women's power over allocative resources increased through greater employment opportunities and changes in the property laws. Second, women's power over authoritative resources increased through the greater involvement of women in 'social' questions (notably child care, housing, poverty, social work, medical provision and welfare) and the determination of taste and style (see Saisselin 1985: 53–74; Wilson 1985; Forty 1986).

These are the central arguments in the chapter. They do not amount to an attempt to replace feminist notions of reproduction and production with circulation and exchange. As Saisellin (1985: 60) notes of the circulation process under capitalism, 'woman was the most expensive jewel men wore'. Nothing that I have to say will cancel the validity of that remark. On the other hand, I will seek to show that the metropolis and the market are as basic to understanding women's experience in bourgeois society as marriage and the home.

My commentary is divided into five sections. It opens with a discussion of women and the passions. My aim here is to ascertain what has traditionally been attributed to 'femaleness' and, by implication, what constitutes 'maleness'. Upon this 'common-sense' division, much official thought about women's capacities and propensities for pleasure and physical and mental exertion rests. Yet it has rarely been the subject of systematic enquiry in the sociology of leisure.

In the second section I will explore the historical experience of bourgeois women in the home. Feminist thought has approached the home as the site of domestic reproduction, and has all too often concluded that it is little more than woman's prison. My discussion seeks to sow how the growth of the vast external world of bourgeois society, the world of the metropolis and the market, opened up the bourgeois interior and produced new opportunities in work and leisure for women. This was not, of course, a one-way process. If the development of capitalism created new life chances for women, it was itself changed by women seizing those opportunities and acting upon them. My discussion will comment on the influence of bourgeois women's standards of taste, on bourgeois values in welfare issues and on interior design.

The third section is devoted to an examination of women and public space. Early capitalism imposed a series of limitations upon the appearance and movement of 'respectable' women in public places. The street was seen as a thoroughfare of moral and physical pollution, where dirt and squalor accumulated. It was part of the double-standard in Victorian moral life that women were thought to risk losing their reputation and dirtying themselves by going out alone in public; whereas for men, the street was regarded to be a place of self-abandonment and self-knowledge. My account will focus on the circulation process in fashion and retail distribution, notably the rise of the department store. My purpose is to show the development of leisure spaces for bourgeois women in the metropolis through the related processes of greater accumulation and increased velocity of exchange. However, I shall also be concerned to demonstrate the active campaigning role of bourgeois women in challenging received male barriers to women's appearance and mobility. Accordingly, the section includes an outline of the emancipation movement in sport and physical recreation. Here many of the most stubborn items of bourgeois 'commonsense' regarding femininity an the 'natural' frailties of the female body, were directly confronted and overcome.

The fourth section continues the theme of the female body by examining the relationship between Victorian medicine and women. Feminists have justifiably railed against the male prejudices in medical practice which permitted, not only the social organization of the female subject, but the mutilation of her body and mind (Jeffreys 1987: 9–57; Showalter 1985). The construction of the hysterical woman and what Foucault (1981: 104, 146–7) called 'the hysterization of women's bodies' will be examined in this chapter as examples of the narrowness of male ideals of feminity. However, it is important to avoid zero-sum interpretations of women's power. Invalidism may have been forced upon Victorian women by men as a way of repressing them, but it was also exploited and developed by women to gain leisure and abstention from the cares of marriage. In this section I will use the concept of the sick role to explore how some Victorian women created enclaves of leisure space and privilege within bourgeois marriage.

The fifth section examines the argument that feminist values have triumphed in Western state formation. Exponents point to 'the nanny state' and 'matricidal culture' as evidence. Feminist values are presented as weakening the fabric of society by undermining independence, self-reliance and motivation. In particular, women's liberation is linked to the decline of the family and the spread of *anomie*. Similarly, the increasing visibility of women's bodies in leisure and travel is presented as a cause of moral decay. In brief, the growth of women's power over authoritative and allocative resources is condemned for undermining Western culture. Typically these arguments culminate in the demand for women to resume their 'natural' role in the home. Such arguments go a long way towards confirming womens' suspicions about 'heavy male theory', and I shall dissociate myself from them in my commentary. On the other hand, it is no part of my argument to replace male sexism with female sexism. 'The common world of women' seems to me to be a false abstraction, as does 'the common world of men'. In the next chapter I will peruse some of the unintended, unplanned social forces which militate against membership and community and support fragmentation and division (among women, as among men).

FEMININE PASSIONS

We saw in the last chapter that classical political economy yoked the passions with Nature. Nothing in man's power was granted to alter their constancy or strength. The sexual division of the passions was defined with equal inevitability. Lloyd (1984) argues that from Plato to the modern day, maleness has been associated with superiority and femaleness with inferiority. However, it is not classical philosophy or political economy but classical biology which supplies the clearest expression of the prejudiced conventional wisdom. For example, Bachelard (1938: 47–8), in his wonderful book on the element of fire, disdainfully quotes the view of Doctor Pierre Jean Fabre, written in 1636:

> If the semen, which is one and the same in all parts and of an identical constitution, is divided in the womb and one part withdrawn to the right and the other to the left side, the mere fact of the division of the semen causes such a difference in it . . . not only in form and figure, but in sex, that one side will be male and the

other female. And it is that part of the semen which has withdrawn to the right side, as being the part of the body which is the hotter, and more vigorous, which will have maintained the force and vigour and heat of the semen that a male child will come forth; and the other part, since it has retired to the left side which is the colder part of the human body, will have much diminished and lessened the vigour of the semen, so that from it there will come forth the female child which, however, in its first origin was all male.

A natural basis then, a *seminal* division, no less, for explaining the differences between men and women. Women's nature was thought to be endowed with modesty, the desire to serve, loyalty and low emotional control. It was animated by weaker passions and a lower capacity to understand itself. 'The reasoning powers are more perfect in [man] than in [woman],' commented the *Christian Observer* (1865: 547). 'The creative powers belong almost exclusively to him . . . it was impossible for her ever completely to know or realize the tempest of passions which held sway in the souls of an Othello or a Faust.'

Larner (1981: 91–2) traces the stereotype of women as inferior creatures back to the Aristotelian view of woman. But she also notes the influence of the Judaeo-Christian view which identified woman as the source of sin and the Fall of Man. This view regarded woman as the source of malice, sensuality and evil. As such it provided a basis for men to fear women. For example, Burton, in *The Anatomy of Melancholy* writes caustically on the wiles of women:

They will crack, counterfeit and collogue as well as the best, with handkerchiefs, and wrought nightcaps, purses, posies and such toys . . . When nothing else will serve, the last refuge is their tears . . . To these crocodile's tears they will add sobs, fiery sighs, and sorrowful countenance, pale colour, leanness, and if you do but stir abroad, these fiends are ready to meet you at every turn, with such a sluttish neglected habit, dejected look, as if they were ready to die for your sake . . . But believe them not. Thou thinkest, peradventure because of her vows, tears, smiles and protestations, she is soley thine, thou hast her heart, hand and affection, when as indeed there is no such matter, she will have one sweetheart in bed, another in the gate, a third sighing at home, a fourth, etc. (1924: 545)

Rousseau also pointed to women's power to charm, captivate and influence male passions and to send men to their destruction. 'Women so easily stir a man's senses,' he wrote in *Emile* (1974: 321), '[that] the men, tyrannized over by the women, would at last become their victims, and would be dragged to their deaths without the least chance of escape.' Later, in my discussion of women's public space I will examine the stereotype of 'the red woman' to show how male fears were externalized.[6] Here it is enough to note that male fears of what women could do to them, existed side-by-side with the male assumption of female inferiority.

The latter belief was embodied in many of the central institutions of capitalist society. Nowhere more so than in the marriage bond. Until well into the nineteenth century, a woman had no status unless she was married (Stone 1979: 136–48; Perkin 1989: 292–310). A book on respectable feminine behaviour, written by a woman (Mrs A.J. Graves), and published in 1858, expressed the conventional wisdom cogently:

> A good woman has no desire to rule where she feels it to be her duty, as it is her highest pleasures "to love, honour and obey"; and she submits with cheerful acquiesence to that order in the conjugal relation which God and nature have established. Woman feels she is not made for command, and finds her truest happiness in submitting to those who wield a rightful sceptre in justice, mercy and love. (Quoted in Klein 1971: 11)

Bourgeois society required woman to lead a vicarious existence (Veblen 1925: 229). It compelled her to find a husband, and once found, to live through him and his children. Hence the importance attached to charm, good manners, cheerfulness, appearances and domestic accomplishments in the education of girls and in women's marriage handbooks and primers. They emphasize that deference and restraint are the way to a man's heart. The leisure of girls and women was organized accordingly around the needs of men and children. Mrs Beeton proffers some typical advice on suitable leisure pursuits for females:

> Light or fancy needlework often forms a portion of the evening's recreation for the ladies of the household, and this may be varied by an occasional game of chess or backgammon. It has often been

remarked, too, that nothing is more delightful to the feminine members of a family than the reading aloud of some good standard work or amusing publication. A knowledge of polite literature may thus be obtained by the whole family, especially if the reader is able and willing to explain the more difficult passages of the books, and expatiate on the wisdom and beauties it may contain. (1861: 17)

Similar passages might be quoted from earlier nineteenth-century handbooks, such as Mrs Parkes's *Domestic Duties* (1825) or Lydia Sigourney's (1838) *Letters to Mothers*. Women are shown to be less robust than men and happiest in repose or in playing with children. As we shall see in the penultimate section of the chapter which explores medicine and women, this view was reinforced by medical opinion which presented women as physically delicate beings, with lower reserves of energy than men.

For Victorian middle-class men, work was the serious side of life, and leisure was secondary. For Victorian middle-class women, the opposite was the case. Although women acknowledged the importance of the male provider in making money, much of their time was spent in refining female accomplishments and managing the complex codes of etiquette that governed relations in the bourgeois household. After the 1850s, the surplus time which accrued to them after discharging their work responsibilities was vastly increased by the growth in the number of domestic servants. Davidoff's (1973) fine study of 'the Season' showed how the calendar of social events worked as a showcase for the aristocracy to make introductions and match marriage partners. Only a few daughters of the bourgeoisie came from families rich enough to qualify for entry to the annual round of events that made up the Season. Instead, most of them relied upon private dinners and parties organized by their mothers or acquaintances of their parents, to make new contacts. These leisure events served single women as opportunities to display their accomplishments and find a mate. They were governed by rigid bourgeois conventions of role distance. For example, an *Edwardian Etiquette Book* (1902: 43–55) laid down rules for respectable female dress, conversation, table manners and requirements of disengagement ('the ladies retire'). Behaviour which broke the received idiom was frowned upon and dire social consequences were predicted to follow from it.

However, even at the time that this advice was being published, things were changing. With the rise of the new woman in the closing decades of the century, the old values of deference and restraint in the female character were set off with new values. Chapters in women's handbooks appeared on 'Etiquette for the Bachelor Girl' which reflected the growing opportunities for women in the labour market and the changes in female lifestyle which followed them. In addition, and interestingly, male and child psychology featured more prominently as vital assets of female character. Women are presented as not only reacting to the needs of men and children but also anticipating and managing them. One can hardly maintain that this was an invention of the period.[7] We have already referred to the long-established male view that women were inferior and incomplete beings. Porter (1982: 37) notes the male horror of 'shrewishness' and 'petticoat government' in the eighteenth century. Women were certainly aware of the situation and had devised ways of dealing with it. However, what was new in women's handbooks after the 1860s was the open recognition of male weakness and vanity. Women were no longer instructed that 'God and nature had made them unfit to command', and that their happiness lay in submitting to those 'wielding a rightful sceptre in justice, mercy and love'. Instead they were now encouraged to question male authority and reject it if necessary. For example, Lady Troubridge's *Etiquette and Entertaining* (1926) rejected the rigidity of received Victorian codes and ideas of relationships. 'Etiquette in those comparatively far-off days', she wrote (7), 'was a *bogy* . . . but, nowadays quite a new spirit has crept into those unwritten laws which we know as etiquette until, in this year of grace, one is almost tempted to say "Anything goes". [Emphasis in original.]

This new spirit of relaxation is further reflected in the growth of frankness about female sexuality.[8] It is generally accepted that Victorian society repressed female sexuality (Bernheimer and Kahane 1985; Showalter 1985; Mendus and Rendall 1989). For example, the conventional wisdom confined female indulgence in sexual intercourse to marriage and described it in dutiful terms as one of the many crosses that women must bear to beget children. As Elizabeth Edson Evans, author of *The Abuse of Maternity* put it:

The pleasure attendant upon the animal function of reproduction shall never be sought as an end, and the sexual act shall be indulged at rare intervals, for the purpose of calling into existence a sufficient number of successors to the joyous inheritance of health wisdom and plenty. (1875: 128–9)

Some evidence exists that Victorian middle-class women departed from this austere code in their private lives and enjoyed mutually fulfilling sexual relations with their husbands (Gay 1984: 71–108). However, the evidence here is not strong. The source material of women's journals and diaries was itself subject to self-censorship. Certainly, there is not enough evidence to support the conclusion that the repression of female sexuality in Victorian society can be passed off as mere rhetoric. For example, consider Krafft-Ebing's (1886) *Psychopathia Sexualis*. This influential work summed up dominant medical opinion in its assertion that women's sexual passions were 'without doubt', weaker than men's. Women, he continued, crave love and protection rather than erotic fulfilment. This was the common view of the time among educated people. Indeed, some writers went so far as to diagnose erotic desires in women as a source of social pathology. For example, John Harvey Kellogg, inventor of the cornflake, argued:

If a child is begotten in lust, its lower passions will as certainly be abnormally developed as peas will produce peas, potatoes potatoes. If the child does not become a rake or prostitute, it will be because of uncommonly fortunate surroundings, or a miracle of divine grace. But even then, what terrible struggles with sin and vice, what frail thoughts and lewd imaginations – the producer of a naturally abnormal mind – must such an individual suffer. (1888: 450)

Female eroticism is here identified with degeneration. The cure, according to Kellogg, was to increase consumption of cereals at the expense of meat and eggs which, he believed, would dampen 'the lower passions'.

By the turn of the century a change is evident. Women's handbooks no longer confine female sexuality to procreation. The importance of sexual fulfilment for men and women in marriage is openly discussed. For example, *The Marriage Book* (nd) refers to women's 'fictitious modesty' in sexual matters. It goes on to outline the creed of the happy wife:

I believe in the rightness and beauty of natural sexual expression as the framework for love, without which no matrimonial romance can be healthy or long-lived. I believe that any sexual gesture, play or craving of my husband or myself is natural, provided only that it demands the participation and seeks the happiness of the mate as well as the self . . . Sex adjustment, like courtship, involves the give-and-take of two persons. I shall not be so naive as to suppose that I can give adequate outlet to my own primal urge, or the highest joy to my mate by playing only a passive role in our physical love-making. I will seek to express my love by taking an active part in the sexual act, using my imagination freely. (50–1)

Nothing like this is to be found in the handbooks of early capitalism. *The Marriage Book* advocates a partnership based upon the recognition of mutual sexual, emotional and intellectual needs. It acknowledges the variety of individual needs and puts the case for negotiation and adjustment in producing a fulfilling relationship. On the other hand, it would be quite wrong to suppose that the new handbooks envisaged anything like an equal sexual relationship. Lady Troubridge (1926: 170), who, as we saw earlier in the chapter, poked amiable fun at the stuffiness of etiquette in Victorian society, was nevertheless capable of making the following announcement:

Let's be quite frank about this, and face up to the fact that friendships with men are the thrill of most girls' lives. Or would you I rather call them the Spice of Life? I'm not suggesting you let such friendships interfere with your work or even with your home life, but there they are, or rather, there he is, this boy-friend of yours, the reason why you simply must get a new summer outfit, and a new permanent wave, and practise up your tennis.

Lady Troubridge continues by offering hints for women on the technique of friendship with men:

Be casual. He'll like that in you. Remember some men are scary of a girl who takes their male privilege of doing the asking out of their hands . . . do not cramp his style . . . Never by word or look, in public or private, hurt his *amour-propre* by hinting how well other men have got on, or suggesting that it is his own fault that he is at the rear end of the success procession (171, 59, 62).

This is hardly the language of female liberation. Many feminists may take it as proof that any changes which occurred in sexual relationships between early and late capitalism amounted to small beer. Women were just as oppressed in the 1930s as they had been in the 1830s. They continued to organize their dress, manners, conversation and leisure interests around their needs of men. All that had changed was the rules of the game.

Such pessimism is not justified. Changes in sexual codes and ideals between early and late capitalism were not superficial. Wouters (1986, 1987) argues that the period was marked by 'the informalization process'.[9] By this he means a process in which established sexual roles of domination and subordination tend towards greater leniency, flexibility and variety. He substantiates his argument by pointing to three crucial differences in sexual codes and ideals between early and late capitalism.

First, gradually but unmistakably, the idea that there is one 'correct' code or ideal of heterosexual dating, written on tablets of stone, collapsed in fragments. Tolerance of difference and diversity grew. Flexible guidelines permitting social actors to interpret the correct manner of behaviour according to circumstances became fashionable. Women developed their own interests in leisure, sport and recreation which were independent of the interests of men.

Second, late capitalist society has dealt a severe blow to the Victorian notion of 'the male protector'. No one can convincingly argue that capitalist society has banished the idea of 'the weaker sex'. On the contrary, feminists have provided countless examples of sexual prejudice from the school curriculum, advertising, the mass media, politics and employment opportunities (see Williamson 1978; McRobbie and McCabe 1981; Coward 1984). At the same time, there has been a trend from male protection to self-protection. For example, women travel in public places and make trips abroad unchaperoned. They openly challenge male authority in the home and public life. As Wouters (1987: 418) puts it, 'where once behavioural codes and ideals based on male protection determined the possibilities and limits of relationships between the sexes, today men and women are invited and compelled to negotiate – with themselves and each other – the borders of each individual's private territory or (right to) privacy and about the balance between formal and informal, between aloof and intimate'.

Third, the taboo against women entering paid employment has been broken. Women are no longer expected to fulfil themselves solely through marriage and the family. Career women and working wives became acceptable roles for women. Wives have greater control over their household income and have legally recognized claims on household capital. Their comparative independence from what the Victorians called 'the head of the household' is reinforced by a wide range of welfare arrangements and simplified legal procedures for divorce.

Most of the rest of the chapter is dedicated to the task of putting flesh onto the bones of the informalization thesis. I want to show why women became more vocal and visible through capitalist accumulation, circulation and exchange, and how women's movements kicked against male domination generally, and specifically in interior design and sport. Feminists have every reason to revile male theories which depict women's liberation as a long and inevitable march of progress. Not only do these theories have a superficial view of women's liberation, they also turn a blind eye to the potency of capitalism in turning the women's liberation movement into a resource for further exploitation and accumulation. For example, Ewen (1976: 159–76) demonstrates in an exemplary fashion how 'the new woman' became a resource for capitalist advertising and marketing in the 1920s. He writes:

> A classic example of commercialized feminism was a 1929 campaign in which the American Tabacco Company attempted "to induce women to smoke [cigarettes] in public places." George W. Hill had contracted Edward Bernays to run the campaign, hoping to expunge the "hussy" label from women who smoked publicly . . . Bernays had a contingent of cigarette-puffing women march in the 1929 Easter parade down Fifth Avenue in New York. "Our parade of ten young women lighting 'torches of freedom' on Fifth Avenue on Easter Sunday as a protest against woman's inequality caused a national stir," Bernays proclaimed. "Frontpage stories in newspapers reported the freedom march in words and pictures". (160–1)

Informalization then was certainly not a one-sided affair. If women became more vocal and visible through the relaxation of behavioural codes and ideals, their relations with men and each other, were increasingly mediated through the stylized images of consumer culture. Several commentators have drawn attention to the currency and power of degraded gender images produced by the capitalist culture industry (Williamson 1978; McRobbie and McCabe 1981; Coward 1984). The profligacy of these images has presented feminists with new challenges in trying to understand women's position in society and combating male oppression. On the other hand, it would be quite wrong to minimize the importance of informalization in changing the balance of power between the sexes. Women's life chances were increased generally and appreciably by the process. The home, the great Victorian symbol of woman's domain, was also a key indicator of informalization. By studying changes in its architecture and meaning for middle-class women we can pinpoint some of the crucial changes in the balance of power between the sexes. The next section is devoted to this task.

WOMEN AND THE HOME

Stone (1977) argues that from the 1770s the family was subject to the revival of moral reform, paternalism and sexual repression. One of the ways in which this was reflected tangibly was in the privatization of the home. Before the 1770s the homes of all bar the aristocracy, were places of work as well as of residence and of leisure. This is not the place to attempt a detailed account of these conditions. Segalen's (1983: 52) few words on the architecture of a house in Normandy in the 1760s must suffice as a general indicative statement:

> The modest dwelling was principally made up of a *chambre à cacher* which served as a bedchamber and dining room: in it were found the loom and spinning wheel, that is to say, the means of production, and also the bed, table, sideboard and stove. The separate kitchen was used only during the summer. The whole of the family was concentrated in the work-room, the only room warm enough to ensure agile fingers.

The rise of industrial capitalism separated the workplace from the residence, the public from the private (Sennett 1977: 89–106; 130–41; Davidoff and Hall 1983: 327–45). The wife who did not need to work in paid employment became a badge of status in Victorian families. Middle-class women were assigned a distinctive sphere of influence; the home. Here they were expected to cultivate gentility, comfort and security as a refuge from the vast, 'unnatural' external world of urban, impersonal bourgeois society. Ruskin, meditating on 'the true nature of the home', ventured:

> It is the place of peace; the shelter, not only from all injury, but from all terror, doubt and division. In so far as it is not this, it is not home; so far as the anxieties of the outer life penetrate into it, and the inconsistently-minded, unknown, unloved, or hostile society of the outer world is allowed by either husband or wife to cross the threshold it ceases to be a home. (1865, quoted in Mackay and Thane 1986: 197)

Women were therefore cast in the role of gatekeepers, gathering the vulnerable family to their bosom and keeping a watchful eye on the moral, economic and physical dangers of the external world. Their 'honorific status' was not confined to an abstention from paid employment. In addition they were required to manage the household with spotless efficiency and the utmost decency in order to signify the probity of their husbands to potential customers or creditors. The home, therefore, acted as the externalization of the inner world of the mistress of the household. Its cleanliness symbolized her virtue; its physical order symbolized her moral gravity. Frances Power-Cobbes, writing in 1869, made the same associations in a remarkable and revealing passage of Victorian sexual psychology:

> The more womanly a woman is, the more she is sure to throw her personality over the home, and transform it, from a mere eating and sleeping place, or upholsterer's showroom, into a sort of outermost garment of her soul; harmonised with her bodily beauty. The arrangement of her rooms, the light and shade, warmth and coolness, sweet odours, and soft or rich colours, are not like the devices of a well-trained servant or tradesman. They are the expression of the character of the woman . . . A woman whose home does not bear her this relation of nest to bird, calyx to flower, shell to mollusk, is in one or another imperfect condition. She is either not really mistress of her home; or being so, she is herself deficient in the womanly power of thoroughly imposing her personality upon her belongings (Quoted in Forty 1986: 106).

The feminist tradition in the sociology of leisure has tended to emphasize the submissiveness and inferiority of the home-making role.

In considering the bourgeois 'separation of the spheres', which maintained that the proper place of women was the home, one can see the historical reason for this emphasis. However, it would be superficial to take the invisibility of bourgeois women in public life, especially in early capitalism, as a pretext for believing that the influence of bourgeois women in the conduct of society was itself invisible. On the contrary, the bourgeois interior was the fulcrum of women's power. From it they made criticisms of the moral disorder and aesthetic ugliness of the metropolis and the market. Under early capitalism, their influence was mainly felt indirectly, through the activities of their husbands and sons. However, as the nineteenth century drew to a close, they took a more active campaigning role in determining the bourgeois order of things in public life. It is very important to note that such campaigns were not necessarily or consistently hostile to male authority. In many respects they were highly conservative, notably in the staunch defence of family values and the sanctity of marriage. Nevertheless, in demanding legally approved rights for women and criticizing male mismanagement of the economy the authentic voice of new bourgeois womanhood was articulated. It would be a mistake to imagine that this voice was self-supporting. It was underpinned by the accumulation of surplus through improvements in economic productivity, and the increased circulation which opened up the exchange of information and ideas and the recognition of interests. The ideological buttress behind much of the disquiet felt by middle-class women in the face of the male conduct of society was the Bible. But here a digression is called for.

A commonplace in accounts of the formation of the bourgeois moral ethos is the recognition of the importance of religious nonconformity and dissent (Weber 1930; Tawney 1937; Ossawska 1956: 184–214). Thompson (1988: 251) argues that evangelicalism ignited a revolution in the moral culture of early capitalism. It imposed the ideal of a Christian home governed by piety, charity, sobriety, filial obedience, chastity and disapproval of luxury upon all middle-class families. Others have commented upon the instrumental role of nonconformist religious voluntary organizations in rational recreation and philanthropy (Stedman Jones 1971: 5–6, 273–4; Yeo 1976: 59–60, 66–8, 154–5; Springhall 1977; Bailey 1987: 57–8, 110–11, 116–17). While the repressive and puritanical effects of religion in organizing the free time of subjects in bourgeois society has received much attention, its effects in empowering the bourgeois wife and mother have not been fully appreciated. The feminist sociology of leisure has argued that male domination in capitalist society marginalized women in public life. While this was true of many of the central institutions of early capitalism, notably the political system, the business world, the judiciary, the media and the education system, it was not true of the Church. Women may have been excluded from the role of ministering religion, but they were prominent in the public life of the Church. Although the Evangelical message contributed to the domestication of women by emphasizing women's special capacities for caring and piety, it also encouraged self-awareness and unflinching scrutiny of this-worldly conditions. There is some evidence that this led directly to the radicalization of bourgeois women. Mathews (1977: 101–24) notes that women's conversion to evangelicalism pitted wives in open conflict with their conformist husbands. The Church played a supportive role in backing women's actions against male authority. Mathews writes:

> Women's conversion could easily be interpreted as an independent action and a personal determination to develop oneself through a new ideology, even against the wishes of one's husband – or perhaps especially against the wishes of one's husband. The intimate bonds of the religious community must have provided some women with care, sense of worth, and companionship they did not receive from their husbands. (105)

However, cases in which the Church figured as a catalyst for open revolt were comparatively rare. The common alliance between bourgeois women and the Bible was found in the home. The physical absence of the husband from the house during work-time projected bourgeois wives into the role of chief moral educator. Bourgeois society accorded formidable respect to mothers. The wise mother who provided helpful counsel, and the *mère terrible* who punished wayward behaviour, were powerful archetypes in Victorian literature on the family (Harvey 1985: 138–9). However, one should not deduce from this that the disciplinary power of bourgeois women stopped short with the moral education of their children. Women also exerted moral force over their husbands. *Pace* the instruction of traditional advice manuals and marriage books which, as we have seen, lectured on the virtues of self-sacrifice, compliance and cheerfulness in women, evangelical wives were quite capable of taking their husbands to task. The moral authority for their criticism resided in the Bible. Here were the words of God on the male respons- ibilities of Christian union, which could be appealed to as a higher source of authority than the words of their husbands. The Church stood ready to support the legitimate claims of injured wives. Mathews (1977: 104) reports that church committees for the investi- gation of allegations of 'child abuse' were not unusual in Evangelical churches.

The dissenting tradition in religion, then, was by no means simply a strait-jacket which reinforced the submissiveness and dependence of bourgeois wives. On the contrary, in the details and manner nominated, it bolstered the moral force of bourgeois women within the home. This was reflected in the growth of leisured women's involvement in social welfare and recreation issues. It was also ex- pressed in the more critical stance that women adopted to the aes- thetic values of industrial society. Let me briefly expand upon both of these points.

By the 1860s, 'good works' and 'deserving causes' had become the forte of leisured bourgeois women. I have already referred to Samuel and Henrietta Barnett's exercise in rational recreation in the Whitechapel art exhibitions. To this a whole list of bourgeois wo- men's 'good works' for the deserving poor might be added. For example, Mary Carpenter was a leading proponent of the 'Ragged School' movement which sought to provide underprivileged chil- dren with the sort of education, based on Christian principles, that would turn them into useful members of society. Housing was cen- tral to the Victorian strategy of working-class moral improvement because the home was thought to give one a stake in society and, through this, to encourage 'respectability'. The home-making ex- perience of bourgeois women made them obvious candidates to participate in this strategy. Baroness Burdett Coutts was a pioneer of private philanthropic effort to provide 'model dwellings' for the urban industrial class. However, of greater influence on the housing problem was the Octavia Hill system. This scheme aimed to com- mandeer overcrowded and run-down streets and train the tenants in punctuality, thrift and respectability through the example and discipline of the landlord or the lady rent collector (Stedman Jones 1971: 183, 193–6). Together with Helen Bosanquet, Octavia Hill was a major figure in the development of British social work. The Charity Organization Society, founded in London in 1869, aimed to develop professional standards for welfare work with the deserving poor. Many of its patrons and volunteer workers were bourgeois women.

They were driven by a sense of social responsibility which was well articulated by Octavia Hill:

> If we are to place our people in permanently self-supporting positions it will depend on the various courses of action suitable to various people and circumstances, the ground of which can be perceived only by sweet sympathy and the power of human love. (Cited in Jones 1983: 78)

For bourgeois society, the cradle of 'sweet sympathy' and 'love' was, of course, the home. In pointing to these values as the foundation of successful social work, Hill was hardly confirming the doctrine of the separation of the spheres. On the contrary, her words show that in late capitalism this separation was no longer hard and fast. I shall expand upon the way in which the erosion between the home and external society occurred in the next section where I discuss the rise of the department store. Before reaching that point I want to show how the doctrine ceased to be tenable in a parallel area of bourgeois society: that of aesthetic values and design.

Under early capitalism, the bourgeois interior was sharply demarcated from the external world of society. It was designed and furnished to encourage total dissociation from the chaos and impersonality of the market, the workplace and the metropolis. The colours, comforts and softness of the home were contrasted with the austere furnishings, utilitarian colours and hard surfaces of the office and the factory. As the showplace of the presiding feminine character, the home was inevitably the receptacle of studied particularity. Rooms were crowded with furniture, needlework, drapery, objets d'art and bric-à-brac.[10] Benjamin (1983: 167) described the bourgeois interior as a 'phantasmagoria'. He continued, 'it represented the universe of the private citizen. In it he assembled the distant in space and in time. His drawing-room was a box in the world theatre' (167–8). The commercial embodiment of 'the distant in space and time' in interior decoration was, of course, the designs of Morris & Co. William Morris was galvanized by a sentimental vision of the Middle Ages. He equated this time with a harmonious society, close to nature, human in scale and steeped in respect for the dignity of labour and creativity of craftsmanship. Morris's designs for wallpaper and furniture aimed to use this repertoire of images to embody the Victorian reverence for the home as a place of feeling, honesty, sincerity, virtue and love.

It is important to recognize that Morris's designs were a reaction to the mass-reproduced objects of interior design which flooded the market in the 1840s, 1850s and 1860s. Saisselin (1985) refers to this period as one of 'bricabracomania'. Because the designers of mass-produced objects could not rely on exclusivity to attract the customer, they were forced to rely on novelty, price effectiveness and utility. This was often the excuse for rather showy design values. Few home-owners were in a position to acquire their furniture, carpets, draperies and domestic ornaments simultaneously. So, in the majority of homes these objects and designs tended to accumulate over a number of years. In addition, since the design values of the mass-produced market tended to concentrate upon novelty and utility, objects and designs tended to be purchased on the basis of their individual attraction or use, rather than their correspondence and resonance with the collection of objects and designs already acquired. This meant that the domestic interiors of bourgeois homes tended to be adorned with designs and objects which did not enhance each other's attraction or meaning through their connection but rather competed furiously with each other for the spectator's attention. The effect was to create an interior which was nothing but a jangling collection of fragments – an exact parallel indeed, of the vast external world of the metropolis.

The leisured men and women who were the main customers of firms like Morris & Co. rejected the crowded rooms and showy design values that predominated in their parents' homes. They associated these with claustrophobia, the lack of refinement and the ugliness of the machine age. Instead they valued exclusivity, uniqueness and the liberation of space in interior decoration. Bourgeois women were to the fore in consolidating these developments. Their traditional home-making role lent them authority as consumers in determining the architecture and appearance of the bourgeois interior. In addition, it is very important to note that they contributed directly as producers of design innovation. The history of women's interior designs in the nineteenth century is too complicated to be fully represented here. Even so, in order to counter the received wisdom of the feminist sociology of leisure, that women were rendered invisible for our period by reason of male domination, it is necessary to give a few positive examples.

Few are more noteworthy than the architectural designs of Catherine Beecher published in her book *The American Woman's Home* (1869).[11] Beecher's designs are widely held to anticipate the design revolution in the American home of the 1920s associated with the work of architects like Buckminster Fuller (the Dymaxion house 1927) and Frank Lloyd Wright (see Banham 1969: 96–101; Hayden 1981: 55–7). Beginning from the 1830s, the fashion in middle-class homes was for compartmentalized rooms designed for specialized activities, e.g. the drawing room, the morning room, the dressing room, the music room, etc. This reflected the rationalization of the market and the metropolis in the external world. Beecher's designs depart from this precedent. They have a unified core of services around which floors are arranged not as a set of compartmentalized rooms, but as free space differentiated functionally by built-in furniture and equipment. Instead of dark, enclosed space her designs favour sunlit, open spaces which assist mobility, flexibility and interaction. In Britain, similar design values were championed by Rhoda and Agnes Garrett, authors of *Suggestions for House Decorators* (1879). The Garretts also ran their own design business and school of interior decoration. Mrs Panton, who wrote an influential weekly advice column on home furnishing in *The Lady's Pictorial* in the 1880s and 1890s, also operated a private design consultancy. In New York, Edith Wharton and Elsie de Wolfe were respected and successful interior decorators (Forty 1986: 111). Edith Wharton was also famous for her book *The Decoration of Houses* (1901),[12] which criticized the bourgeois interior of early capitalism for its cluttered, tasteless design values in furniture and decoration. Wharton argued for interior designs based on 'cultivation and judgement' (187). She wanted interiors which 'suggested a mellower civilization – of days when rich men were patrons of the "arts of elegance" and when collecting beautiful objects was one of the obligations of noble leisure' (ibid).

Such sentiments, it might be argued, reflected changes in the course of capitalist accumulation, but hardly threatened the system itself. What did the criticism of the aesthetic values of capitalism amount to if not new opportunities to generate more surplus through the commercialization of taste? Equally, where do the 'good works' and 'deserving causes' in which bourgeois women immersed themselves so vigorously after the 1860s lead, if not to the ideology of 'caring capitalism' and hence the strengthening of the system of class exploitation? The field of leisure studies is strewn with examples like this of forceful-sounding but basically over-simplified and tendentious arguments.[13] We no longer take orthodox Marxists and feminists at their word in asserting that the key to understanding capitalism is the class struggle or women's oppression is patriarchy;

we see a mix of enduring structures and discontinuities where twenty to thirty years ago all seemed evolutionary. So it is with the greater participation of bourgeois women in public life after the 1860s. The growth of the design industry and the commercialization of taste undoubtedly created new opportunities for capitalist exploitation and accumulation. On the other hand, it also paved the way for collective organization and action among feminists who disapproved of the superficiality and sexism of consumer culture (see Ewen 1976: 200–1; Wilson 1985: 208–13). Similarly, the voluntary welfare work of bourgeois women certainly contributed to the ideology of caring capitalism. On the other hand, it also promoted the recognition among women of the social and environmental damage caused by unregulated competition and possessive individualism. Hayden's (1981) outstanding study of the 'material feminists' in the USA shows the remarkable experiments made by bourgeois women in our period to combat the divisive, exploitative tendencies of capitalism. They established housewives' co-operatives, promoted new building types such as the kitchenless house, the day-care centre, the public kitchen and the community dining club, and proposed ideal feminist cities.

In general, throughout our period, the privacy of the bourgeois home remained intact. On the other hand, the increased velocity of commodity circulation and the expansion of advertising and retailing increased the importance of material, monetary accumulation as indicators of status distinctions between families (Lowe 1982: 70). The identity and practice of the bourgeois wife became defined not simply as the home-maker, but increasingly as the arbiter of domestic taste. This was reflected in the purer design values which became popular by the turn of the century. Plain surfaces, simple wallpaper designs, less furniture, white panelling and the deliberate creation of open space in rooms was thought to bring harmony and moral balance into the home (Forty 1986: 112-13). Bourgeois women had to keep abreast of the latest thinking on domestic elegance to be good taste-makers. This involved greater contact with the design industry, through the trade media and design specialists.[14] The pressure to keep in touch with the most advanced thinking did not stop with matters of design. Others have shown that bourgeois wives in our period devoted large amounts of spare time to the latest thinking on the scientific management of the family and society, especially childcare, mental health and social welfare (see Donzelot 1979: 18–21, 64–6; Sussman 1981: 161–88; Soloway 1982: 70–155; Hardyment 1983: 89–155).

The increased involvement of bourgeois women with the mechanics of the 'unnatural', external world of society reinforced changes in the balance of power between the sexes in the home. The power of women was advanced by virtue of their educative usefulness (Donzelot 1979: 18). The 'gendered alliance' between women and male experts in medical practice, psychoanalysis, social welfare and commodity aesthetics 'provided women with a means of representation into the male-defined world of public political debate' (Mort 1987: 118).

It would be difficult to argue that women's leisure was increased by these historical changes. The pressure to be a 'thoroughly modern woman' in the scientific management of the family and society may have enhanced women's status, but it was also time-consuming and it bred new anxieties in women, e.g. keeping up with one's neighbours and trying to anticipate the fashions of the day. In addition there is evidence that women's 'thoroughly modern' interests in the latest labour-saving devices for the home actually increased their domestic workload in the long run. This was because essential housekeeping tasks were transferred from domestic servants to the housewife. It should be noted that the attraction of the self-service domestic economy was greatly enhanced for penny-conscious housewives as the cost of domestic labour-saving devices declined rapidly relative to the cost of domestic servants (Gershuny 1978). On the other hand, the cultivation of leisurely qualities and accomplishments did become more important in the identity and practice of bourgeois women. Leisureliness, simplicity of manner and self-confidence were associated with a modern outlook. '*Simplicity*,' Lady Troubridge (1926: 9) declared stoutly, 'that's the key word for social demeanour nowadays'[15] (emphasis in the original). Simplicity and a relaxed manner were part of the behavioural components of the informalization of relations between the sexes which occurred between early and late capitalism. They were evident not only in relations between the sexes within the home but also in women's deportment in public spaces. The next section of the chapter takes up this question and examines it at length.

WOMEN AND PUBLIC SPACE

Early capitalism restricted the movement of bourgeois women in public space. There were several reasons for this. Among them, it was claimed was the fear of robbery or sexual attack. The metropolitan street was regarded as a place of menace. Unchaperoned women tempted fate by going out alone. Poorly lit, unpaved and littered with nuisances, the metropolitan street was also seen as a place where injury and disease might befall 'the angel of the household'. The cholera epidemics of the 1820s and 1830s were explicitly seen as plagues of the street (Mort 1987: 13–16). The bourgeois association of menace and plague with the metropolitan street were also symbols of deeper, class-based fears of degradation and pollution. For the street was the habitat *nonpareil* of the working class. It was part of the 'exterior', part of the unnatural, chaotic world of society, and its inhabitants were seen as nomads, wanderers, and primitives. Mayhew (1861: 29–30), in his famous survey of London streetfolk, identified six 'genera or kinds':

I   Street Sellers
II   Street Buyers
III Street Finders
IV Street Performers, Artists and Showmen
V   Street Artisans, or Working Pedlars
VI Street Labourers

Streetfolk were assumed to be bound by morals and manners which were looser and rougher than those of 'civilized' society. Contrary to all empirical evidence, they were assumed to be physically robust, and, by reason of their lower intelligence, to possess strong sexual desires (Marsh 1986: 79; Thompson 1988: 258).

Bourgeois anxieties about 'the residuum', the mass of seasonal labourers and unemployed bodies, immigrants, low purveyors of vice and sedition, have already been mentioned (see pp. 37–9). What should now be added is that these anxieties concerning the alleged immorality of the lower classes were ambivalent and contradictory. Behind the outward disapproval was a fascination with the endlessly growing, ever-changing body of working-class life. Both Benjamin (1983: 45–6) and Bataille (1962: 164) have commented that the crowded metropolitan street was experienced as a place of erotic possibility. In the male bourgeois mind, the street held the promise of chance encounters with romantic or sexually knowledgeable women. On the other hand, it was precisely male awareness of the seductive possibilities of the street which motivated them to restrict the movements of their womenfolk in public. For the street threatened to pierce the male monopoly over the emotional and erotic dependence of the wife upon her husband. The association of the street with assignation, seduction and sexual opportunities made it figure prominently in the erotic fantasies of bourgeois men and women (de Swaan 1981: 364).

In trying to understand the place of the metropolitan street in the sexual fantasies of the bourgeois class it is helpful to follow a distinction made by Theweleit (1987: 90–228). He argues that bourgeois male fantasies about women centred on two archetypes. 'The White Woman' served man's needs, supported his endeavours and withdrew into the home. The 'Red Woman' threatened male composure, tormented male self-control and rejected female submissiveness. Before 1850 the iconography of the 'Red Woman' was indelibly established in the male Romantic tradition. For example, Keats's enthralling vision of *La belle dame sans merci*, Heinrich Heine's pitiless siren, the Lorelei; and Prosper Mérimée's diabolical gipsy, Carmen, were all destroyers of men (Gay 1984: 201). They figured prominently as alluring images in male middle class daydreams and sexual fantasies, (and also, perhaps, in the demonology of bourgeois women). What do these images of women have in common? They are all young, beautiful, independent, intensely sexual, manipulative, untrustworthy, captivating, heartless and foreign. The latter quality may be regarded as the key to the others. For in being foreign, they were of a different style and a different nature to the middle-class 'White Woman' whose restrained and disciplined feminity typified the bourgeois interior.

The quest for the erotic power and licence of 'Red Woman' was not, of course, confined to the pages of literature. The history of travel shows that the Western association between the Orient and sex was uniform and longstanding.[16] The lure of 'sexual promise, untiring sensuality, unlimited desire, deep generative energies,' drew a stream of male travellers to the Orient (Said 1978: 188; Kabbani 1986: 26–7). They yearned for the experience of unrestrained sexual desire, which only an infidel, alien culture was thought fully to provide. By the same token, they sought to escape what the Victorian adventurer and explorer, Sir Richard Burton called, 'the life of European effeminacy' (Brodie 1967: 106).

However, long-distance travel was only a realistic option for the rich or those who were not committed to the professional or business life of bourgeois society. Middle-class men of humbler means raked for 'Red Women' in the 'foreign' cultures of their own society, the cultures of the 'exterior' which the bourgeoisie had not succeeded in 'making after their own image' (Marx and Engels 1848: 39).[17] The spatial location of these cultures was, of course, the street. Prostitutes and proletarian women were the definitive women of the streets. In the bourgeois mind the fact that these women were forced to work for a living meant that they were closer to degradation. There is no doubt that they were the embodiment of the 'Red Woman' for middle-class men. It is difficult to give accurate figures on the scale of sexual contact between middle-class men and proletarian women. A Metropolitan police survey of 1857, published in Acton's famous book *Prostitution*, estimated that there were some 8600 prostitutes active in London. However, this is almost certainly an underestimate. Police estimates depended on data assembled from court cases and therefore ignored prostitutes who traded successfully, discreetly and without police detection. An estimate published in the medical journal, *Lancet*, also in 1857, put the number of prostitutes at 80 000 out of a total population in the city of 2 362 000 (Heath 1982: 12). Thompson (1988: 257–8) submits that the overwhelming majority of their clients were working-class men. However, he goes on to note that middle-class clients were a sizeable minority.[18] Whatever the real size of the figures, bourgeois male curiosity and sexual fantasies at the prospect of 'slumming' with proletarian women is undeniable. For example, the anonymous, memoirs published in *My Secret Life* (1888), show a ravenous bourgeois interest in the male use and abuse of lower-class women. Similarly, Arthur Munby's remarkable diaries and photographic studies of 'labouring women' testify to the same appetite.[19]

How did the 'Red' and 'White' archetypes influence the leisure of bourgeois women? The main point is that they limited the potential for recognition and membership between women of different classes. The restricted movement in public of bourgeois women meant that they had little direct contact or understanding of working-class conditions. The lady of the household could rely on servants to deal with tradespeople. It is striking that when contact began to increase after the 1860s,[20] the archetype of the Red Woman underwent a subtle change. Its class and racial character loosened somewhat and, to some degree, it was replaced by the scapegoating of independent women, regardless of their class. For example, Theweleit (1987: 63–70, 171–90) vividly describes male bourgeois and petit-bourgeois revulsion at female socialists and communists who dared to speak out against the ruling order of things. Another point is that the archetype of the 'Red Woman' reinforced bourgeois women's respect for work, thrift and sobriety. This was visible in the staid and restrained fashions of dress adopted by bourgeois women. For example, it was deemed to be intolerable for a respectable woman to be on the streets without a bonnet or a veil to protect her from prying eyes and to hide her blushes (Wilson 1985: 34). Reinforced respect for work, thrift and sobriety was also evident in the moral climate of the home. By the 1840s and 1850s the triumph of the bourgeois ideology of the family ensured that prostitutes in particular, were stigmatized as the most shameful incarnations of the female sex. The moral fervour against them also drew on the Puritan teachings of evangelicalism. Prostitutes were luridly described as debauched women whose lifestyle led inevitably to disease and early death. The irony is that, in addition to being relatively well-paid and well-dressed, most prostitutes enjoyed an independence and freedom from male control that would have been unheard of in the average bourgeois household. As the noted feminist historian, Jan Marsh remarked:

> Indeed, it is sometimes hard to understand why more girls did not take to the streets. Those who did, it may be noted, often lived together and supported each other in various ways, and it was not until late in the century that pimps and the oppression of 'organized vice' appeared, partly in response to the moralists' determination that any woman not visibly under the protection of a man could be defined as a prostitute. (1985: 145)

Be that as it may, the fallen woman certainly loomed larged as a spectre of female disgrace in the morality tales of the bourgeoisie. She symbolized the certain end of erring feminine ways, irresponsible conduct and the lack of moral fibre. Similarly, she cast a long shadow over the deportment and manner of women in public, constantly reminding them of the dangers involved in being too relaxed or over-familiar with men.

There are dangers in judging one century by the standards of another. Even so, the exercise can sometimes bring to focus points which might otherwise remain obscure. Today, the formalist sociology of leisure asserts that the *sine qua non* of leisurely practice is freedom, spontaneity, self-determination and flexibility.[21] From the standpoint of respectable feminine opinion in the early nineteenth century this assertion would be condemned. It would be seen not only as too venturesome, but also as sailing dangerously close to what was understood by the phrase 'loose woman'. For it was exactly the free, spontaneous, self-determining and flexible woman who was seen as being thriftless, irresponsible and dangerous: the Red Woman of bourgeois demonology.

We know that the restrictions on the movement of bourgeois women in public have dissolved. We also know that freedom, self-determination, spontaneity and flexibility have become esteemed attributes of the modern woman. How did this come about? The processes which contributed to the expansion of surplus in capitalist accumulation, and the increased velocity of commodity and data circulation and exchange, are too complicated to attempt to analyse here. They were connected to demographic, political, medical and social impulses in the development of capitalist society which present an even more formidable challenge for political economists to explain adequately. Some of the symptoms of change are less complicated to discuss. Among the most relevant, not to say double-edged, with regard to the emancipation of bourgeois women, was the rise of the department store.

At first sight one might ask what the rise of the department store has to do with the emancipation of bourgeois women's leisure time and leisure space? After all, shopping may be technically considered as an extension of women's work in managing the home. In most middle-class households the housekeeper did the buying, and the lady paid the accounts. The movement of the middle class to the gentility of the suburbs after the 1820s and 1830s, meant that goods tended to reach customers via a delivery system operated by retailers (Winstanley 1983: 53, 127). All of this implies that shopping in bourgeois society was a well-organized routine which obeyed the principle of minimum contact between the classes.

What the department store did was to break down the impersonality of exchange and make shopping a social event for leisurely women. The first department store is generally agreed to have been Bon Marché in Paris, which Aristide Boucicault took over in 1852. It was followed by Macy's in New York (1860), and Whiteley's (1863) and Harrod's (1868) in London[22] (Hamish Fraser 1981: 130-1; Winstanley 1983: 35).

It took time for the stores to acquire the reputation of luxury shopping. For example, *Bon Marché* was organised on the principle of bringing a variety of commodities under one roof. But its policy of high volume sales, low mark-up and rapid turnover meant that initially it was more like a warehouse than a temple of bourgeois culture (Sennett 1977: 142–3). However, retailers realized that the profits lay in attracting a loyal and wealthy bourgeois clientele. They did so by turning the store into a spectacle (Sennett 1977: 142–5; Chaney 1983: 24). The placement and display of commodities, the use of plate-glass and spotlights to frame desirable items, and the employment of specialist, deferential, trained staff in large numbers,[23] contributed to the association of department-store shopping with excitement, sensation an the *haut monde*. Sennett comments insightfully on the mythical aspects of this process:

> By mystifying the use of items in their stores, giving a dress "status" by showing a picture of the Duchesse de X wearing it, or making a pot "attractive" by placing it in a replica of a Moorish harem in the store window, these retailers diverted buyers, first, from thinking about how or even how well the objects were made, and second, about their own roles as buyers. (1977: 45)

Illuminated window displays contributed to the impact, sensation and excitement of the stores by projecting commodities from the interior of the stores to the exterior of society. Metropolitan experience of movement and association in the city centre began to approximate to the now-familiar context described by Schivelbusch (1988: 148) as, 'the illuminated window as stage, the street as theatre and the passers-by as audience'. The circulation of commodities as signs became part of the texture of big city life.

Once the style of department-store shopping became defined its attraction for the leisured class grew potent. Four points must be made. In the first place, as early as 1870 the leading stores had become the acknowledged showplaces of high fashion. Leisured ladies were drawn to them for examples of the latest and most elegant styles. Women's fashions between the 1870s and 1918 became more streamlined and less fussy. Designers and women became preoccupied with the total look of women's clothes, whereas before the fashion focus had been on the quality of each individual garment which was worn to produce separate, slow appreciation in the viewer. As opportunities for women grew in the employment market and sports participation, shorter skirts became more fashionable. This had more to do with making the female body more active-looking and mobile than increasing women's sexual attraction. Exposing a woman's legs emphasized her body as a means of locomotion rather than as a study of repose. Art nouveau and Art deco defined the look of the new woman (Hollander 1980: 328–38). The increased velocity and circulation of information brought about by developments in media technology and distribution, especially the greater use of fashion photography in women's magazines, made knowledge and expression of the latest fashions an important part of the modern bourgeois woman's self-image. However, the shop windows and the women's departments in the most prestigious stores became the places where women inspected the latest designs, tried them on, and purchased them.

The second point that must be made is that department-store shopping had an image of not only being leisurely but also 'civilized'. The prices were fixed, and women were encouraged to enter the store without any obligation to buy. So bourgeois women had no fear of the vulgar and unseemly practice of haggling. In addition, the stores had provided new employment opportunities for large numbers of women from middle-class and lower-middle-class backgrounds. So bourgeois customers had the expectation of being served by 'decent' people, rather than by representatives of the untrustworthy and dangerous lower orders (Chaney 1983: 25, 28–9).

The third point is that access to department stores became relatively easy and safe after the 1860s. The rail services from the suburbs and provinces, the greater use of street lighting, paving and police patrols, combined to make travel to the leading stores quite hazard-free. Some train services virtually eliminated the possibility of bourgeois travellers coming into dangerous or degrading contact with the lower classes. For example, in the closing decades of the century the businessmen's express trains linking Brighton to London admitted only first class passengers (Chaney 1983: 26; Schivelbusch 1980: 188–97).[24]

The fourth and final point is that the department store contributed to the erosion of the bourgeois 'separation of the spheres' and promoted opportunities for recognition and membership between women of the same class. As Wilson puts it:

> In a very real way the department store assisted the freeing of middle-class women from the shackles of the home. It became a place where women could meet their women friends in safety and comfort, unchaperoned, and to which they could repair for refreshment and rest. (1985: 150)

Retailers encouraged the association of leisureliness with depart-ment-store shopping by providing cloakrooms, lavatories and re-freshment rooms.

Although there can be little doubt that the rise of the department store liberated bourgeois women in some ways, it is equally true that in other ways it reinforced women's traditional role in bourgeois society. Hence, my comment made above that the department store was one of the most relevant but double-edged symptoms of wo-men's emancipation. For what was the effect of cultivating leisureli-ness in store service and decor if not to create a 'home from home'? That is, an extension of the bourgeois interior to the public realm in which women's traditional role as home-makers, consumers and objects of male desire were stressed over their capacities as produc-ers and independent agents. Whatever escape the department store offered women from the routine of the bourgeois interior, and as we have seen, the experience of escape *was* genuine, it never really challenged the sexual division of labour authorized by the dominant male culture. This was one reason why department stores lost their reputation for being at the vanguard of the latest thinking on fashion and desirable objects after 1910 to specialist luxury retail outlets. By the time that Selfridge's opened in 1909 the heyday of the depart-ment stores had passed. They adopted the role of quality emporia of artefacts for the middle class that we know today.[25]

Sociologists are often criticized for being over-deterministic in their explanations of social events and relations. My discussion of the opening-up of public space for women after the 1860s may be taken to invite the same charge. For what does my emphasis on capitalist accumulation, circulation and exchange in freeing bour-geois women bring to mind if not the image of social actors being carried along helplessly by unplanned, unintended processes which were not of their own making? Reification is undoubtedly one of the most common faults in attempts to understand society. In opposing it one must stress with Garfinkel (1967) and other writers, the prac-tical knowledge and skills of human actors in 'making their own history'.[26] Thus, the changing balance of power between the sexes in the bourgeois home after the 1860s and the breaching of the bour-geois 'separation of the spheres', involved women in making prac-tical choices, negotiating gender alliances and acting deliberately against male power. Women accomplished nothing in these areas without organization and struggle.

To underline the point it is useful to consider briefly the example of sport and women. Few types of male public space in early capitalism were protected more exhaustively and fiercely from female entry and participation than sport. According to McRone (1988: 147) the received (male) wisdom was that 'women who played men's games would jeopardize their femininity and physical and moral health'. The variety of risks that women faced by playing male games was extensive. For example, cricket was thought to make women deep-voiced and wide-shouldered; cycling was held to produce bow-legs, overdeveloped leg muscles, varicose veins, nasal disorders, depression, headaches, lassitude and coarse complexions; football was regarded to pose danger to the reproductive organs and breasts because of sudden twists and turns; hockey was alleged to inhibit breast-feeding (McRone 1988: 148, 179–8, 201; Mason 1988: 7). The source of these prejudices was the male belief that women were naturally more delicate and frail than men. Repose, not action, was felt to be the appropriate state of the female body and mind. Women were thought to be most emotionally fulfilled in cultivating the finer feelings rather than aping the male passions through participation in aggressive and competitive sports. A hard, taut, muscled female body conflicted with bourgeois ideals of women as soft, expansive creatures. To the bourgeois mind a prominent bosom and hip in a woman indicated her affinity for childbearing and nurturance. A narrow waist symbolised a capacity for self-control and self-denial (Ewen and Ewen 1982: 139). Where Nature erred, in not equipping women with the standard ideal, feminine art and guile were called upon to rectify matters. Several authors have commented upon the grotesque lengths to which women went to push, truss and deform their bodies in order to conform to the requirements of the male gaze (Hollander 1980: 108–14, 120, 121, 153; Sennett 1977: 187–9; Wilson 1985: 97–8). Sport, with its respect for aggression, assertiveness and courage ran against the grain of received bourgeois notions of women as graceful, submissive and gentle (Hargreaves 1989: 140).

All of this has been highlighted by feminist commentators on sport and leisure (Deem 1986; McRone 1988). They show that sexual physical differences were translated by men to mean the sexual superiority of men and the sexual inferiority of women in sport and leisure activity. On the other hand the struggle of men and women to overcome male barriers against female participation in sport and leisure should not be minimized. The convening of women and men, conducted to the purpose of rebutting male prejudice, did open up opportunities for women. For example, the Ladies All England Lawn Tennis Championship was introduced at Wimbledon in 1884; the Ladies Cricketers Club was founded in 1893; the Ladies Golf Union followed in the same year; and in 1897 the first Ladies International hockey match was held. If changes in the structure and distribution of capitalist accumulation after the 1860s created new opportunities for the growth of female participation in sport, it was nonetheless human actors who exploited and developed these opportunities through their choices and actions.

WOMEN AND MEDICINE

Feminist historians have argued that the traditional medical view was that woman's passions were influenced by her sexual organs (Showalter 1985: 101–66; Digby 1989: 200–8). Nervous complaints, tension and irritability were diagnosed in terms of over-active sexuality. As Professor Laycock observed in his *Treatise on the Nervous Diseases of Women* (originally published in 1874):

> Women in whom the generative organs are developed or in action are those most liable to hysterical disease. Indeed, the general fact is so universally acknowledged, and so constantly corroborated by daily experience, that anything in the nature of proof is unnecessary. (Quoted in Digby 1989: 202)

The cure was 'voluntary' reduction in, or abstinence from, sexual activity. In extreme cases surgery was used to correct the symptoms. For example, Gardella (1985: 60) and Jeffreys (1987: 2) refer to the practice among some Victorian physicians of performing clitoridectomies as a cure for masturbation which was thought to be at the root of some forms of female mental disturbance.

The rise of the medical profession in the eighteenth and nineteenth centuries was associated with new perspectives on the body. Foucault (1981: 104, 146–7) wrote of 'they hysterization of women's bodies'. By this he meant the reconceptualization of the female body in terms of the new social responsibilities which women had for the moral development of their children, the continuity of the family and the preservation of society. Feminists have described the power of male-dominated medical ideology to regulate the conduct and freedom of women (Showalter 1981, 1985; Bernheimer and Kahane 1985; Jeffreys 1987; Digby 1989). The burden of the feminist case is that Victorian physicians did not so much discover the symptoms and causes of female pathology as produce them through male prejudice, ignorance and misunderstanding. For example, the most dreaded disease of the nineteenth-century leisured woman, the bourgeois wife and daughter, was hysteria. Why was it so dreaded? Because it signified the failure of self-discipline and symbolized excess and disorder in a society founded upon self-control and proper appearance. Hysteria, which has now virtually disappeared, is seen by feminists as a consequence of unrestricted sexual inequality.[27] Women, who were denied independent views, hopes and voices by men, were driven into states of madness. The luxury of the Victorian medical profession was to attribute this collapse in women's reason to the disorders of the female reproductive system. For in doing do, male doctors avoided confronting the brutal injustice of male power.

The feminist analysis of writers like Showalter (1985) and Jeffreys (1985, 1987) is brilliantly insightful. They expose the knots and binds of medical ideology and practice in the treatment of womens' complaints. Their work shows that our understanding and care of even such a personal object as the body is political. It reflects social values and social inequalities. The achievement is all the more remarkable when set against the background of the long tradition of male dominance in the academic study of history and society – a tradition which quite unequivocally operated to marginalize women's experience.

On the other hand, some feminists have warned against the sort of mechanical thinking which treats every nineteenth-century female patient of the medical profession as a victim. Thus, Mendus and Rendall (1989: 133) point out that although medicine was dominated by males, women were not entirely denied entry into practice. The growth in recruitment of women physicians helped to corrode the complacency of male prejudice in the profession. Although many counter-examples might be adduced to qualify the argument, it became more difficult for physicians to nominate the female sexual organs as the culprit in cases of female madness.

There is also the important question of the responses of female patients to consider. Not all of them accepted the diagnosis and labels attributed to them by their doctors. In order to clearly understand the mechanisms of counter-action and rebellion a brief digression into the field of medical sociology is called for. Sociological analysis of sickness and medical treatment has been influenced by the sociology of Parsons (1951). In particular, his concept of the sick role has received much attention. According to Parsons, all forms of sickness involve a social dimension as well as a biological dimension. He formulated the concept of the sick role in order to clarify this social dimension. It consisted of four features. The first feature of the sick role is that it involves the legitimate withdrawal from the obligations of everyday life. Withdrawal is presented as the necessary condition for recovery. The second aspect of the role is that the sick person volunteers responsibility for treatment and cure to professional helpers, e.g. doctors and nurses. The third feature is the acceptance by the sick person that withdrawal and the answer of responsibility for treatment are motivated by the goal of getting better. Embracing the sick role means accepting the professional recommendations of helpers. The fourth feature is contacting a qualified doctor and asking for help.

Criticisms of Parsons's concept have centred upon four points (see Turner 1987: 45–9). In the first place, the concept of the sick role falsely isolates the doctor–patient relationship from the network of social relationships in which a sick person is involved. The crux of the matter here is that lay referrals by the sick person with friends, relations or other contacts may carry more weight than the doctor–patient relationship in effecting treatment and cure. The second point is that Parsons assumes that all of the power in the sick role lies with the doctor. Patients are presented as the passive recipients of professional care. In fact, patients always have a degree of power to deflect, redefine, marginalize or reject professional advice. I will come back to this point when I consider the case of nineteenth-century female invalidism later in the section. The third critical point is that Parsons's assumption that the sick person must believe that treatment will lead to recovery simply ignores the wide range of chronic illnesses which cannot be cured. These range from terminal illnesses to illnesses of progressive disability such as multiple sclerosis or incipient blindness. The fourth and final criticism is that Parsons is rather too generous in assuming that social factors like class, gender or status do not enter the doctor–patient relationship. They influence treatment and cure in ways which Parsons simply never discusses.

If one were to search for an example of Parsons's concept of the sick role, one could find none better than the nineteenth-century rest cure. As described by Bassuk (1986: 139–51), this was developed in the 1870s by S. Weir Mitchell to treat soldiers suffering from battle fatigue. However, its medical reference to nervous complaints meant that it was soon taken up by physicians dealing with mental disorders in women such as hypochondria, hysteria and neurasthenia. As Parsons's concept of the sick role suggested, the rest cure was based in the patient voluntarily surrendering control to the physician. Treatment consisted of the withdrawal of the patient from everyday life, and providing rest and seclusion. This was accomplished, in the first instance, by confining the patient to bed for six weeks to two months. Doctors assumed responsibility for the diet, cleaning and toilet of the patient; they also determined the number of visitors she could have. As the patient improved she was subject to a programme of moral re-education into normal life. Physicians determined programmes of order for the day, including set times and periods for rest, leisure, meals and sleep.[28] The abuses of the practice are not lost on Bassuk:

> Imagine such a treatment. Under the paternalistic, authoritarian control of a male physician, the Victorian woman regressed physically and emotionally. Isolated from her family and children and her usual responsibilities, she was put to bed and taught complete submission; even her arms and legs were moved for her. Every orifice was invaded – by vaginal douches, enemas and milk feedings. Then when she was fatter and ruddier, she was told what to think and how to express her thoughts. (146)

Whatever metaphorical significance such a line of argument has, it is open to the same major criticisms made of Parsons's concept of the sick role. That it, it exaggerates the power of the doctor (for example, by ignoring the lay referral system) and underestimates that of the female patient to manipulate the situation. Indeed the role of hypochondria, hysteria and neurasthenia in mid-nineteenth-century class and gender relations was far more complicated than Bassuk's discussion of the rest cure suggests. Given the conventions of bourgeois domestic life, bourgeois women could use the excuse of nervous illness to escape from an unwanted suitor or unpleasant family duties. For example, it is widely agreed that Florence Nightingale, who took to her bed for virtually the rest of her life after returning from the Crimea, did so to avoid being assailed by her demanding

family. Her retreat from the responsibilities of family life enabled
her to organize campaigns for the reform of public health provision
and military organization. Similarly, Christina Rossetti, the poet and
sister of the Pre-Raphelite painter Dante Gabriel Rossetti, confirmed
in later life that her adolescent illnesses had been a ruse to prevent
her parents from sending her away to become a governess – a station
in life which she loathed. Jan Marsh, the feminist historian, sums up
the situation of the mid to late nineteenth-century female invalid
with an admirable sense of balance:

> While it may be that invalidism was foisted on Victorian women
> to prevent them from asserting themselves, it is also true that it
> could be used to secure a position of leisure and privilege. The
> chief forms of treatment prescribed and taken were often pleasent
> ones: 'special diets', continuous rest and frequent 'changes of air'
> or holidays at spas and by the sea. Illness of this kind was not of
> course faked, nor consciously sought: most sick women must
> undoubtedly have suffered genuine and sometimes severe pain.
> But there could be compensations and in some cases it may be
> said that by succumbing to the notion of the immobile, incapable
> invalid, some Victorian women freed themselves from other prob-
> lems and disabilities. Sickness conferred status, and a gratifying
> degree of attention. It offered protection from household chores
> and from criticism, especially, if embellished with a saintly refusal
> to voice any complaints or fear. (1986: 80)

Marsh is pointing to the contradictions of male power. For example,
there is a contradiction between the attempt of male doctors to limit
autonomy and self-control in their female patients, and the use that
some invalids made of this situation to gain autonomy, control and
leisure, not least from the demands of their husbands, children and
other family members. Marsh shows that helplessness was not the
inevitable lot of the female invalid. Her discussion emphasizes the
variety in nineteenth-century class and gender relations, and suggests that received ideas of dependence and authority in the bourgeois marriage were exploited by women to expose the injustices
and anomalies of male power. And this is something that emerges
only tenuously in, or is entirely absent from, mainstream feminist
accounts of medicine and women, to say nothing of the mainstream
in the feminist sociology of leisure.

CONCLUSION: FEMALE FORCE/MALE RESISTANCE

In tagging the growth of the market and the metropolis to the empowerment of women as I have done in this chapter, there is a danger. The danger is that the narrow male ideas of leisure, which feminists have done so much to discredit, will be vindicated. Already there is evidence of male resistance to feminism in mainstream social theory. A case in point is John Carroll's (1985: 178–90) troubled discussion of 'matricidal culture'.[29] He defines modern Western culture as anxious, guilt-ridden and insecure. Like many right wing critics, he diagnoses the welfare state as the cause of these symptoms. Its attempts to produce universal financial security and care from the cradle to the grave has produced chronically dependent personalities who lack initiative, will and the ability to stand on their own two feet. Carroll equates the welfare state with the triumph of feminism:

> The Welfare State is the leading example of the female value of compassion having run amok, in a perverted form . . . Matricidal culture produces men who do not stand anywhere, who therefore cannot take responsibility: these men force their frustrated women to take a whip to them. (1985: 175)

A legitimate question from feminists to this thunderous argument might be, why should the triumph of the female produce guilty, anxious and insecure personalities? Carroll anticipates the question, and answers it in the following terms:

> The fundamental feminine anxiety is of inner barrenness, of being dirty, polluted or ruined inside. This anxiety is biologically determined, although its surface symptoms vary from culture to culture. A women will project this anxiety on to her external environment, especially on her own body and her home and family. She thus tries to ensure that the outside for which she is responsible is clean and pure, in the hope that the inside will be the same. A fresh complexion, a beautiful body, clean and healthy children, and a lovely home are all encouraging counters to her fear of inner barrenness. (1985: 90–1)

Carroll's solution to what he sees as the malaise of Western culture is predictable. He wants to retract the influence of feminine values in public life and usher women back into their 'natural' habitat: the home. Interestingly, sport is one area that he singles out for special attention:

> Women should once again be prohibited from sport: they are the true defenders of the humanist values that emanate from the household, the values of tenderness, nurture and compassion, and this most important role must not be confused by the military and political values inherent in sport. Likewise sport should not be muzzled by humanist values: it is the living arena for the great virtue of manliness (1986: 98).

Feminists have rejected this argument (Hargreaves 1986); and so would many men. There is an alarming gap between the limited evidence which Carroll marshals to support his case, (and here one must note that much of his 'evidence' is highly speculative), and his ostensibly universal conclusions. Where Carroll's evidence is weakest, the readers' suspicion that sexism and elitism are the forces which carry his argument along is strongest. After all, what scientific evidence exists to support the assertion that the fundamental feminine anxiety is of inner barrenness? And where is the cast-iron defence for a fastidious view of 'manliness' and 'feminity' in a period in which not only sexuality, but identity, practice and association, are widely seen as fragmented, decentred and plastic?

We come then, to the question of identity, practice and association today. It is the question of the condition of *society*.[30] Anyone who has understood my discussion of the history of bourgeois women's leisure correctly, will know that the cultivation of leisureliness in the bourgeois household required a great deal of work. This was evident in the expenditure of labour by domestic servants which bought the leisure class free time. However, it was just as true of members of the leisure class who kept one eye on the financial accounts and the other on the fashions and styles circulating in the world beyond the brassbound door.

The reasons for this were unplanned and unintended. The growth of industrial capitalism increased the velocity of circulation of capital, ideas and bodies. Increased velocity of consumption was itself connected to structural changes in production and distribution. The effects on identity, practice and association were so penetrating that we are only now beginning to comprehend them. Simmel's (1907: 324–39) essay on 'The metropolis and mental life' provides a remarkably precocious guide to this matter. He pinpoints diversity and ceaseless activity as the key to understanding metropolitan existence. To enter the city is to enter the field of inexhaustible, rapidly changing stimuli. The social effect is twofold: selves experience a sense of liberation and possibility through the environmental dissolution of traditional, time-honoured restraints on behaviour; on the other hand, selves become levelled by the onslaught of impersonal standards, dehumanization and reification which accompanies big city life. Simmel identified various psychological responses to the ever-changing backcloth of the metropolis. They ranged from the quotidian fare of passing excitement and exhaustion to the extremes of neurasthenia (the permanent, crippling feeling of tension and unreleased desires) and the blasé attitude of continuous indifference and colourlessness.

Although in many respects Simmel's discussion remains profoundly illuminating and suggestive, he can hardly be allowed to have had the first word on the condition of nervousness in metropolitan life. For example, Marx and Engels (1848: 38) clearly identified nervousness, uncertainty and agitation as springing from the demolition of 'all fast, fixed, frozen relationships'; and they nominated the bourgeois metropolis as a forefront of the assault upon Nature (ibid 1848: 39–40). Similarly, Durkheim's (1897: 241–76; 1902: 353–73) discussion of anomie clearly harnessed psychological feelings of unease and self-destruction with the rapid, transitory character of metropolitan social relations.

Not surprisingly, the quest to make sense of these psychological and social effects emerged as the pre-eminent theme of social theory in the late nineteenth century. Marx, Durkheim and their successors aimed to build theoretical systems which would reveal the hidden laws of motion which governed the social totality. Moreover, these systems were not devised with a mere hermeneutic purpose in mind. They were also, quite unabashedly, managerialist in the scale of their ambition. The laws of motion governing the social totality were to be deciphered in order to diagnose the real nature of its ills and thus to effect remedies.

The spirit of this quest is very much intact in the feminist contributions to the sociology of leisure considered in this chapter. These contributions use male domination as a 'totalizing' concept to explore social reality. They locate pathologies in social reality and diagnose them as stemming from male power. Finally, they advocate remedies (positive discrimination/consciousness raising/imposing genuine equal rights and opportunities) to cure the ills of the social body.

Of course, feminist contributions are not unique in pursuing these objectives. Social formalists and neo-Marxists, albeit in diametrically opposed ways, have also approached leisure and society with the values of totality, the diagnosis of pathology and planned intervention, at the centre of their concerns.

What is odd is that these contributions should continue to champion these late-nineteenth-century values at a time in intellectual life when the values themselves have little credibility. Notions of social totality, *the* diagnosis of pathology and planned remedies for society was widely discredited for confusing social reality with ideology or metaphysics (Harvey 1989: 44–54). These notions are criticized for outliving the social conditions which gave rise to them. The social conditions of the present, the critics continue, are incompatible with strategies of central planning and regulation. Indeed, the very idea of a social totality which can be centrally acted upon is now seen as objectionable because it glosses over the diverse interests, values and norms that actually make up 'society'.[31]

If these criticisms are correct there is much in not only the feminist sociology of leisure, but also in formalist and neo-Marxist accounts that must be dispensed with. In particular, the received idea of leisure as freedom from work looks decidedly unconvincing, as does the whole work/leisure distinction. For 'work' and 'leisure' can no longer be seen as terms whose meanings are unambiguous. Instead they must be seen as terms in which a variety of meanings, none of them authoritative, merge and collide. Once this is allowed it becomes harder to make arguments of class domination and sexual repression prevail. For one can no longer assume that the 'working class' or 'women' constitute integral entities with common needs, wants, moods and interests. However, this is to make several important and controversial points in a compressed and unsupported way. The next chapter is given over to the task of beginning to make amends for these defects. It points to the inadequacies of notions of social totality, pathology and planned remedies of total change, by considering what they are said to have outlived: Modernity.

3
Disorganized Leisure?

Bourgeois culture was wedded to a rational view of work and leisure. It identified a structural dichotomy between work and leisure
in the organization of individual life-space and society. Work was
seen in every sense as the dominant partner. Through it, the individual was said to develop the disciplines of attention, application
and perseverance, and also to husband the dexterity necessary for
dealing with the affairs of ordinary life. As for society, work was
viewed as the fundamental principle of well-being and growth.[1] In
contrast, leisure, though of secondary importance, was seen as necessary for the health of the individual and society. Most commentators regarded leisure to be the reward for work. Furthermore, a
balance in favour of leisure over work was castigated as a moral and
social danger. In the words of Samuel Smiles:

> Leisure cannot be enjoyed unless it is won by effort. If it have not
> been earned by work, the price has not been paid for it. There
> must be work before and work behind, with leisure to fall back
> upon; but the leisure without the work, can no more be enjoyed
> than a surfeit. (1894: 93)

Marx recognized this view as a distinctive characteristic of capitalism. In the feudal mode of production work dedicated to self-
interest is not the fundamental principle of life. Work and pleasure
are tied more closely to the rhythms of life in the community. They
are not so polarized and the time given to them is not so regimented.
However, under capitalism:

> Pleasure is only a side issue – recreation – something subordinate
> to *production*; at the same time it is a *calculated* pleasure. For (the
> individual) debits it to his capital's expense account, and what is
> squandered on his pleasure must therefore amount to no more
> than will be replaced with profit through the reproduction of
> capital. Pleasure is therefore subsumed under capital, and the

97

pleasure-taking individual under the capital-accumulating individual. (Marx 1964: 157; emphasis his)

The subsumption of 'the pleasure taking individual' under 'the capital accumulating individual' serves as a powerful metaphor of the quality of work and leisure relations under capitalism. It is one which Weber (1930) was to echo later in his discussion of the protestant ethic thesis.[2] However, it was by no means exclusive. Marx himself compared bourgeois society to 'the sorcerer, who is no longer able to control the powers of the nether world whom he has called up by his spells' (Marx and Engels 1964: 41). And this consciousness of the bourgeois order of things gradually becoming more disordered and irrational became more pronounced under late capitalism (Sayer 1991: 122–51).

This consciousness is often illustrated with reference to the dramatic events of late capitalism, notably the mass slaughter in Europe during the two world wars. However, it is essential to understand that it was also part of the quotidian, ordinary relations of life. For example, as we saw in the last chapter, the authority of the bourgeois patriarch was increasingly weakened by the resistance of women, especially bourgeois women, and the circulation processes of capitalism (see 56–77). As for leisure, a parallel deviation from the bourgeois order of things under early capitalism can be observed. After the 1840s, the bourgeois class had sufficient capital to educate its children according to aristocratic principles of taste. Although their principles were redefined to conform to bourgeois standards of sobriety and industry they nevertheless recognized the notion that leisure activity is a crucial resource in the business of self-making. The revival of the Grand Tour for the sons of the industrial and commercial entrepreneurs reinforced the aristocratic view of travel as a means of broadening the mind and of developing the personality. Similarly, the growth of interest in collecting paintings, building libraries and acquiring property of distinction, and in accumulating cultured experience, served to increase the importance of cultivated leisure in the struggle for self realization.

By the turn of the century fears were being raised that the more pronounced role for leisure in bourgeois culture was weakening the fabric of society. For example, Veblen (1925) attacked the emptiness and wastefulness of free time activity in the bourgeois leisure class. He maintained that emulation by the lower orders would make the economy less productive and society less stable. The same sense of encroaching disintegration is evident in the critical commentaries on the growth of leisure by Cutten (1926) and Jacks (1932). They called for a return to the values of rational recreation. But this time these values were to be applied to the degenerate leisure class as well as to the lower orders. As Cutten (1926: 132) warned, 'a civilization which creates a leisure which it did not use in a rational manner is in greater danger of annihilation than one that has never obtained leisure'.

To put matters concisely, in the period of early capitalism bourgeois culture sought to lay down simple moral principles designed to achieve self-realization. Work was divided from leisure, private life from public life, the nation state from other nation states, men from women, in an attempt to produce a rational, stable order of things. But the development of bourgeois society ceaselessly undermined this order by turning principles into contradictions and divisions into chaos. To understand how this happened it is necessary to consider Modernity analytically. If it is correct to describe bourgeois culture as *the* culture of Modernity, it must also be noted that the tranquility of bourgeois culture was obstructed by the progress of Modernity. For by insisting on the necessity of continuous innovation as the spearhead of Modernity, bourgeois culture wrecked its claim to impose a secure and rational order of things in society.

The discussion that follows is split into three main sections. The first aims to clarify what we mean by the term Modernity and to show how bourgeois culture was bonded to it. The second section explores how the various circulation processes associated with modernity operated to undermine the bourgeois order of things. The third section describes the arguments recently made by many writers that we are currently living at a time in which Modernity is being replaced with Postmodernity. Throughout the discussion examples from leisure and travel practice it will be used for illustrative purposes.

MODERNITY

As Frisby (1985: 12) and others have pointed out, Modernity is an oblique concept, rich in paradoxes. Charles Baudelaire, who is credited with introducing the term in his 'The Painter of Modern Life', declared (1962: 13) that 'by "modernity" I mean the ephemeral, the fugitive and the contingent'. For Baudelaire, the distinctive quality of modern life is that the shock of the new has been incorporated as the continuous experience of the present. As Benjamin (1983) noted, several motifs emerged in Baudelaire's works to convey this quality of experience — the *flâneur*, the arcades, and the metropolitan crowd. However, the dominant motifs of modernity in Baudelaire's work are all abstract – restlessness, circulation, fragmentation and mystification.

Baudelaire was not alone in viewing modern society as riddled with change, opposition and illusion. As Frisby (1985: 11–37) observes, these themes emerged as the leitmotifs of modern social theory, linking the work of writers whose thought is in other respects diverse – Marx, Nietzsche, Weber, Durkheim and Simmel (see also Berman 1982: 87–111). Many contemporaries would have agreed with Marx and Engels (1848: 38), that the modern epoch is distinct from former times by 'constant revolutionizing of production, uninterrupted disturbance of all social conditions, everlasting uncertainty and agitation'. However, not everyone followed Marx and Engels in viewing these conditions as amenable to rational control by means of the extirpation of the bourgeois class through proletarian revolution. Baudelaire (1962: 12) recognized that the inevitable accessory of change, opposition and mystification under Modernity was a type of consciousness which desired to 'distil the eternal from the transitory'. But the expressions of this consciousness in the nineteenth and twentieth centuries took many different forms. For example, bourgeois culture was managerial and interventionist. It posited a universal ontology in society which emphasized individualism over collectivism and rationalism over irrationalism. Life was compartmentalized. The Interior was separated from the Exterior, Nature from Culture, Mind from Body and Work from Leisure. Maturity in the person was seen to be a matter of the atomized individual reaching consciousness of the 'rationality' of these divisions, and using this knowledge to pursue self-realization. Of course, bourgeois culture also recognized that change was fundamental to modern experience. Its heroic character lay in the perception of change as the opportunity for the exercise of firm leadership.

However, just because bourgeois culture took the from of speaking on behalf of others, it generated counter-cultures which refused to defer to the 'authorial' voice of the bourgeois class. In the late nineteenth and early twentieth centuries the most important counter-culture was, indisputably, socialism. It emphasized collectivism over individualism, labour over capital, and planning over the market. Bourgeois culture held that the pursuit of self-interest by the individual would advance the interests of all. Socialist culture rejected this argument. Instead, it insisted that the pursuit of self-interest ultimately simply intensified exploitation and the disorder of things. Socialists called for the application of science to discover and regulate the laws of motion in modern society.

Although both cultures were antithetical to one another, they occupied the same plane of consciousness in thinking about and acting upon Modernity. Both approached Modernity in technical terms as a set of social, economic and political processes which required the imposition of rational order. What is largely missing from both is the detailed investigation of the phenomenal forms of everyday life under Modernity. On this question, the claims that Georg Simmel should be considered as the first sociologist of Modernity must be taken seriously (Frisby 1985, 1990).

Simmel's sociology centres upon the inner life and the disruption of stable forms of experiencing time and space. In the metropolis and in the money form he finds haunting metaphors for the ceaseless circulation of bodies, values, commodities and information, the colourless acts of exchange, and the endless, superficial distractions which preponderate in modern experience (1907; 1971: 324–39). The metropolis, Simmel writes (1971: 329), 'stimulates the nerves to their utmost reactivity until they finally can no longer produce any reaction at all'. The city dweller becomes punchdrunk on an excess of stimulation and retreats into what Simmel (1971: 329) calls 'the blasé attitude'. The essence of this is 'an indifference toward the distinctions between things' (ibid.). Money reinforces this torpor by annihilating subjective distinctions between use-values and replacing them with exchange values. We experience a sense of invalidity and feel estranged from society. In Simmel's words:

> We feel as if the whole meaning of our existence were so remote that we are unable to locate it and are constantly in danger of moving away from rather than closer to it . . . The lack of something definite at the centre of the soul impels us to search for momentary satisfaction in ever-new stimulations, sensations and external activities. Thus it is that we become entangled in the instability and helplessness that manifests itself in the tumult of the metropolis, as the mania for travelling, as the wild pursuit of competition and as the typically modern disloyalty with regard to taste, style, opinions and personal relationships. (1907: 484)

Bourgeois culture in early capitalism sought to compartmentalize leisure time and leisure space from work time and work space. The design of the workplace and the management of work relations aimed to minimize distractions from the task of adding value through the expenditure of labour. At the end of the century this approach was formalized by F.W. Taylor in his principles of scientific management. In contrast, Simmel's discussion of the circulation processes in money and the metropolis suggests that compartmentalization is unsustainable. The one-sidedness and uniformity of the division of labour is at odds with 'the heterogeneous impressions' and 'the hasty and colourful change in emotions' in the streets and display areas of the metropolis.[3] The assertion of individuality and differentiation through fashion is in contradiction with the homogeneous style of life demanded by the work group.

In Simmel's sociology then, there is the acknowledgement that the attitudes and impressions formed outside the workplace crucially influence work relations. Work is not seen as an irresistible force, at the centre of life and totally insulated from home and consumption activity. Rather, Simmel (1971: 188) sees it soberly as part of 'the interlocking of life links' that make up modern everyday experience. There is surely a basis here for regarding Simmel as one of the first sociologists to criticize the conventional wisdom that leisure activity is of secondary importance. However, it would be wrong to conclude that Simmel associated leisure activity with personal fulfilment and life satisfaction. I have already referred to his discussion of the blasé attitude in response to metropolitan experience (see pp. 101). For Simmel, the tumult and distractions of the metropolis contributed to an increase in nervous life. It intensified the lassitude of modern human beings, which developed pathological forms in agoraphobia and neurasthenia (Frisby 1989: 80). The fragmentation of activities and spaces found a parallel in the internal fragmentation of the individual. The blasé attitude of the city dweller may be interpreted as a defence mechanism. Through inward retreat and remoteness the individual seeks to blockade the external stimuli which clamour for his or her attention. Simmel's work suggests that the ceaseless exchange and circulation processes within Modernity produce colourlessness and indifference in social relations. However, as Frisby (1989: 87–9) notes, his analysis of Modernity does recognize loopholes of escape. Through sociability and the adventure the individual can oppose the flatness of modern experience.

Sociability refers to the very simple interactions in which people engage positively. Examples, include the pleasure one experiences in the company of one's friends; the coquetry that occurs between the sexes; and the art of conversation. These activities are organized simply around the qualities of personality. They contrast with the flatness and colourlessness of Modernity.

The second form of experience which Simmel suggests runs counter to dominant movements in Modernity, is the adventure. The imagined possibility of adventure is identified by Simmel as part of the common stream of daily life. However, the experience of it is regarded by him as quite rare. It contrasts with everyday life, but it does not quite break free of this context. As Simmel puts it:

> While it falls outside the context of life, it falls within this same movement, as it were, back into that context again . . . it is a foreign body in our existence which is yet somehow connected with the centre. (1971: 188)

The adventure enables the individual to slip momentarily through the reality net of everyday life.[4] But if modern everyday life is to be at all possible the adventure must be momentary. The continuous experience of adventure would exhaust the nervous system and have pathological consequences. Significantly, the only examples which Simmel (1971: 190–1) gives of this are the gambler and the promiscuous personality – two types driven by a chance-ridden, endless quest.[5]

Simmel's discussion of Modernity conveys a clear sense of the disruption of traditional, stable forms of experiencing time and space. Modern culture, he remarked:

> Overcomes not only space but also time . . . this means that definite periods of time no longer determine the compelling framework for our activities and enjoyments, but rather they now depend only upon the relationship between the will and our ability and upon our purely objective conditions for carrying them out. Thus, the general conditions of life are freed from rhythm; they are more even and provide individual freedom and possible irregularity. The elements of regularity and diversity that are *united* in rhythm are now separated by means of this differentiation. (1907: 488; emphasis original)

As examples of disruption Simmel mentions the conquest of space through the communications and transport revolution and the increased control over Nature (1907: 476–91). More generally the compression of time and space influenced our perceptions of geographical and historical distance. In the discussion of heritage sites and time-space compression attractions which occurs in the next chapter I will try to illustrate how the leisure industry has exploited and developed these modern tendencies.

Simmel died in 1918. He therefore missed the full development of the telecommunications revolution and the improvements in transport, notably air travel, which occurred in the interwar period. These developments further disrupted our sense of the traditional necessities of time and space. Above all the cinematic image contributed to the dissolution of traditional categories of time and space. Appreciation of the antinomies of the mechanical reproduction of images through film received its first and in many ways, its sharpest expression in Benjamin's work (1955: 217–53). He certainly recognizes the liberating effects of moving images in opening up the world to our gaze. For example, he comments:

> Our taverns and our metropolitan streets, our offices and furnished rooms, our railroad stations and our factories appeared to have us locked-up hopelessly. Then came the film and burst this prison-world asunder by the dynamite of the tenth of a second, so that now, in the midst of its far-flung ruins and debris, we calmly and adventurously go travelling. (1955: 238)

The advent of mass communications is here seen as part of the democratization of objects and experiences, because it makes distant objects and experiences available to everyone.[6] Yet Benjamin's metaphors of liberation are unsettling: film 'bursts' our 'prison world' asunder by the 'dynamite' of the tenth of a second; we travel in its wake through 'far-flung ruins and debris' of a shattered world. These are metaphors of destruction. At the heart of Benjamin's troubled view is the concept of aura. In his study of Baudelaire, Benjamin (1983: 148) defines aura as 'the unique manifestation of distance'. The journey is therefore the indispensable requirement for maintaining aura. This is true in both the literal and metaphorical senses of the term. That is, Benjamin's discussion assumes that the particularity of the object or experience may require us to travel over great physical space to grasp its aura; likewise it assumes that we must be prepared to make an inner journey, to discharge everyday reality, in order to capture the aura of the object or experience that we seek. For Benjamin, the degenerative effect of mechanical reproduction is that simulacra inevitably make auratic objects and experience accessible. Once an object or experience becomes readily, effortlessly available it loses its capacity to make us question reality. Instead it becomes part of our reassuring grey background knowledge. It ceases to be challenging, precisely because it can be assumed that we already 'know' about it, or that we can 'possess' it with ease.

Simmel and Benjamin, albeit in very different ways, can be seen as developing phenomenologies of 'the ephemeral, the fugitive and the contingent' which, Baudelaire claimed, defined Modernity. For Simmel, money with its unavailing indifference to subjective culture, symbolized the blasé attitude. While the metropolis, the phantasmagoria of Modernity, symbolized the fractious, restless, irregular qualities of modern conditions. For Benjamin (1983: 165) Modernity is a dreamland dominated by 'the enthronment of the commodity and the glitter of distraction'. Where 'reality' is subject to so much embellishment, duplication and reproduction, the question of what is real and what is false cannot be resolved. Subjective experience is beset with doubt, melancholy and boredom. Although Simmel and Benjamin equip us with much of the necessary building blocks to produce an accurate picture of Modernity, they are not quite sufficient. Their work encourages us to view Modernity in terms of the disruption of stable, universal order of things. However, it does not pinpoint this order in any comprehensive way. If we are fully to understand the pathos of Modernity, we have to confront the comedy of bourgeois culture. For in both its bourgeois liberal and socialist incarnations, it sought to discover the alchemical principle that would 'distil the eternal from the transitory'. It shaped the experience of Modernity by attempting to impose a project upon Modernity. Whether the unfinished, mobile qualities of modern experience were understood in terms of the advance of bourgeois individualism or in terms of the forward march of labour, Modernity was presented as following a direction ordained by historical necessity.

What did it mean to possess experience in bourgeois culture? Bourgeois culture held that sober, rational consciousness was the only viable form of being. Of course, contrary forms of consciousness were recognized. Four, in particular, stand out. First, the experience of childhood: the 'polymorphous perversity' in the child which Freud discovered, outraged the bourgeoisie because it challenged the bourgeois myth of childhood as the stage of innocence in 'Man'. On the other hand, Freud's work also reinforced the bourgeois belief that childhood is a stage which must be overcome. The unpredictable mobility of childhood experience is a threat to the ordered existence of society because it undermines discipline and routine. Bourgeois society therefore organized childhood, into a series of evolutionary stages through which the 'healthy' child was required to pass. The vital rite of passage in the child's progress through these stages was the demonstration of receptivity to external discipline and the internalization of rational order.

A second contrary state of mind was recognized in adult life and was associated with fevered and distempered states of mind which were thought to be transient. Examples include states of mind associated with dreams, hypnosis, drugs, physical fevers and trances. A strong fringe interest in bourgeois society existed in the pursuit of 'the second self' in Man. This sunken existence was thought to be free of the normal restrictions of Reason and normal perception. It was evident, for example, in the interest shown in the writings of De Quincey and Coledridge in the liberating effects of opium (Berridge and Edwards 1987: 50–8); and also in the mania for Mesmerism (Tartar 1988: 121–271).[7]

A third contrary state of mind which came to increasingly fascinate bourgeois society, referred to madness. Traditionally, madness was understood as 'a mark of Man's fallen state, vitiated by sin, folly and pride' (Porter 1981: 110). Foucault (1975) asks us to consider the eighteenth century as the age of 'the great confinement'. To the bourgeois mind, the woe of madness was that it incapacitated the adult individual from playing a full part in everyday life and therefore condemned the individual to idleness. The mad were therefore incarcerated, removed from the market of opportunities and temptations, and subject to the rule of Reform.

The fourth and final contrary state recognized in bourgeois society referred to inter-personal forms of consciousness such as collectivism, nationalism and religion. It might be thought that these forms conflict with the premise of the atomized individual for they point to supra-rational forms of consciousness. However, this would not be correct. This is because bourgeois culture regarded these supra-individual forms not as preceding individual consciousness nor as being external to it. Rather they were perceived in terms of collective agreements that rational, sober individuals reached in struggling to come to terms with the 'facts' of life. What rational man, asked bourgeois theorists, can look at the innate order of Nature and see in it anything other than the hand of God? And what rational man can see in the interests of his country something which is contrary to the interests of himself?

These four forms of consciousness were seen as subordinate and inferior to the sober, rational form through which experience was organized and mediated. It reached its highest expression in the ideology of scientism which dominated society from the 1840s to the early 1900s. Knight (1986: 5) defines scientism as 'the idea that science is the guide to all reasoning and will provide answers to all questions which can reasonably be asked'. Underlying it was the belief that scientists would gradually uncover all of the eternal truths about Man, Nature and the Universe. Scientific consciousness, it was argued, would produce knowledge which is more certain and of more practical use in controlling the world than any other form of consciousness.

It is important to emphasize that scientism represented a sharp break with traditional forms of association and thought. The prescientific mind placed Man at the centre of the universe. All of the values, from the base elements of the dark and imperfect earth to the sublime heavenly spheres, were arranged in perfect, immovable hierarchical unity. The purpose of life was imposed upon Man by divine will. Man lived to realize the God-given spark of divinity within him. This essentially static model of existence was, of course, reinforced by the social hierarchy which consisted of fixed estates and the economy which was based in agriculture and therefore obeyed time-worn seasonal rhythms (Huizinga 1924: 30–64; Pirenne 1936: 58–84, 169–89; Lovejoy 1964: 59–60, 101–3). Scientism defined itself in opposition to all of this. Man acknowledged no fixed order in society. A relativistic view of values, including values of time and space, replaced the absolutist one of the prescientific mind. Man ceased to regard himself as the vehicle of divine purpose, or as bound by ritual and tradition. Instead he regarded the purpose of life as acting upon the world in order to bring it into line with the priorities of the mature rational self. 'One's life,' remarks Oestereicher (1979: 614), 'is now defined as an individual responsibility. Man is what he makes himself.'

Nowhere was this process of self-making more evident than in the bourgeois attitude to Nature. The Enlightenment *philosophes* identified Reason as the active principle in human evolution. The development of bourgeois society did not merely divide Reason from

Nature, it required the former to dominate the latter. Land, sea, air and the animal world were viewed as objects upon which the mastery of Reason must be exercised.

We considered some of the effects of this division in the last chapter when we examined the bourgeois construction of the respectable 'white' woman and the management of the bourgeois interior. However, the division between Reason and Nature exerted a comprehensive effect in bourgeois society in shaping experience. Bourgeois culture committed itself to the goal of governing Nature and imposing Rational order upon society. It aimed to harness the ceaseless change of Modernity as an asset in the realization of character and the advance of society.

The comedy and, ultimately, the tragedy of this project lay in the assumption that the voice of bourgeois culture was nothing less than authorial. That is, it was viewed as having the right to speak for everyone because bourgeois Reason was seen to be exclusive in leading civilization forward. Upon this premise, the whole ideological might of the bourgeois machine of moral regulation was constructed. Its purpose was to stifle difference, to transform the working population into a mass of docile bodies fit for regular, efficient labour and to legitimate the bourgeois programme of living as the sole means of improvement.

Let us now look at two examples of how bourgeois Reason organized subjects, transforming history into 'nature' with ease, and asserting bourgeois dominance without pause: education and travel. Bourgeois culture possessed a keen appreciation of the political and personal advantages of education. For example, the Clarendon Commission, charged with the brief of examining the strengths and weaknesses of the public schools, concluded:

> These schools have been the chief nurseries of our statesman, in them, and in schools modelled after them, men of all the various classes that make-up English society, destined for every profession and career, have been brought up on a footing of social equality, and have constructed the most enduring friendships and some of the ruling habits of their lives; and they have had perhaps the largest share in moulding the character of an English gentleman. (1864: 56)

The Commission's stress on the equality and openness of the public schools was at odds with the perceptions of educational reformers who saw in the working class 'a mighty body of people' unable to awaken to 'the consciousness of the giants' power' of industry, for want of a capable intellect 'to regulate and direct it' (*Fraser's Magazine* 1849: 39).[8] Educational reform was seen as the method of raising the skills and capacities of the masses and promoting social harmony. As Robert Owen (1857: 130) declared in his *Autobiography*, 'no people or population can be made good, intelligent and happy, except by a rational and natural education'. Dance, music and military drill were taught to the children in the new model community that Owen founded in New Lanark, in order to give 'grace to the body' and create peace and happiness in the mind' (Owen 1857: 142). However, the early experiments in educational reform rarely took so sanguine a view of the slumbering capacities of the masses. Rather, they tended to stress that education was the means of teaching obedience, deference, and discipline. For example, a Nottingham day school, founded in 1810, asserted that its task was to teach basic reading and writing and to accustom 'the children to habits of cleanliness, subordination and order'. The same loyalty to teaching deference to the masses was evident in the 1889 *Report* by the Nottingham School Board which set out the aims of the new working-class evening schools. The report claimed that the schools would bring about 'less crime and poverty, quieter streets, more self respect and more respect for others' (Wardle 1970: 25–6). Similar claims were made by exponents of rational recreation after the 1870s. They bemoaned what they saw as the excess, indulgence and violence of lower-working-class leisure activities. They attempted to regulate these activities by licensing laws for the consumption of alcoholic beverages, for the playing of music and dancing, and for the censorship of what could be performed in music halls (Cunningham 1980: 168–70). Organized sport and leisure, they argued, would impart a sense of duty, discipline and *espirit de corps* to the boys of the streets (Gibbon 1934: 46; Springhall 1977: 22–36, 71–84). Educational reform and rational recreation were geared to managing consent and conformity in the masses. They conveyed a spirit of self-improvement which was useful because it gave the workers something to aim for. However, in reality, it taught the masses to be stoical rather than ambitious, and to cleave to respectability rather than revolution.

But what of the place of leisure in the schooling of the middle-class child? How did their education equip them to experience 'free time'? Here, the cases of bourgeois prodigies are revealing. Bourgeois society loved success, especially when it was accomplished through self-discipline and self-denial. Prodigies like John Stuart Mill and John Ruskin were used by Victorian parents as parables of what self-help could accomplish. Yet when one examines the auto-biographies and other personal statements of these prodigies the picture becomes more equivocal. For example, by the age of three Mill (1937: 27) was 'committing to memory lists of common Greek words'. At eight years he was commencing to learn Latin and work-ing his way through Herodotus, Xenophon, Diogenes, Laertius and parts of Lucian and Plato; he was also becoming acquainted with the historical works of Hume, Robertson, Gibbon and Hook. As for Ruskin, at three years old he was given daily Bible readings and instruction in the Classics. By his eighth birthday, he was allowed academic history and the philosophy of religion (Abse 1980: 21–9; Hunt 1982: 28–35). The amassing of facts left little time for play or contact with other children. As Mill remarked:

> No holidays were allowed, lest the habit of work should be bro-ken and a taste for idleness acquired. I had ample leisure in every day to amuse myself; but as I had no boy companions, and the animal need of physical activity was satisfied by walking, my amusements, which were mostly solitary, were, in general, of a quiet, if not a bookish turn, and gave little stimulus to any other kind of mental activity than that which was already called forth by studies. (1937: 27–8)

This sense of solitariness was nothing but the expression of bour-geois individualism which counted self-reliance and rational sobri-ety among the essential virtues of civilization. Yet it should not be allowed to obscure the fact that the bourgeois prodigy was, in fact, never alone. The idea of the self-made prodigy was a myth. Behind every prodigy stood an industrious, and occasionally, tyrannical parent who guided, cajoled and pushed the child along the path of excellence. As Mill wrote of his father:

> He used, as opportunity offered, to give me explanations and ideas respecting civilizations, government, morality and mental cultivation, which he required me afterwards to restate to him in my own words. He also made me read, and give him a verbal account of, many books which would not have interested me sufficiently to induce me to read them myself; among others Millar's Historical View of English Government, a book of great

merit for its time, and which he highly valued; Moshiem's Ecclesiastical History, McCrie's Life of John Knox, and even Sewell and Rutty's Histories of the Quakers. (1937: 11)

Where guidance stops and indoctrination begins is, of course, a question that has to be faced in any system of education. Mill's experience suggested an ambitious father who always knew best – pushing his enthusiasms, convictions, judgements and prejudices down the throat of his dutiful son. However, on the other hand, one should not underestimate the degree to which these parents saw themselves as acting out of a sense of responsibility for the common good. The parents of prodigies often held lofty views about where the accomplishments of their children might lead. Thus, John James Ruskin addressed his son on the occasion of his tenth birthday in these portentuous words:

> You are blessed with a fine capacity and even Genius and you owe it as a Duty to the author of your Being and the giver of your Talents to cultivate your powers and use them in his Service and for the benefit of your fellow Creatures. You may be doomed to enlighten a People by your Wisdom and to adorn an age by your Learning. It would be sinful in you to let the powers of your mind lie dormant through idleness or want of perseverance when they may at their maturity aid the cause of Truth and Religion and enable you to become in many ways a Benefactor to the Human Race. (Quoted in Abse 1980: 24)

Bourgeois culture was forever going on about the value of rest and the importance of taking time off for one's peace of mind. However, the experience of Mill and Ruskin suggested that when bourgeois education was distilled in its most concentrated form it vaporized the ideas of rest and relaxation. Their leisure did not consist of the suspension of activity, but rather the mediation of activity into a different mode of being. Above all, their leisure was self-conscious activity affixed to the purpose of self-development and ultimately, self-realization. Moreover, this interpretation is confirmed if one examines the ethos of training which prevailed in the public schools and later the voluntary and state sector working-class schools. When one examines leisure in these institutions it is not rest and the absence of activity that strike one, but rather the intensity of activity. The games ethic, informal play practice and the plethora of clubs

and associations point to the educational value of leisure as a supplement to work activity, another arena of self improvement (Wardle
1970; Mangan 1981).

The same sense of self-consciousness is evident in the bourgeois
attitude to travel. The aristocratic tradition of the Grand Tour established the idea of a period of 'intelligent wandering' in Europe as the
indispensable part of a Gentleman's education. Travel was expected
to confer polish, sophistication and grace to the young nobleman
(Vale 1977: 73–82; Feifer 1986: 95–136). The Napoleonic wars broke
the tradition of the Grand Tour and the aristocratic travel culture
which surrounded it. However, after the 1830s a wealthy, ambitious
bourgeois class anxious to acquire culture and sophistication was
poised to restore the tradition. The aristocratic Grand Tour associated Greece and Italy with cultural elevation and enlightenment.
Although the general view in bourgeois society was that bourgeois
culture had nothing to learn from the 'backward societies' and everything to teach, it made exceptions with Greek and Roman culture.
Greece and Italy were the only countries in which the bourgeois
class allowed that 'the graces of superior civilization were acquired
rather than imparted' (Pemble 1987: 60). They figured prominently
in most tourist itineraries. The only serious rival to these destina-
tions was, of course, the Holy Land. What did the bourgeois traveller
expect to find in these places? In a world of increasing tumult, hurry
and uncertainty they expected to find the infinite and the eternal.
These locations were endowed with theological significance in bourgeois culture. Visiting them was seen as being tantamount to directly
encountering the origins of Western civilization. Goethe, upon entering Rome in 1786, wrote of his first encounter with the Holy City
in terms of stunned self-consciousness:

> All the dreams of my youth have come to life; the first engravings
> I remember – my father hung views of Rome in the hall – I now
> see in reality, and everything I have known for so long through
> paintings, drawings, etchings, woodcuts, plaster casts and cork
> models is now assembled before me. Wherever I walk, I come
> upon familiar objects in an unfamiliar world; everything is just as
> I imagined it, yet everything is new. It is the same with my
> observations and ideas. I have not had a single idea which was
> entirely new or surprising, but my old ideas have become so
> much more firm, vital and coherent. (1962: 129)

Thousands of bourgeois travellers who followed him in the nineteenth century to Rome, Greece and the Holy Land testified to the same feelings of going inside oneself towards some original point of being. People write of landscapes 'speaking' to them and of being 'drawn in' by a place. They attest to 'holy feelings' and 'overwhelming sensations' which remain in the memory for life. A passage from the notes of Piere de Coubertin, the founder of the modern Olympic games, upon visiting the ancient site of Olympia in 1896 may be referred to as an example:

> I kept watch for sunrise, and as soon as its first rays had crossed the valley, I rushed towards the ruins. Their smallness – owing on the one hand to the restrained proportion of the buildings and, on the other, to their crowdedness (this absence of open spaces so characteristic of Greek and Roman civilization, which is in striking contrast to Persian conceptions) – neither surprised or deceived me. It was a moral architecture I was going to gather lessons from, and it magnified every dimension. My meditation lasted all morning, while only the noise of the bells of the flocks on the way to Arcadia disturbed the silence. All morning long I wandered in the ruins. (Quoted in MacAloon 1981: 191)

Visiting these places was part of one's sentimental education.[9] It placed one at a distance from the mobile, unfinished qualities of modern life and offered the vividly felt charm of permanence.[10]

However, one should also remember that the bourgeois tourist visited ancient sites as a child of a culture dominated by Reason and the quest for rational order. It was not enough for them to visit a place, they had to authenticate it scientifically. Captain Charles Warren's excavations of the Holy Land (1867–70) and Heinrich Schliemann's (1870–90) archaeological digs in Ancient Greece, turned these landscapes into work-pits of science. The disruption met with the approval of an avid bourgeois readership who followed the progress of the digs in their daily newspapers. 'Those green mounds,' mused the Reverend Andrew Thomson in response to Warren's labours in the Holy Land, 'which every traveller may see in Palestine and in the Lebanon valleys, in all likelihood preserve ruins which only need the divining rod of science to bring them to surface, startling expectation, confirming faith (and) casting new gleams of light upon many an inspired sentence' (quoted in Pemble 1987: 193).

The anxiety about scientifically establishing the authenticity of a place reveals the bourgeois concern to acquire *real* experience through travelling. Bourgeois culture, with its fondness for parables, saw travel in terms of a story. Travel, it was thought, led to the accumulation of experience and wisdom. One began with nothing, but through guidance, diligence and commonsense one gained knowledge and achieved self-realization. The examples of Rome, Greece and the Holy Land imply that the bourgeois tourist sought self-discovery only in the ancient sites of Western civilization. While this was a very evident motive in bourgeois travel it would, of course, be exaggerating the point to suggest that it was the only motive. Hegel (1807), in *The Phenomenology of Spirit*, posited self-consciousness as an unfolding of rationality through a series of dialectical negations which confirmed identity in relation to 'otherness'. Similarly, the self-discovery of the bourgeois traveller was often attempted through a confrontation with what was viewed as the antithesis of Western culture: the Orient. The sirens of imagined sexual licence, architectural splendour and the secrets of the East, all lured the bourgeois traveller. A convincing case can be made that bourgeois culture's view of the Orient was nothing but a mass of Western-invented racial and sexual stereotypes (Said 1978; Kabbani 1986). But this mattered not a jot to the typical bourgeois tourist. Rather, like Nerval and Flaubert,[11] they wanted the imaginative experience that they believed the East would give them. The prize was not to get to know the people of the East, but to discover oneself. Thus, Flaubert (1983: 21) after encountering negro sorcerers, the Pyramids, abandoned temples, snake charmers, to say nothing of the 'ferocious *coups*' he engineered with Arabian courtesans, during his trip to Egypt in 1849–50, decided that he began his tour with the self-knowledge of a 'cadaver', but ended it with the self-knowledge of a 'surgeon doing an autopsy'.

One conclusion seems to be inescapable. Bourgeois culture regarded leisure and travel as activity for the stimulation and development of character. 'Spare' time experience was part of the project of self-realization, part of the world of action. As Smiles put it in his book on 'Character':

True happiness is never found in torpor of the faculties, but in their action and useful employment. It is indolence that exhausts, not action, in which there is life, health and pleasure. (1894: 92)

Where did this leave rest and relaxation in bourgeois society? The most powerful symbol of rest in bourgeois culture was the grave. In death, the individual was emphatically, incontrovertibly, 'at rest from earthly cares', 'all labours done'.[12] In life, the leisure of bourgeois men and women was driven by rational, respectable, self-conscious *activity*, and the sober consciousness that 'spare' time must not be wasted or squandered in idleness. Of course, since leisure did not involve the selling of one's time and labour to an employer, it was conducted in a different mode of sociation to work activity. However, just like work, leisure was seen as part of the self-conscious programme by which 'man makes himself'.[13]

Within bourgeois culture there was a degree of equivocation over the question of how far self-making could be applied to the lower orders. As we saw in Chapter 1 (see 00–00), 'the residuum' haunted the bourgeoisie as a horrifying image of Nature impervious to rational will. Even among enlightened bourgeois opinion there were profound misgivings about the capacity of the working class in general to benefit from the example of civilized Reason. Ruskin, who taught voluntarily and regularly at the Working Men's College in London between 1854 and 1858, eventually resigned from his post on the grounds that:

I ascertained beyond all question that the faculty which my own method of teaching chiefly regarded was necessarily absent in men trained to mechanical toil, that my words and thoughts respecting beautiful things were unintelligible when the eye had been accustomed to the frightfulness of modern city life.
(Ruskin's resignation letter of F.D. Maurice, 2 November 1867, quoted in Finke 1985: 125)

Is this not tantamount to a confession of defeat? And can one not detect in it echoes of the turmoil at the heart of bourgeois culture, namely the fear that the bourgeois order of tings could not be universally applied? Certainly, within the ranks of the working class, notably among skilled workers, there was recognition of the violence implicit in the bourgeois project of self-realization. For rational recreation not only forced a uniform set of values upon the subordinate class, it offered a nebulous state of self-improvement instead of the redress of material inequalities. Byington, in her ethnography of the Carnegie steel plant at Homestead near Pittsburgh, found widespread disaffection among the workers at local programmes of rational recreation. 'When speaking of the Carnegie library,' observed Byington (1909: 651), 'men often said to me "We didn't want him to build a library for us, we would rather have higher wages and spent the money ourselves."' However it is misleading to explain the tendency of experiencing leisure as disorganized, imposed or irrational in bourgeois society solely in terms of class conflict. Class conflict was less the agent of change than the symptom of inherent tendencies in Modernity to erode the foundations of bourgeois order. The next section of the chapter considers the decomposition of the bourgeois order of things. It does so with special reference to three examples relating to leisure and travel experience: the ordering of nature as an escape area; the organization of tourism as a means of fleeing the routine, predictable order of daily life; and the decay of the interior as a sanctuary of privacy and escape. The analysis does not discount the proposition that subjectivity was thoroughly organized in the bourgeois period. However, it does question the belief that this organization can be traced back to a centralized source, whether it is conceived of in terms of a ruling class or dominant state. Implicit here is the notion that subjectivity is organized and disorganized on a number of fronts. And, by extension, that it is the relationships between these fronts rather than the action of any single front which shapes development.

DECOMPOSITION

Bourgeois culture was certainly aware of the destructive effects of capital upon nature. Conservatives and Romantics were united in fearing that the headlong dash for profit threatened sensuous, social and spatial particularly, bludgeoning the external work into a monotonous stupour of urban-industrial conformity. They saw nature as inviolate. Its inaccessibility was seen as a symbol of its majesty. The threat posed to nature sprang from the tendency of capital to homogenize space through its 'total 'pulverization' into freely alienable parcels of private property to be bought and traded at will upon the market' (Harvey 1985: 13). Ludic space, in the form of parkland and wilderness, commanded high cultural value because it symbolized escape from the concrete jungle. As land values increased through commercial development, the exchange value of these 'free' spaces increased. The Conservative and Romantic tradition developed preservationism as an ideology for protecting Nature from the property developers. Ancient Footpath Societies, Footpath Preservation Societies, and Rights of Way Societies were formed as early as the 1820s (Donnelly 1986: 219). The Commons and Open Spaces Preservation Society was formed in 1865 as a direct result of the threats to enclose the remaining London commons. It campaigned successfully to retain large areas of commons around the metropolis as open spaces for public access: Hampstead and Putney Heaths, Epping Forest, Burnham Beeches and Wimbledon and Berkhampstead Commons. Its example inspired Octavia Hill, Sir Robert Hunter and Canon Hardwicke Rawnsley to found the National Trust in 1895. 'The central idea,' wrote Hunter (quoted in Wright 1985: 51) 'is that of a Land Company formed . . . with a view to protection of the public interests in the open spaces of the country'. Its success paved the way for the foundation of twentieth-century pressure groups like the Ancient Monuments Society (1924), the Council for the Protection of Rural England (1926) and the Civic Trust (1957). Outside the voluntary sector, planning for preservation and the development of open spaces became a feature of municipal government policy in London, Paris and New York from the 1850s (Theobald 1984: 192–3; Wilkinson 1988: 136–41).

The philosophy of preservationism raised crucial questions of power and authority. Two points must be made. In the first place, preservationism involved value judgements about what was worth preserving. Preservation societies were essentially aristocratic and middle-class organizations. They were attached to ideals of 'natural beauty' and 'historic importance' which were formulated in the golden age of private property relations (Wright 1985: 51–87). These ideals devalued peripheral cultures, and supported a depoliticized, deracialized view of nature and history. They symbolized a tradition to which we all 'belonged', but from which many were manifestly excluded or treated as second-class citizens.

The second question raised by preservationism relates to the quality of experience associated with preserved spaces. The creation of natural space for leisure and recreation depended upon the exploitation of agricultural and genuinely natural space beyond the boundaries of preserved land (Williams 1973: 124). Nature was not so much saved by preservationists as arranged to fit the requirements of bourgeois culture which demanded 'natural' escape areas to contrast with the artificiality and restlessness of the metropolis. Preservationism imposed a physical, social and economic order upon space. In terms of experience, it contributed to the estrangement of culture from Nature by turning the latter into a stylized spectacle. As Simmel, commenting upon the modern love for the monumental in Nature, expressed it:

> If modern man finds his highest enjoyment of nature in the snow-bound regions of the Alps or on the shores of the North Sea, then this can be . . . explained by the fact that this inaccessible world actually rejects us, represents the extreme enhancement and stylization of what nature as a whole still means to us . . . a promise that is never fully kept and an entity that responds to our most passionate devotion with a faint resistance and strangeness. (1907: 478)

The same sense of estrangement is evident in the relation of bourgeois culture to the animal kingdom. Travelling exhibitions of exotic animals, usually of the ferocious type, were a common amusement attraction in England from the late seventeenth century. However, bourgeois culture invented the zoo in which a permanent collection of wild animals was created for scientific study and public display. Regent's Park Zoological Gardens was opened in 1828; others followed rapidly, e.g. Birmingham Zoological Gardens (1837), Rosherville Zoological Gardens in Kent (1837), Manchester Zoological Gardens (1837), Leeds Zoological Gardens (1840). Zoos symbolized the domination of Nature by culture. As Ritvo (1987: 218) comments, 'animals were arranged taxonomically, the exhibits showed nature not only confined and restrained, but interpreted and ordered'. Signs of proprietorship emerged rapidly through the development of feeding rituals. for example, bears and monkeys were taught to perform tricks in return for food supplied by zoo-keepers and members of the public. In addition, the more docile animals, such as elephants, camels and llamas were used to give rides to adults and children.

The commodification of spectacle in bourgeois society constantly required new supplements in order to maintain itself. In the case of the zoos, the quest for ever more exotic animals was remorseless, even to the point of condoning the calculated extermination of some exhibits. For example, in 1861 the American showman P.T. Barnum conceived the idea of displaying live whales in his American Museum in New York.[14] He embarked upon an expedition to the mouth of the St Lawrence river and successfully captured two whales for exhibition. Barnum, in his *Autobiography* takes up the story in these words:

> I bulletined in front of the Museum and sent copies to the papers. The excitement was intense and, when at last, these marine monsters arrived and were swimming in the tanks that had been prepared for them, anxious thousands literally rushed to see the strangest curiosities ever exhibited in New York. Thus was my first whaling exhibition a great success, but I did not know how to feed or take care of the monsters, and, moreover, they were in fresh water, and this, with the bad air in the basement, may have hastened their death, which occurred a few days after their arrival, but not before thousands of people had seen them. (1869: 276)

Undeterred, Barnum embarked upon another whaling expedition. This time the captive whales were exhibited in a tank, twenty-four feet square, built of slate and French plate-glass. It was supplied with 'fresh' sea water. 'It was a very great sensation,' wrote Barnum, 'and it added thousands of dollars to my treasury. The whales, however, soon died – their sudden and immense popularity was too much for them' (276). Ever conscious of the dollars for his treasury Barnum despatched another expedition which returned with two more whales and subjected them to the same ordeal.[15]

Bourgeois culture's insistence upon the necessity of rational order entailed the subjugation of nature. In creating 'natural spaces' and grand menageries, bourgeois culture transformed nature into an object of display and consumption. One no longer lived in nature, one visited it as a tourist from the real world of the metropolis and the money economy. The cruelty of Barnum's whaling enterprise illustrates the distance between culture and nature achieved through bourgeois development. The suffering of the animals was secondary to the self-consciousness of the observer as the master of the natural world – a self-consciousness for which, as Barnum proudly trumpets, 'thousands' were willing to pay. I want to come back to the question of the limits of bourgeois consciousness later in the chapter in which the matter of postmodernism is addressed. However, at this point in the discussion I want to give a second example of the decomposition of the bourgeois order of things as it applied to leisure and recreation experience by examining the organization of tourism as a means of escape.

'Foreign travel', declared the self-made Victorian millionaire and moralist, Andrew Carnegie (quoted in Wall 1970: 233), 'I have found to be more than all that is said of it and to the enquiring mind, no mode of collecting knowledge can be compared with it.' For Carnegie, tourism was part of the process of self-making, the development of one's self as a capable, complete person. The bourgeois tourist followed the aristocratic precedent of regarding foreign travel as adding refinement and maturity to the personality.[16] Travel was pursued as a status asset, as well as an enjoyable and exciting experience.

Another reason for foreign travel was health. This became increasingly common as the nineteenth century developed. The climate of the Mediterranean was seen as a cure for the *ennui* of the cold northern metropolitan life. The experience of the young Benjamin Disraeli was not unusual (Blake 1982). The son of financially independent parents, he found himself afflicted, between the ages of twenty-three and twenty-five, with a troublesome psychosomatic illness. The symptoms were lethargy, exhaustion, depression and inertia. In 1830, at twenty-five, he determined to restore his health by embarking on a tour of the Mediterranean and Near East. The warmer temperatures, it was hoped, would heat up his blood and repair his weakened nerves. The association of the Mediterranean with therapy was very strong in northern bourgeois culture. An ideology of invalidism grew up around the reputed restorative properties of the Mediterranean climate (Pemble 1987: 84–97). It attracted people with bronchial troubles, weak hearts, consumption and the much larger, amorphous category of 'the highly strung'.

It was never enough for the bourgeois class simply to visit a place of escape. In addition they required that certain domestic standards and modern conveniences should be provided so as to make their stay comfortable. These requirements included railways, roads, hotels, shops, hospitals, churches and the other basic necessities of modern existence. The consequence of these material developments was to annihilate the 'unspoilt', 'natural' qualities of life which had drawn the tourists to the escape areas in the first place. The late Victorian and Edwardian tourists were fearfully aware of the destruction wrought on the Arcadian prospect of Mediterranean harmony, simplicity and beauty by the onslaught of the tourist industry. In particular, the democratization of travel achieved by cheap fares and package holidays of the type offered by Thomas Cook filled the inveterate traveller to the south with loathing. In the words of Pemble:

> The organized tour particularly menaced the fragile magic of art and atmosphere, and despising Cook's tourists (or 'Cookites') became a mannerism of the cultural elite. Charles Lever wrote in horror of 'cities of Italy deluged with droves of these creatures' and of 'the Continental bear-leader who conducts tribes of unlettered British over the cities of Europe', and Gissing referred with pain to 'the Cook's Tourist type' who made the exquisite precincts to Italy unbearable. (1987: 170)

By the end of the nineteenth century, patrician despair at the perceived corrosion of the ancient cultures and 'eternal' landscapes of the south, invested the democratization of travel with the taint of destruction of culture and the obliteration of escape areas. In these circles, travelling to the Mediterranean 'to get away from it all', no longer carried with it the old exclusivity, and they were forced to fortify themselves against the hordes by constructing villas and elite tourist accommodation. At the same time the tourist industry began to introduce administrative technologies designed to make the experience of travel an extension of life back home. Couriers and guides were trained and employed by travel companies like Thomas Cook, to domesticate the experience of foreign travel. Where to go, what to see, what to eat, became administrative principles pursued by successful tourist companies. Gradually the tourist became divided from the vital experience of foreign travel which is being in a foreign place. Tourism became reduced to a series of supervised appointments and controlled experiences with little room left over for novelty or autonomy. The accumulation of sights produced parallel experiences with the accumulation of money through paid employment. Carnegie, hurrying across Europe on one of his self-improving holidays in the 1860s, observed that 'there is no work so exhausting as seeing picture galleries, churches, etc' (quoted in Wall 1970: 233). It is significant that Carnegie, a man rich enough to avoid the trappings of the package tour, nevertheless viewed tourist experience as becoming more regimented and more like work.

Bourgeois culture pursued foreign travel for 'pleasure' as part of the technology of self-improvement. The aim was to accumulate experience in order to develop the personality and to attain maturity. However, the superiority complex of bourgeois society meant that the bourgeois tourist confronted peripheral cultures with the self-consciousness that he had more to teach than to learn. The self-realization of bourgeois culture demanded that peripheral cultures and peripheral peoples should be annexed and subjected to the bourgeois programme of self-improvement. To propose that the effects of the bourgeois project were all bad is as extreme as asserting that the Enlightenment simply negated human freedom. In both cases, one confronts a mixed bag of effects. However, what emerges unequivocally from the bourgeois experience of tourism is that the incursion of the bourgeoisie onto foreign soil for the purposes of pleasure negated the values which originally motivated the desire to travel. Pemble (1987: 168–82) vividly conveys the air of fatalism which oppressed the bourgeois traveller to the Mediterranean more intensively as the hotels went up, the railways opened and the people turned up in ever increasing numbers. The ordering of travel contributed to the disordering of tourist experience. The search for adventure and self-realization was frequently neutralized by a sense of anti-climax and the impression that things were not really so different from home. The rapid and stark disordering of experience is a modern condition. It is Modernity's revenge on bourgeois culture which always endeavoured to maintain rational order and the rule of Reason. I want to return to the subject later in this section. However, before doing so it is worth considering another example of disordering, another example of the decomposition of bourgeois culture: the dissolution of the interior as a place of escape.

Benjamin (1983: 167–8) remarked that the interior is 'the universe of the private citizen'; while Bachelard (1964: 4), in his phenomenology of space, described the interior as 'our first universe, a real cosmos in every sense of the word'. These statements reflect the exalted state of the interior in bourgeois culture. It was seen as a place where the reality of existence was located.[17] Family life, relaxation and intimate experience, it was believed, were concentrated in the home. With regard to leisure experience, the interior was the most important area of escape. In it the individual pursued hobbies and pastimes which were absent from the world of work.

The division between interior and exterior provided one of the fundamental structural dichotomies in bourgeois culture. However, as bourgeois society developed it found it increasingly difficult to maintain. Two forces came into play to weaken the dichotomy. In the first place, as we saw in Chapter 2, the integrity of the interior depended upon the full-time expenditure of domestic labour. With new opportunities in the labour market after the 1850s, women became increasingly less willing permanently to resign themselves to the role of the housekeeper. At the same time, their capacity to liberate themselves from their role was enhanced by the development of new labour-saving technologies which mechanized many of the most time-consuming tasks of household management (Gershuny 1978). The second point is that the private character of the interior buckled under the increased flow of information entering the bourgeois citadel. Working wives were an important agent in this respect. Their increased contact with the exterior often involved being exposed to and developing new forms of medical, sociological and psychological knowledge which challenged bourgeois patriarchy (Donzelot 1979). Another important agent in mobilizing and multiplying information was the media. After the 1880s cheaper printing techniques, changes in retail distribution and rises in real incomes combined to increase the influence of the serious and popular press. In the next century, the development of audio-visual forms of entertainment, notably the radio, the gramophone and television, further reduced the capacity of the bourgeoisie to shut out the world from the interior.

From the Marxian standpoint, the weakening of the division between the interior and the exterior is explained as the fulfilment of capital's need to exploit the workers at home as well as at work. For example, Andrew (1981) contends that patterns and forms of leisure became subject to principles of scientific management at the same time as scientific management became popular in the workplace. The aim in both home and work was to standardize the behaviour of workers to conform to the accumulation requirements of capital. It follows that the escape experience provided for the masses under capitalism is bogus because the system cannot permit consumers to escape from dependency upon the commodity form.

Andrew's approach seeks to unmask the illusory forms of freedom and escape which leisure in capitalist society presents to us. What is largely missing from his account is a discussion of the experience of leisure in everyday life and the ambiguities of modernity. The history of the weakening of the division between the interior and the exterior illustrates this very well. Let me focus on two examples: the effects of electric lighting in domesticating the exterior and the concern with 'leisureliness' in industrial design.

Public electric lighting was introduced in the 1870s and 1880s. Before then, street lighting in the metropolitan areas of Europe and

North America had been largely confined to lanterns and gaslights. They provided pale and uneven illumination which left many places in the street in half-light or cloaked in menacing darkness. The introduction of public electric lighting has been likened to bringing 'a flood of light' into the nocturnal public exterior (Schivelbusch 1988: 114).[18] Electric light made transport more manageable and interaction more visible. Shop windows ceased to be inefficiently lit, or draped, shuttered and bolted at nightfall. The development of shopping arcades and shop window displays used electric light to enhance their spectacular quality. Window arrangers aimed to create simulacra of the interior in the exterior of the metropolitan streets. However, these simulacra were designed to be more lush and extravagant than anything that could be found in the bourgeois home. Egyptian, Persian, Greek and Roman architecture and art were to create a sense of the distant in space and in time. Temples, columns, urns, garlands, vines, swathes of silk flowers, topiary and stuffed peacocks were employed as artefacts radiating confidence and splendour. Mannequins for display had been introduced at the Paris exhibition of 1894. The prototypes were exceptionally primitive by today's standards. They were made of wax and iron, weighed between 200–300 pounds, and displayed genuine hair and eyelashes, glass eyes and false teeth for 'authenticity' (Wood 1982: 13-15). Mannequins enabled window arrangers to create tableaux of private life, e.g. families at play, lovers gazing into each others eyes, children feeding animals, etc.

What were the psychological and sociological consequences of public electric lighting upon the experience of modernity? Three points have to be made. In the first place, the old bourgeois distinctions of space and privacy were violated. 'Street lighting,' remarked Schivelbusch, 'created an "interior" space out of doors' (1988: 150). It enabled new forms of public space to emerge.[19] For example, Benjamin (1983): 37) defined the arcades as 'a cross between a street and an *intérieur'*. In other words, they were a space in which the public and the private soaked into each other, so weakening and invalidating former distinctions. The second point is that public electric light increased opportunities for sociability. The metropolis lost is nocturnal hermetic and menacing qualities and became more open and exciting. The time for exposure to, and experience of, society was increased. This brings me to my third point. The domestication of the metropolitan exterior did not necessarily result in the co-option of the spectator to the commodity form. Both Baudelaire and Benjamin have drawn attention to new forms of leisureliness associated with the illuminated metropolis. These forms were realized, above all, in the character of the *flâneur* who, as Benjamin (1983: 36) put it, 'goes botanizing on the asphalt'. The *flâneur* is a metropolitan observer *nonparaeil*. Strolling, browsing, listening, watching and reflecting is his *métier*. Benjamin suggests that something of this character is present in all city dwellers. One's movement through the boulevards and past the shops and 'buildings for transitory purposes' (exhibition halls, cafés, railway stations) in the metropolis is englobed with a sense of leisureliness (Benjamin 1983: 138–9).

By the turn of the century 'leisureliness' was also being self-consciously incorporated as a design value in industrial architecture. Partly as a result of Taylor's methods of 'scientific management', industrial designers began to pay more attention to ergonomics. Furniture and equipment were designed to optimize the workers productivity and to reduce workers' fatigue. After the Hawthorne experiments (1927–32) industrial designers began to experiment with schemes to domesticate the workplace. An atmosphere of comfort and security was introduced into the workplace through the use of relaxing colour schemes, pictures on the walls and potted plants. The goal was to create a more worker-friendly work environment. This was taken much further in the postwar period by designers who sought to 'landscape' industrial areas. Landscaping was based on scientific principles designed to optimize work flows. However, the primary design details emphasized openness, flexibility, comfort, choice and authenticity. The design references were clearly rooted in an idealized view of the home. Landscaping used the image of the domestic interior as a place 'in which people are authentically themselves' and 'as the source of all sincere relationships' (Forty 1986: 144).

These changes in leisure and tourism were, of course, part of much wider changes in industrial society. Lash and Urry (1987: 310–12) argue that by the 1950s there was open recognition that the bourgeois order was in a state of disorganization. A considerable body of literature documents the key indicators of disorganization: the décline of staple industries like coal, iron, steel and shipbuilding in the capitalist core and the partial transfer of these functions to the periphery and semi-periphery; the growth of a service class based in knowledge and communication industries; the globalization of finance and culture which promoted a handful of metropolitan centres in the West as global trend-setters; the fragmentation and differentiation of labour along lines of occupation and community; the diffusion of ex-colonial ethnic populations to the capitalist core; the decline of class-based politics and institutions; the increasing independence of large monopolies from state regulation; the growth of challenges to centralized state bureaucracy and power; and the increases in resources devoted to leisure and travel.

Within sociology the first coherent response to the disorganization of the bourgeois order of things was to posit the emergence of a new, higher level of socio-economic integration. Riesman (1958) was one of the first sociologists to use the term 'post industrial society' in this connection. However, by the 1960s and early 1970s the term had entered common currency (Touraine 1971; Bell 1973). It was generally argued that postindustrial society would consist of higher standards of living, an economy based on automated production, enhanced education provision and political pluralism. As a corollary, it was argued that leisure values would become more pronounced in social and economic relations. Leisure in post industrial society theory was generally associated with freedom and personal growth.[20] However, some critics raised the spectre of 'empty leisure time', 'programmed', in the words of Gorz (1983: 87) by the 'distractions of the mass media and the oblivion merchants'. To correct this possibility, Gorz (1983, 1985) advocated 'post industrial socialism', by which he means a planned approach to achieving 'the realm of freedom'. The point to emphasize is that in both its liberal and left-wing forms the postindustrial society thesis assumed that the new conditions would cohere into a few integrated order based upon rational principles.

In the 1980s and early 1990s the debate on industrial and post-industrial society ceased to be central in intellectual life in Western social science.[21] It was replaced by the debate on modernity and postmodernity. Postmodern authors agree with the central tenet of the post-industrial society thesis; namely, that social and economic conditions in society have changed so drastically that modernist categories and distinctions of thought and action are now defunct. However, they break sharply with the proposition that society is moving towards a new rational integrated order. Instead postmodernism emphasizes the discontinuities of change and the irregularity of association and practice. The next section is devoted to describing the main arguments of postmodernism and showing how these arguments can be connected with leisure and tourism.

POSTMODERNITY

Postmodernity is a multi-faceted concept. However, at the heart of the matter is the rejection of modernist universal categories of ontology and epistemology. Lyotard (1984) provided one of the first and most influential statements of this position. He argues that the development of postindustrial technology has transformed knowledge. More specifically he submits that computer technology has encouraged the transfer of resources in knowledge from traditional speculative philosophical purposes to pragmatic techno-economic purposes. Knowledge production has become steadily subject to commodification. The new pragmatic attitude has had several consequences. Lyotard mentions the increasing impatience with traditional inter-disciplinary boundaries in scientific practice; the emergence of new analytic spaces; and the growing reputation of forms of instability and undecidability in knowledge. The modernist belief that scientists are gradually uncovering underlying truths about the nature of reality is now openly scorned. Instead postmodern scientists are more conscious of the gaps and inconsistencies in knowledge and the absurdities involved in positing grand universal theories. For Lyotard the delegitimation of many traditional scientific methods and theories is paralleled by similar processes in the social, economic and political world. The traditional modernist faith in the capacity of rational-humanist intervention to provide universal solutions to social, economic and political questions has imploded. The notions of a new deal for society or a scientific revolution in the means and relations of production are now treated with considerable scepticism – even by commentators who feel strongly that society *should* be changed. 'We no longer', concludes Lyotard (1984: 60), 'have recourse to the grand narratives – we can resort neither to the dialectic of the Spirit not even to the emancipation of humanity as a validation for postmodern scientific discourse.' This conclusion does not lead Lyotard to abandon the concept of truth. Instead he argues that truth is a condition of 'language games'.[22] Language, as it were, 'makes' reality.

Formal science has traditionally been concerned with producing a rational view of the world which is capable of supporting law-like statements. Against this Lyotard's discussion emphasizes the mobility and elasticity of language and the messiness and inconsistency of knowledge. He discounts the realist belief that there is an objective, material world which exists independently of consciousness, yet which is, nonetheless, ascertainable by consciousness. Instead his arguments are in the philosophical tradition of idealism which agues that reality is nothing but the outcome of our language, ideas and interpretations.

In pointing to the crisis of legitimation in the sphere of knowledge, Lyotard identifies a key characteristic of postmodernist approaches. On a wide number of fronts it is argued not only that received rational categories and distinctions have ceased to be legitimate, but also that there is no prospect of transcending this situation. For example, Huyssen (1986) argues that cultural relations under Modernity were constructed around a great divide between high and low culture. The former was valued as authoritative, accurate and significant; the latter was dismissed as vulgar, brash and inconsequential. According to Huyssen the years since the 1960s have witnessed the disintegration of the great divide. So far from being polarized, high and low culture now connect with each other in an exhaustive, incestuous way. More generally postmodernists argue that the globalization of culture has weakened the salience of many former geopolitical distinctions between nation states and power blocs. The old devotion to universalistic concepts such as 'class', 'religion', 'race' and 'nation' has been replaced with the celebration of particularity and difference. Postmodernists argue that we should read praxis in terms of the aleatory and the contingent and not in terms of necessity and determinism.

Although some of these arguments invite comparison with late-nineteenth-century nihilism,[23] they are relieved by a consistent emphasis on irony and playfulness. Postmodernists do not see the collapse of former divisions as opening up an abyss of meaninglessness and despair. Instead what is stressed is the liberation of feeling which derives from realizing that we are no longer bound by universal necessity. The term 'universal necessity' is open to misunderstanding. Postmodernists do not claim that necessities have disappeared. Rather they hold that *universal* necessities which can be construed as making totalizing claims are no longer supportable. Examples include the modernist conviction that Western culture is necessarily at the vanguard of progress; or the Marxist concepts of historical necessity and dominant ideology. The focus of postmodern analysis is upon a plurality of necessities. It recognizes no basis for declaring priority for any one of them. One corollary of the postmodern emphasis on delegitimation and anti-determinism is the notion that depthlessness is now a generalized quality of cultural relations. The reasoning here is quite simple. If it is now implausible to see ourselves as representing the pinnacle of human evolution or the deedholders of universal scientific truth, we lose the basis for looking down upon others. Both Jencks (1984) and Jameson (1984) comment that depthlessness is an obvious characteristic of postmodern architecture. Modernist architecture was absolutist. It refused to acknowledge historical or local references, irrationality, fantasy or emotionalism. Instead the determinate principle was rational purity of style. Against this, architects who figure in the postmodern canon such as Robert Venturi, Charles Moore, Aldo Rossi, Richard Rogers, Rob Krier and Arata Isozaki, incorporate fictional and local references, playfulness and irony into their building design. Instead of a purity of style these architects aim at eclecticism. As Richard Rogers wrote of his design for the Lloyd's building in the City of London:

> Our intention in the design of the new Lloyd's building has been to create a more articulated, layered building by the manipulation of plan, section and elevation which would link and weave together both the over-simplified twentieth-century blocks and the richer, more varied architecture of the past. Approaches to buildings in cities are often along narrow streets, so they can be seen obliquely. Lloyd's is designed to be approached on the diagonal and viewed in parts. As the viewer approaches the building, the form gradually unfolds, the overlapping elements of its facade opening up to reveal spaces related to pedestrian scale, spaces that are sheltered from the passing vehicles. Contrast is thereby created by the juxtaposition in depth of different layers and elements . . . These techniques enable the viewer to participate in the dialogue between the different parts, between surface and depth, between tension and compression, horizontal and vertical, solid and void. (Quoted in Appleyard 1986: 266)

Lyotard (1984) finds the quality of depthlessness realized most obviously in the electicism of postmodern lifestyle. 'One listens to reggae,' he writes of the archetypal denizen of postmodernism, 'watches a western, eats MacDonald's food for lunch and local cuisine for dinner, wears Paris perfume in Tokyo and "retro" clothes in Hong Kong' (1984: 76). Other observers, notably Korker and Cook (1986) and Baudrillard (1990) find a more tangible example of depthlessness in television culture. TV beams out a stream of information, spectacle and entertainment, collapsing time horizons effortlessly and coalescing spaces with ease. As a medium it conveys simultaneity and equivalence upon all of the happenings, dramas, advertisements and news reports which it broadcasts. According to Kroker and Cook:

> TV is, in a very literal sense, the real world, not of modern but *postmodern* culture, society and economy – of society typified by the dynamic momentum of the spirit of technicisme triumphant and of real popular culture driven onwards by the ecstacy and decay of the obscene spectacle (emphasis in the original). (1986: 268)[24]

Baudrillard (1983: 55) also refers to 'the dissolution of TV into life, the dissolution of life into TV'. For these writers television is the clearest embodiment of the replacement of reality with representation. Baudrillard (1983: 2) describes this as a condition of 'hyperreality' which he defines as 'the generation by models of a real without origin or reality'. He is one of the few commentators in the debate on postmodernity to give an historical perspective to his argument. It is worth briefly recounting the main details of this perspective.

Baudrillard (1983: 83–152) posits three orders of simulacrum since the Renaissance. The first he terms *Counterfeit* and identifies as the dominant scheme of the 'classical' period from the Renaissance to the industrial revolution. The second he calls *Production* and locates as the dominant scheme of the industrial era. The third and present order he calls *Simulation*. Baudrillard is not particularly interested in situating his work in the context of an academic history of ideas. However, it is plain that Benjamin's essay 'The Work of Art in the Age of Mechanical Reproduction', and McLuhan's (1967, 1973) work on the media, were decisive influences in the construction of his ideas. Putting it simply, what are the key features of Baudrillard's three orders of simulacrum?

The Counterfeit only has meaning in terms of its anterior mode of production and representation: the medieval mode. In this relatively static mode there was general equivalence between the sign and the object to which it referred. Counterfeit was only possible through magic or sacrilege. However, with the development of mechanical reproduction processes society 'passed from a limited order of signs which prohibits "free production" to a proliferation of signs according to demand" (Baudrillard 1983: 85). In the fashion of stucco and baroque art Baudrillard finds evidence of the self conscious theatricality of the Renaissance. At this moment collective representations began to move from the ambition to reflect nature, religion and society to the desire to remodel them. Artefacts like concrete trees with real leaves printed in them, a hog made out of concrete but with a real hog's skull inside, concrete sheep covered with real wool, begin to appear (Baudrillard 1983: 90).

The order of Production is based on the methods of serial production developed in the industrial revolution. Here reproduction becomes an end in itself. The fecundity of the system means that reproduced objects cease to refer to an original (the opposite was the case under the order of the Counterfeit). Instead in the glut of innovation and production reproduced objects relate to each other with 'equivalence' and 'indifference'. 'In a series,' writes Baudrillard (1983: 97), 'objects become undefined simulacra one of the other'; and so do their producers.

The present order is termed the order of Simulation. Here the distinction between medium and reality has been erased. Action and reaction become a matter of calculated media stimuli 'mediated with designer bodies and processed through computerized imaging-systems' (Kroker and Cook 1986: 15). These stimuli work in the form of a binary sign system of question and answer. Responses are called for, but the responses, insists Baudrillard, are already preconditioned by the form of the question. For example, we are presented with images of tropical beaches, palm trees, sun, surf and sun-tanned bodies, and we are asked, would we not like to go there? Similarly, we are given images of luxurious hotel rooms, filled with laughing glamorous people and we are asked, would we not like to make a reservation? In both cases our response is calculated on the basis of media representations of 'reality'. The point is that the information which we use to make our choice is already packaged, thereby compromising the status of our 'decision'. I have chosen examples from the holiday industry for obvious reasons. However, Baudrillard's argument is that present day society in general belongs to the order of *Simulation*. As he puts it:

Objects and information result already from a selection, a montage, from a point-of-view. They have already tested "reality" and have asked only questions that "answered back" to them. They have broken down reality into simple elements that they have reassembled into scenarios of regulated oppositions, exactly in the same way that the photographer imposes his contrasts, lights, angles on his subject. (1983: 120)

Meaning has not vanished. On the contrary, Baudrillard repeatedly makes the point that we are awash with meaning. However, at the same time, he insists that there is a 'fatal' quality to it. This is because we have reached an historical juncture with the third order of Simulation, where the fate of meaning is always to conform to the model. Critics of Baudrillard claim that this argument leads to political acquiesence (Kellner 1989). But this is hardly the case. Baudrillard's (1983) view is that under the order of Simulation it is unrealistic to believe that an historical actor, such as the proletariat, is poised to leap centre-stage to alter the course of history. For the proletariat is itself a simulation, in Baudrillard's terms, and not a 'real' agent. To accept this is not to lapse into a state of acquiesence. On the contrary, Baudrillard (1988: 22) submits that the silence of the masses constitutes a political 'reply' to the seductions of the media.

Neo-Marxist and feminist writers see hope in cultural production and leisure relations. There is still room, they claim, for critical discourse, consciousness-raising and progressive action (Deem 1986; Talbot 1988; Critcher 1989). Against this, Baudrillard (1990: 68) maintains that contemporary culture has moved from forms of organization and practice based upon 'expression and competition' to 'aleatory and ecstatic' forms. Radical theorists believe in the possibility of utopia based upon humanistic principles of planning and administration. They invoke the ideal on the foundations of a 'scientific' analysis of the real. Baudrillard's key point is that this act of invocation was never valid. Even under the orders of the Counterfeit and Production the real was nothing but a matter of appearance. Under the order of Simulation, the condition of generalized hyperreality, the status of the real has become more tenuous: representation *is* the real. The implication is that utopia has ceased to be a destination worth travelling towards. Rather it is part of the network of representation through which identity, practice and association is mediated. 'Everything is here', claims Baudrillard (1990: 71), 'heaven has come down to earth, the heaven of utopia . . . We're in paradise'.

In this depthless, transparent 'paradise' the progressive, evolutionary concepts developed under modernity, such as 'self-realization' and 'social improvement' deconstruct. Leisure ceases to have any connection with self-actualization. Instead it reflects the aleatory, decentred and restless conditions which obtain everywhere. As Baudrillard writes:

> The man of leisure looks desperately for a nail to hammer, a motor to dismantle . . . at a loss for something to do with his free time, he nevertheless urgently "needs" to do nothing (or nothing useful), since this has distinctive social value. (1981: 77)

Modernist theory characteristically viewed leisure to be primarily an *activity*. In contrast, Baudrillard typically sees it as a *sign*. Following Veblen (1925), he argues (1981: 76–7) that the social value of leisure is that it signifies unproductive labour. Leisure activity is conditioned by its sign value as unproductive labour. As Baudrillard puts it:

> (Leisure) time is not . . . "free", it is sacrificed, wasted; it is the moment of production value, of an invidious production of status, and the social individual is not free to escape it. (1981: 76)

In answer to the neo-Marxist and feminist argument that leisure is a site of struggle and transformation, as well as one of control and incorporation, Baudrillard emphasizes the intractability of unproductive activity as the main site of leisure.[25] 'What `claims the average individual,' writes Baudrillard, 'through the holidays and during his free time, is not the liberty to "fulfil" himself (in terms of what? What hidden essence will surge to the fore?). He must verify the uselessness of his time' (1981: 77).

Postmodernism then, reveals contemporary culture to be dominated by depthlessness, fragmentation and reproduction. It emphasizes particularity and difference over uniformity and totality. Life is seen as contingent and not determined by objective forces. Postmodernism also argues that reality is not independent of social consciousness but, on the contrary, reality is merely the expression of social consciousness. The historical condition of the present is one of hyperreality, in which identity, practice and association are organized around processes of simulation.

The inferences of this position for leisure and tourism are not hard to specify. Four points must be made. In the first place, leisure and tourism are now equivalent to mere consumption activity. The modernist quest for authenticity and self-realization has come to an end.

Instead we are in a stage of post-leisure and post-tourism in which we can relax enough not to bother about self-improvement or capturing the essence of every sight.

The second point is that post-leisure and post-tourism are part of a social situation made up of generalized de-differentiation. De-differentiation refers to a condition in which social and economic distinctions are redefined to denote a contrary but not necessarily permanent rearrangement of elements. So old workspace becomes reallocated to leisure functions; patriarchal rule becomes associated with male weakness and not male strength; leisure activity acquires some of the characteristics of work activity.

The third point is that post-leisure and post-tourism question the state's moral density, its right to rule over others. The licensing of leisure forms, the official management of recreation space, and the policing of leisure and sport are intensely politicized. Different identity groups stake claims on the collective representations of the state. For example, in Britain the ancient site of Stonehenge has become an object of civil disobedience. The issue centres on the claims of a group of hippy travellers that the monument is an essential element in their rites of group renewal. Since the early 1980s on the summer solstice there have been regular clashes between the police and what one Home Secretary called 'these medieval brigands'.[26] More generally Gold (1980) suggests that a general divergence has opened up in US inner city areas between the supply of recreation providers and the needs of recreation users. The point to emphasize is not that conflict in leisure provision is new. As we saw in the discussion of leisure and moral regulation in Chapter 1 (see pp. 10–50), conflict in leisure has a very long history. Rather the point is that objective principles of legitimation have become so discredited that there is extreme difficulty in reconciling disputes.

The fourth point is that post-leisure and post-tourist forms celebrate fictive and dramaturgical values. Since authenticity is no longer an issue under postmodernism, it is reasonable to expect that these forms would be preoccupied with spectacle and sensation. The consumption experience is accompanied with a sense of irony. One realizes that what one is consuming is not real, but nonetheless the experience can be pleasurable and exciting, even if one recognizes that it is also 'useless'. Eco, in his discussion of hyperreality in American leisure, contends that:

The American imagination demands the real thing and, to attain it, must fabricate the absolute fake; where the boundaries between game and illusion are blurred, the art museum is contaminated by the freak show and falsehood is enjoyed in a situation of "fullness". (1986: 8)

Eco's account drew on the debate around postmodernism. He argued that as early as the mid 1970s post-leisure and post-tourism forms were evident in American culture. The next two chapters discuss forms of leisure and tourism in the 1970s, '80s and early '90s. The aim is to mount some evidence to test postmodern claims of depthlessness, de-differentiation, fragmentation, simulation and delegitimation in contemporary culture. Following Eco I want to explore whether our demands for the real thing in leisure and tourism can only be achieved by fabricating 'the absolute fake'. And, following Baudrillard, I want to consider if hyperreality is already accepted as normality in contemporary leisure and travel experience.

4

Fatal Attractions

Fatality is a striking feature in the landscape of postmodernism. The 'excremental culture' which Kroker and Cook (1986) and Baudrillard (1990) negotiate, is choking with mass-produced commodities, simulated images and self-negating utopias. Meaning has been replaced with spectacle and sensation dominates value. What evidence is there in contemporary leisure forms to support this assertion?

The 1970s and '80s certainly witnessed gigantic capital investment in escape areas organized around spectacle and sensation. From private sector initiatives, like the Alton Towers leisure park, to local government tourist projects, like South Tyneside's 'Catherine Cookson Country' or Nottingham's 'Robin Hood Country', new leisure space was constructed around fictional and mythical themes (Urry 1990: 144–53). The specific theming of space was often eclectic, fusing, for example, references of locale with artefacts of the culture industry. However, meta-themes can be detected which enable us to classify these new escape areas into four types:

(1) *Black Spots*: these refer to the commercial developments of grave sites and sites in which celebrities or large numbers of people have met with sudden and violent death. Examples include the recreation space constructed at the junction of Highways 466 and 41 near Cholame, California, where James Dean died in an automobile crash; Graceland where Elvis Presley died and is buried; the Grave Line Tour of Hollywood which takes in the suicide sites, assassination points and other places of death involving stars of the movie and pop worlds; Auschwitz, the Bridge over the River Kwai, and the Killing Fields in Cambodia.

(2) *Heritage Sites*: these refer to escape areas which attempt to recreate events and the ways of life of former times. Two subtypes can be identified in this category: (i) *Performance sites*, in which actors and stage sets are used to re-enact the past, e.g. the staged attractions at Beamish Open Air Museum, Newcastle; the Wigan Pier Heritage Centre, the Plymouth Plantation, New England, and the village of Waterloo, New Jersey; (ii) *Tableaux*, in which models, audio-

animatronics and laser systems simulate the past, e.g. the Jorvik Centre in York, the Crusades Experience, Winchester, the Oxford Story, Oxford, and the Disney Hall of Presidents.

(3) *Literary Landscapes*: these refer to escape areas which are themed around the lives of famous novelists and the characters from their fiction. Hotels, tour companies, gift shops, refreshment centres and museums all exploit these imaginary landscapes. Examples include, 'Hardy Country', Dorset; 'Dickensworld', Rochester; 'James Herriot Country', Yorkshire; 'Bronte Country', Yorkshire; 'Lorna Doone Country', Somerset; 'Land O' Burns', Western Scotland; 'Steinbeck Country', the Monterey Peninsula; 'the landscape of the Beats', North Beach, San Francisco; 'Hemingway Country', Key West, Florida and Sun Valley, Idaho.

(4) *Theme Parks*: these refer to themed leisure parks organized around serialized spectacles and participant attractions. Common features include fantastic and bizarre landscapes, exotic regions and 'white knuckle' rides. Although the origins of many of today's most popular theme parks lie before the 1970s and '80s, it was during this period that many engaged in a vigorous and sustained dash for growth involving vast capital outlay and the dramatic expansion of attractions. Examples include the Alton Towers complex in the Midlands, the Chessington World of Adventures, Surrey, De Efteling Park in Eindhoven, southern Netherlands, Phantasialand, western Germany, the Disney Parks in California and Florida and the Universal Film Lot in California.

In what follows I shall expand upon each leisure form, describing its attractions and giving examples. Although I shall comment upon how these forms relate to postmodernism in passing, my considered remarks on this subject will be postponed until the final section of the chapter. The order of my discussion will follow the listing above.

BLACK SPOTS

When news of the explosion of Pan Am Airlines Flight 103 over Lockerbie in Scotland on 21 December 1988 was broadcast, one of the immediate effects was the arrival of scores of sightseers to the scene of the catastrophe. Next day newspapers reported a six- to seven-mile traffic jam on the main road to Lockerbie; and the AA were quoted as estimating that they had received over 2000 enquir-

ies from people asking for the best route to the crash site.[1] The
incident is not isolated. For example, in March 1987, the media
reported that crowds of sightseers had flocked to the shores of
Zeebrugge where the ferry *Herald of Free Enterprise* had capsized a
few miles out to sea drowning 193 people. 'Some motorists,' reported one newspaper,[2] 'left their cars in neighbouring towns and
walked several miles to Zeebrugge, complete with sandwiches.' Likewise, in April 1988, the press reported police criticism of sightseers
who had travelled to Larnaca Airport to view the siege on board the
Kuwait Airlines Boeing 747 (Flight 422). It was reported that ice-
cream vans had arrived on site to supply the onlookers with snacks.[3]

The interest in catastrophes and disasters might seem to be dis-
tasteful. However, it would be foolish to deny that it is widely
shared. Death sites and places of violent death involving celebrities
or large numbers of people, almost immediately take on a monumental quality in our culture. One commercial expression of this is
the death tours now offered by increasingly large numbers of tour
operators. For example, the Dallas Tourist Board offers visitors an
itinerary which explores the essential geography of the shooting of
President John F. Kennedy. The visitor, the witness of the a monumental scene, is taken down the route to the junction of Elm and
Houston. He or she is asked to stand in the spot where the Presid-
ential motorcade passed the Texas Book Depository, and to scru-
tinize the sixth-floor window where the alleged assassin, Lee
Harvey Oswald, fired the fatal bullets. One is asked to project oneself into the past. Another example of a commercially successful
death tour is Grave Line Tours in Hollywood, California which takes
tourists on a two and a half hour trip around the 'Deathstyles of the
Rich and Famous'. The tour, which is conducted in a converted
Cadillac hearse, lingers over suicide sites, assassination spots, and
the terminal patients wings of Los Angeles hospitals.[4] In addition
to action tours, a large 'tourist' literature has grown up around
celebrity black spots. Kenneth Anger's *Hollywood Babylon* (1975) and
Hollywood Babylon II (1984), are arguably the best-known examples
of the genre. They cater for the connoisseur with promotion stills,
open-casket mug-shots and police and press photographs of the
scene of death. Herman's *Rock 'n' Roll Babylon* (1982) repeats the
formula for famous rock stars.

One of the most prominent examples of Black Spots as tourist
attractions are metropolitan and national cemeteries. Here one can
almost speak of a league table of the most famous cemeteries in the

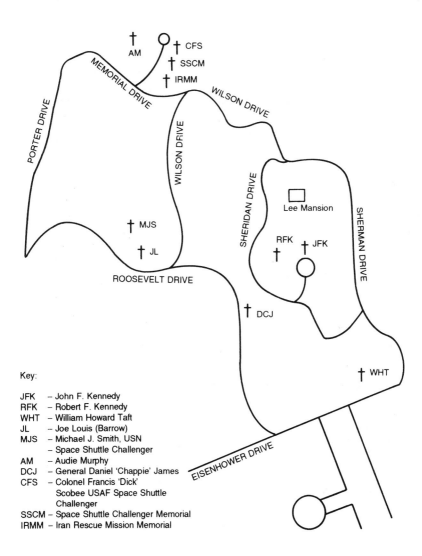

Key:

JFK – John F. Kennedy
RFK – Robert F. Kennedy
WHT – William Howard Taft
JL   – Joe Louis (Barrow)
MJS – Michael J. Smith, USN
     – Space Shuttle Challenger
AM   – Audie Murphy
DCJ – General Daniel 'Chappie' James
CFS – Colonel Francis 'Dick'
     Scobee USAF Space Shuttle
     Challenger
SSCM – Space Shuttle Challenger Memorial
IRMM – Iran Rescue Mission Memorial

Figure 3: Arlington National Cemetery, Washington DC

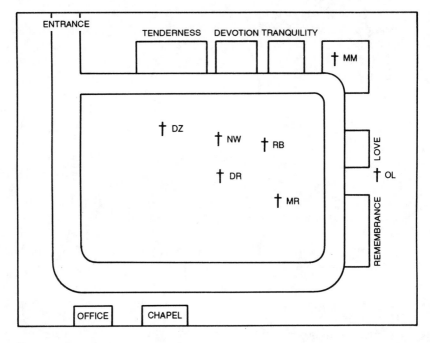

Key:

MM – Marilyn Monroe
OL – Oscar Levant
RB – Richard Basehart
DR – Donna Reed
DZ – Darryl Zanuck
NW – Natalie Wood
MR – Minnie Ripperton

Figure 4: Westwood Memorial Park, Los Angeles

world: the Arlington National Cemetery in Washington where the remains of President John F. Kennedy, Senator Robert Kennedy, Joe Louis, President William Taft and Audie Murphy lie buried; Westwood Memorial Park in Los Angeles, where stars including Marilyn Monroe, Natalie Wood, Donna Reed, Richard Basehart and Oscar Levant are interred; Hollywood Memorial Park where the graves of Douglas Fairbanks Senior, Rudolph Valentino, Peter Finch, Nelson Eddy, Tyrone Power, Nelson Riddle, Bugsy Siegel and John Huston can be found; the *sepulture* of Père Lachaise in Paris where lie the remains of Apollinaire, Balzac, Sarah Bernhardt, Chopin, Doré, Eluard, Max Ernst, Ingres, La Fontaine, Nadar, Gérard de Nerval, Piaf, Pissaro, Proust, Raymond Radiguet, Seurat, Signoret, Visconti and Oscar Wilde; the Montparnasse Cemetery in Paris, where, among others, Baudelaire, Tristan Tzara, Guy de Maupassant, Cesar Franck and Saint-Saens are interred; the San Michele Cemetery in Venice where Stravinsky, Diaghilev, Ezra Pound and Frederick 'Baron Corvo' Rolf are buried; the Protestant Cemetery in Rome where one can find the graves of Keats, Shelley and Gramsci; and, of course, Highgate Cemetery (East and West) in London where lie the remains of Karl Marx, George Eliot, Ralph Richardson, Jacob Bronowski, Michael Faraday, Radclyffe Hall, Sir Edwin Landseer and Christina Rossetti.

Bourgeois culture constructed the cemetery as a place of dignity and solemnity. Visitors were expected to show proper respect for the dead. The vast scale of Victorian mausoleums and statuary was intended to reinforce this message. However the action of Modernity operated to break down the barriers between the sacred and the profane, the closed world of the cemetery and the outside world of commerce and spectacle. With the rise of mass tourism, the metropolitan cemetery, with its collection of illustrious corpses, became a sight to see just like any other monument. Today, the most regular visitor to the star cemeteries is in fact the tourist; and the most common accessory they bear with them is not a bunch of flowers, but a camera.

Jim Morrison's grave in Père Lachaise illustrates the extent to which the search for spectacle has replaced the respect for solemnity. Morrison, of course, was the Rimbaudesque lead singer and rock poet with the influential sixties band, *The Doors*. He died suddenly and unexpectedly in Paris in 1971.[5] His grave has become a *cause célèbre* among the old-style Parisian establishment who wish to maintain the sacred aura of the city's leading cemetery. It is easy to find. Graffiti – JIM with an arrow underneath – is daubed into various tombstones *en route*. A newspaper report from 1990 described the gravesite as 'a defaced, urine stained Mecca'.[6] Certainly, empty wine bottles and beer cans are regularly deposited on the site. The surrounding crypts are scrawled with graffiti. A bust of the singer which adorned the site was stolen in the 1980s.[7] The headstone is now strewn with dead flowers and empty wine and tequila bottles. The aura of this site depends upon its distance from the conventions of the bourgeois cemetery. As we saw in the last chapter, Benjamin proposed that distance was the indispensable requirement of the auratic object (see p. 104–5). However, in Benjamin's sociology aura tends to be associated with cultural elevation and the refinement of sensibility. Against this, the aura of the Morrison gravesite stems from the palpable degradation which it conveys. The site is socially organized precisely as the derangement of the stock bourgeois values of dignity, solemnity and respect.

One of the characteristic themes in postmodernism is that duplication and reproduction abound in contemporary culture. The simulation of objects and experiences call into question the status of history and reality. Cinematographic and televisual technologies are crucial in bringing about the vapourization of reality. The representations which they promote are more real than reality itself (Baudrillard 1983, 1988; Kroker and Cook 1986: 268–79).

The leisure forms constructed around black spots certainly give signs of repetition-compulsion and seeking the duplication of experience. Three examples may be referred to at this stage in the discussion. To begin with, take the case of the James Dean fan club. James Dean died in a car crash near Cholame on 30 September 1955 at 5.59 p.m. Every year on that day a procession of 1949 Mercs and 1950 Fords, driven by fans of Dean, arrive at the spot where the crash occurred in time for the exact moment of the crash. Not only do the fans visit the black spot, but they fastidiously take the same route that Dean followed from Los Angeles on his last day. Mile for mile, and moment for moment, they try to repeat the sights, sounds and experiences that their hero experienced on the journey. Here the black spot functions not only as a monument to the dead hero, but also as the touchstone to a whole way of life which has been submerged in time. The fans take pride in the period authenticity of their automobiles and their fifties style of dress (Beath 1986: 10).

The second example is provided by the twenty-fifth anniversary of John F. Kennedy's assassination. Kennedy, the 36th president of the United States, was shot at approximately 1.56 p.m. Central Standard Time on 22 November 1963. He was pronounced dead about thirty minutes later. Kennedy's death conferred the patina of invulnerability upon the landscape of the assassination site and its immediate surroundings. Little has been allowed to change. The Book Depository, from which the alleged assassin, Oswald, fired the shots has been preserved from demolition and is now a museum. However, the attempt to preserve the memory of 22 November 1963 goes much deeper than that. On the occasion of the twenty-fifth anniversary of the assassination, at precisely 1.56 p.m., a Dallas cable television channel replayed four full hours (uninterrupted by commercials) of NBC's original assassination coverage. The tragedy was replayed as spectacle. Viewers were invited to follow the events as they unfold – or rather, as they unfolded again. The sign and the real were treated as equivalent. The presence of events in the contemporary-life world was not compromised by their material absence. The simulation was presented as a 'live' event.

The third example refers to Graceland, Tennessee. Elvis Presley died in Graceland on 16 August 1977. He was buried in the grounds. Every year on the anniversary of his death, thousands of people take part in a Candlelight Vigil. They take the journey to Graceland, along the Elvis Presley Boulevard, and file past the Meditation Gardens where Elvis is buried along with his mother, father and grandmother. Hundreds linger on until the dawn breaks on the actual anniversary of his death, lighting a succession of candles. Throughout the year, tour operators present visitors with the Elvis experience. Tourists are invited to walk where he walked, sit where he sat, see what he saw. His personal cook has been employed to prepare Elvis's favourite dishes. Tourists are therefore given the chance to actually enter Elvis's bodily experience. By consuming the food that he consumed, by being catered to by the same cook that catered to him, one receives the illusion of knowing what it was like to be Elvis. In Graceland, one is shown the dining-room where Elvis customarily had his dinner; the actual television set where Elvis watched football; the Buckingham china which Priscilla and Elvis favoured when they married; the den which Elvis decorated with his own hand; and the 200 guns which Elvis liked to fire. It is as if his death were of incidental importance. Graceland radiates with Elvis's presence, or, at least the Presley Estate's version of what Elvis actually was. And this sense of Elvis's presence in contemporary life is hardly apocryphal. Sightings of him occur constantly. For example, as the space shuttle landed in the night sky over Edwards Air Force Base late in 1989, Elvis's kindly face was sighted with arm outstretched to guide the craft back home. On the night when he died, people have reported that an angel appeared above the clouds in Graceland. Call 900–246–ELVIS from any American home and you are connected with the Elvis hotline which carries bulletins of the latest sightings and best wishes to Elvis. In 1989, 1.5 million callers used the service. On the 900 telephone exchange each caller was charged $2 for the first minute, and 95 cents for each minute after that. 1.5 million calls represented a minimum income of $3 million for the California-based company which runs the service. The US, in the 1980s, was deluged with books which claimed that Elvis had faked his death and retired from the spotlight to Alaska, Hawaii or Key West. In 1989 the sightings became so persistent that the *Sun* newspaper in London offered £1 million to anyone who could prove that Elvis was still alive.[8]

Baudrillard, writing on the omnipresence of simulation in contemporary culture, submits that,

> the unreal is no longer that of dream or fantasy, of a beyond or within, it is that of a *hallucinatory* resemblance of the real with itself. To exist from the crisis of representation, you have to lock the real up in pure repetition. (1983: 142)

The leisure forms described above are indeed activities of pure repetition. The commercial development of black spots encourages the tourist and the fan to project themselves into the personalities, events and ways of life which have disappeared. But this projection could not be accomplished at all unless the personalities and ways of life were not so omnipresent in our culture through audio-visual media. 'What is real,' comments Tagg, 'is not just the material item but also the discursive system of which the image it bears is part' (1988: 41). Electronic audio-visual culture emphatically presses the past upon us. Through bio-pics, drama documentaries, mini-soaps, re-packaged recordings and re-released movies, the past is rendered 'contemporaneous' with the present.

The cult of nostalgia was, of course, the inevitable consequence of the progress of modernity. The 'constant revolutionizing of the instruments and relations of production' (Marx and Engels 1848: 38) which the nineteenth century established as 'normality', made the flight into the 'calmer', 'resplendent' pre-modern past seem like a magnetic attraction for large numbers of the Victorian intelligentsia. In the Pre-Raphaelites' return to medieval England, Tennyson's popular cycle of poems organised around the Arthurian legends, and the 'classicist' photography of Francis Frith, Julia Margaret Cameron and James Craig Annan, do we not find evidence of strong aesthetic and ideological associations with the past as a place of peace and splendour? Simmel's essay on 'The Ruin' (1965) recognized the prevalence and force of nostalgia in modernity. 'The ruin,' he wrote, 'creates the present form of a past life, not according to the contours or remnants of that life, but according to its past as such' (1965: 265). Simmel rejects the idea that nostalgia is a cultural effect, a matter of technique, staging or re-enactment. If the ruin infuses us with a sense of nostalgia it is, he wrote, because 'where the work of art is dying, other forces and forms, those of nature have grown' (1965: 260). Nothing illustrates the contrast between human work and the remorseless effect of nature so unequivocally.

Of the Black Spots described in this chapter it is perhaps, only cemeteries that meet Simmels' criterion of nostalgia. They are clearly on the edge between culture and nature, and the physical decay of headstones, effigies and epitaphs only serve to make the contrast more poignant. Perhaps this is one reason why people visit cemeteries in such large numbers.[9] The other Black Spots described above have a staged, sensational quality which corresponds with Debord's discussion of the spectacle. Debord writes:

> The spectacle presents itself as something enormously positive, indisputable and inaccessible. It says nothing more than "that which appears is good, and that which is good appears". The attitude which it demands in principle is passive acceptance. (1967: 12)

Debord goes on to anticipate an argument which postmodernist authors elaborated in the 1970s and '80s. That is, contemporary society is permeated with spectacle to such an extent that modernist distinctions between the real and the imaginary are no longer valid. I shall return to this argument in the final section of the chapter. However, before doing do I want to shed more light on the blurring and elimination of distinctions between the real and the imaginary by examining contemporary attempts by the leisure industry to display and re-enact the past: Heritage Sites.

HERITAGE SITES

'Robin Hood is alive and well and living in Sherwood Forest,' declares the Nottinghamshire County Council's Leisure Services Department 'Special Break' brochure for the Spring and Summer of 1989. Robin is the lead item in the city's tourist attractions. A colour picture of his statue near the city castle appears on the cover of the complimentary Nottingham 'General Information and City Centre Map'; and a cartoon of his smiling face (evidently a simulacrum of the face of Errol Flynn who played the famous outlaw in the successful Hollywood film of Robin Hood in the 1930s), dominates the Council's 'Special Breaks' brochure for Spring and Summer 1989. Robin's image has also supported several private sector leisure initiatives in the city. Among the most ambitious is the 'Tales of Robin Hood' centre which opened in 1989 at the cost of £1.9 million. 'Here', the 'Souvenir Guide' reports, 'in the City where England's best loved outlaw waged war against his arch enemy, the Sheriff of Nottingham, we invite you to step back into a long-gone world of story-telling and adventure'. The 'Guide' continues:

> Come with us to the days when good was good and evil was most foul. When the king ruled the land with justice. When the Sheriff of Nottingham oppressed the people with greed and corruption. When heroes fought oppressors with courage and cunning. Ride through Nottingham in our unique adventure cars. Meet its people. Smell its smells. Join its daily life. Come with us to the greenwood.

The exhibition uses a mini ski-lift system to transport visitors through scenes from medieval Nottingham, and audio-visual effects such as talking heads, holography, soundtracks, lighting and costumes to create the sense of a journey back in to the world of Robin Hood.

But there is a problem with this hawking of civic pride. Historical authorities submit that Robin existed in folklore rather than fact. 'Robin's activities', declares Holt flatly, 'were not recorded by any contemporary chronicler. No one says that he knew him or had seen him. No one could point to authentic records of his activities' (1982: 40). Holt argues that Robin Hood was the mythical expression of the interweaving of numerous medieval and Tudor folktales, ballads and romances. The most powerful of these emanated from the north of England and locate Robin's activities in the Barnsdale region of

Yorkshire; which is many miles from Nottingham's Sherwood Forest (Holt 1982: 188). Even historians who are more sympathetic to the proposition that Robin did exist as a real person, insist that his relationship with Nottingham is dubious. For Bellamy (1985: 136), the 'archetypal' Robin Hood was Robert Hud, *fugitivus*, apparently arraigned and outlawed at the York sessions of 1225, and active in the Barnsdale region of Yorkshire.[10]

However, as a myth, as a discursive system which has real effects on the way in which community and free time practice and association are organized, the legend still has enormous power in Nottingham. For example, in 1988 the city council issued a new tourist leaflet. It conceded that the legend of Robin Hood would always occupy a special place in the history and life of the city. At the same time, the leaflet pointed out that many aspects of the legend were questionable. Robin Hood and Maid Marian, it alleged, were never sweethearts and never even met; Friar Tuck was pure invention, a product of the romantic imaginations of Medieval balladeers and minstrels; to be sure, the leaflet implied that the whole Robin Hood legend had been embroidered by travelling minstrels and glamorized further by the Hollywood film industry. The leaflet was the object of ferocious criticism in the city. The Nottingham Robin Hood Society was reported as stating that, 'the city has a golden egg which they should be making the most of, not trying to spoil', while the City Council Conservative group tabled members of the Tourism Committee 'to destroy the offending leaflet after world-wide protests'.[11]

Eco (1986: 7), in his inventory of hyperreality, comments upon the organization of new leisure forms based upon simulation, spectacle, impact and sensation, in which 'absolute unreality is offered as real presence'. The aim of these leisure forms, continues Eco, is to supply a 'sign' which will immediately be accepted as reality. This preoccupation is very evident in the planning and commercial development of heritage sites. 'Reality' is 'convened' by the use of two methods: (1) the employment of actors and stage sets to reenact the past; (2) the design of tableaux in which holography, soundtracks, moving 'time cars', trick lighting and other special effects 'transport' the visitor back in time. In fact they are often mixed in heritage sites to add variety to the attractions. However, for the present purpose I will treat them in an ideal-typical way as separate categories. First, let me give some examples of 'performance sites', in which actors and stage sets operate to create a sense of historical reality.

One of the chief attractions in 'Plymouth Country' New England, where the Pilgrim Fathers landed in 1620, is the artificially constructed Plimouth Plantation heritage site. This 'outdoor museum' aims to recreate the 1627 settlement of the Pilgrims. Aboard *Mayflower II* which is docked in Plymouth harbour, 'interpreters' play the parts of the crew and passengers who made the 1620 voyage. Visitors are encouraged to pay to go on board and meet them. As the Plymouth County Development Council heritage leaflet for the site puts it:[12]

Their authentic dress, speech, manner and attitudes enhance their description of the 66-day voyage from England aboard the cramped, leaky vessel. In the same manner, interpreters in the Pilgrim Village portray actual residents of 1627 Plymouth. Visitors meet the likes of Gov. William Bradford, John and Priscilla Alden, Myles Standish, Elizabeth Hopkins and Bridget Fuller. Villagers demonstrate period crafts, cooking and gardening skills while answering questions in 17th century English dialects.[13]

Thousands of miles west in contemporary America, at the MW ranch in Hudson, Colorado, a more strenuous heritage scheme is in operation. This aims to recreate 'the old West adventure' by an 'authentic' 1870s full-scale cowboy cattle drive. The six-day journey on horseback involves moving 200 head of cattle over 65 miles of varied terrain, including low mesa and high alpine forest. 'Drovers', dressed in period costume, sleep on bedrolls, eat from the chuckwaggon and work two hour shifts to control the herd. The average age of the drovers is the late 30s to early 40s.[14]

At Wigan Pier, Lancashire, 'The Way We Were' heritage centre employs a team of seven actors to recreate life in the north-west at the turn of the century. The centre is financed and administered by Metropolitan Wigan Council and its tourist leaflet for the site invites you to:

Enter the world of 'The Way We Were' and step back into the year 1900. This is how the people of Wigan, Leigh and other local communities were at the turn of the century; how they lived, loved, worked, played and died. Start in the fantasy world of the Wigan Pier joke or join Wiganers on their all-too-brief annual Wakes Week holiday . . . experience life below ground at the coalface, see the work of the famous Lancashire pit brow lasses and feel the horrors of the Maypole colliery disaster . . . Above all, talk to the people of 1900. In the schoolroom become a child once more and experience the rigours of a strict Victorian education. In the collier's cottage speak with the family, hear their hopes and share their sorrows. Peep into the Mayor's parlour as he tries on his ceremonial robes for the coronation of Edward VII; bargain in the markets with stall holders or talk with the young volunteer, off to South Africa and the Boer War.

Wigan Pier is presented as 'part theatre, part museum'. In common with many other heritage performance sites, for example, the Black Country Museum (Dudley) or the Beamish Open Air Museum (near Chester-le-Street), the educational role of the centre is stressed. Wigan Pier employs three full-time teachers to lead up to 200 children in project work. More generally, the exhibitions of life are designed to fulfil an educational purpose for adults. Many of the staged events focus on actors performing vanished or marginalized crafts. For example, the Black Country Museum invites you to 'witness the traditional skills of nailmaking, chainmaking, glasscutting, brass founding or boatbuilding' and to 'see how people lived in days gone by'.

I want to return to the educational purpose of heritage sites, and also to speculate on the reasons why vanished or marginalized crafts are presented as attractions, later in the section. However, before doing so it remains to consider the next main growth area in heritage sites: *tableaux*. 'Canterbury Pilgrims Way' is a tableau which offers 'modern pilgrims' the experience to 'tread again in steps worn 600 years ago in Chaucer's pilgrims'. In the words of the travel brochure:

As your journey unfolds you experience authentic, unforgettable sights, sounds and smells of 14th century life. Along the dusty stretches of road, five of your companions, the bawdy Miller, the Courtly Knight, the Wife of Bath, the Nun's priest and the Pardoner will recount their colourful stories of chivalry, romance, jealousy, pride and avarice.

The leaflet also emphasizes the educational purpose of the exhibition.

Everything you encounter, [it maintains] in The Canterbury Pilgrims Way enthrals as well as explains. Students discover a living world not found in study programmes about Chaucer. People fascinated by the past find the textures of life that books alone cannot convey.

The Canterbury Pilgrims Way experience is far from being the only major capital investment heritage project themed around a tableau which was developed in Britain in the 1980s. For example, in Windsor, 'the Royalty and Empire' heritage centre offers tourists 'the experience of another lifetime'. The theme of the centre is the Diamond Jubilee of 1897. On-site attractions include a replica of the Royal train 'exact in every detail'; a reproduction of the Royal wedding-room; mannequins of 70 Coldstream Guardsmen on the parade ground; mannequins of selected members of the Royal family of 1897; and an audio-visual show called 'Sixty Glorious Years' in which computer technology is used 'to present famous Victorians who actually move and talk'. Similarly, Winchester offers 'The Crusades Experience' featuring 'the Battle of Acre' in which models of Richard the Lionheart and Saladin speak their respect for each other, before the siege machines activate and crusader bowmen appear with arrows drawn. While *The Black Country Museum* in Dudley offers visitors *Into The Thick*, a tableau themed around the underground mining experience in Victoria's reign. 'Take a trip "Into the Thick",' urges the tourist leaflet, 'through dark tunnels to the coal face and the pit bottom; see miners at work; hear the timbers creak and the coal drop off the roof. Meet "Lija Wedge" and his workmates in this reconstruction of a Black Country mine in the 1850's'.[15]

In Disneyland, California, the 'Great Moments with Mr Lincoln' attraction boasts 'the most sophisticated lifelike robot in the world' (Birnbaum 1989: 70). 'Honest Abe' was completely reprogrammed in December 1984 following a joint three-year research project at the University of Utah. The university, with a worldwide reputation in the development of artificial limbs, was given the task of enhancing the reality of the audio-animatronic figure. The result was the development of 'the compliance system', a technology which allows Lincoln to shift his body weight 'as naturally as a human and enables him to sense when he is near another object' (ibid). The Lincoln robot, nods, gestures, turns and 'discourses on liberty, the American spirit, the changes facing the country, respect for law, faith in Divine Providence, and duty' (ibid).[16]

'Postmodernism,' asserts Foster, 'is marked by an eclectic historicism, in which old and new models and styles . . . are retooled and recycled' (1985: 121).[17] Eclectic historicism has certainly been the style of the performance sites and tableau developed by the heritage industry in the 1980s. For example, the Jorvik site in York is generally regarded as one of the most successful heritage attractions developed in Britain during the 1980s. The site consists of a tableau representing the sights, sounds and smells of the Viking city of Jorvik. One is 'whisked back through the centuries' by 'time cars' into 'a journey to real-life Viking Britain'. Adjacent to the tableau is a reconstruction of the archaeological dig 'exactly where it took place'.[18] The contemporary excavation and the re-erected tenth-century buildings and objects found in them are preserved together in absolute equivalence. Similarly in major performance sites in Britain, like the Beamish Open Air Museum and 'The Way We Were' exhibit in Wigan Pier, authentic historical buildings and artefacts are preserved and actors in period costume present themselves as real living people from the past. The authentic and the inauthentic are displayed as equivalent items.

The staging and display of heritage sites in the 1970s and '80s through performance sites and tableau, involved not only the preservation of items from the past, but also simulating a context for them. Invented people were produced to personalize history. For example, 'Lija Wedge' in the 'Into the Thick' tableau in the Black Country Museum, and the teachers, collier's family and young Boer War volunteer in 'The Way We Were' site in Wigan Pier. The aim was to increase the attraction value of heritage. Design values of impact, drama and sensation were particularly important at a time in which government funding of public sector museums and heritage sites was being cut back. Self-finance was the buzz-word in the heritage industry in Britain during the 1980s. This meant not only that heritage had to be preserved, but that it had to look right (Lowenthal 1985: 263, 293; Wright 1985: 69; Urry 1990: 128–34).

Some of the complexities involved in presenting inauthentic 'sights, sounds and smells' as authentic are explored by MacCannell (1973; 1976: 92–102) in his discussion of 'staged authenticity'. MacCannell uses this concept to refer to the use of dramaturgical and other presentational devices to simulate 'real life' for tourists. The concept has an obvious application to tableau and tourist sites discussed above. However, interestingly, MacCannell invests it with deeper theoretical resonance. He submits that modernity dislocates our attachment to work, neighbourhood, town and family. We become interested in 'the real lives' of others. As touristic examples, he mentions the development of tours to society's 'back regions'. That is, areas normally closed off or concealed from our view: factories, coalmines, fire-stations, farms, the stock exchange, bank vaults, ghetto areas, etc. One ironical implication of this is that as economies de-industrialize, and more flexibility and leisure is created for people, the workplace where we can observe others at work, increases its attraction value as a leisure and tourist destination. This certainly helps to explain the attraction of displaying vanished or marginalized crafts in contemporary heritage sites like the Black Country Museum, the Plimouth plantation, the village of Waterloo and Beamish. The action of modernity, it might be said, destroys traditional crafts only to restage them as objects of display in the heritage industry. The example also illustrates the tendency of modernity to undercut the divisions and dissolve the boundaries which it initiated: back regions are turned into front regions, hidden areas of life become items of exhibition, the past which is 'lost' is 'recreated' in the present.

The personalizing of leisure and tourist space, and the use of devices of staged authenticity, is not confined to heritage sites. The same methods have been used widely and intensively in the marketing and organization of literary landscapes. It is to this area that I now wish to turn.

LITERARY LANDSCAPES

Number 221B Baker Street in London is now a branch of a leading national building society. It was also, of course, the home of the fictional detective, Sherlock Holmes, invented by Sir Arthur Canon Doyle in 1854. One of the duties of the marketing staff employed by the building society is to answer the regular letters written to Holmes at the Baker Street address. 'Please write back and tell me what you think about the Loch Ness Monster,' requests one correspondent from Idaho. 'Dear Holmes,' writes another correspondent from Texas, 'every time I go outside my window I see strange things, I see footprints with three toes and blood on the house. Please come quick.' The marketing staff write back explaining that Holmes has retired to the Sussex countryside to pursue his hobby of bee-keeping, and that he no longer undertakes detective work.[19]

The Holmes myth shows no sign of withering away. All of the stories are still in print. Between 1900 and 1980, 60 actors played him in 175 films. Holmes is, in fact, the most frequently recurring character on the screen. Off Trafalgar Square the Sherlock Holmes restaurant features a museum including a reconstruction of Holmes's study. Sherlock Holmes societies organize mystery week-ends in the locations of his most famous stories and tours to the Reichenbach Falls in Switzerland where Holmes disappeared in his final conflict with Moriarty and where actors re-enact the drama. The Holmes myth has even received official sanction through the decision to decorate London Transport's Baker Street Underground station with reproductions of his silhouette, complete with deer stalker and pipe.

The landscape of Atlanta, Georgia is peppered with references to the fictional characters of Rhett Butler and Scarlett O'Hara created by Margaret Mitchell in her famous novel *Gone With The Wind*. Tours of the essential geography of the novel are combined with tours of the main Civil War battle-sites in the area. At the CNN Center in downtown Atlanta, the film of *Gone With The Wind*, featuring Clark Gable and Vivien Leigh, plays every day of the week. The advertisement for the Center shows a colour illustration of Rhett and Scarlett locked in a passionate embrace against the backdrop of CNN TV monitors. The dialogue underneath reads:

I declare Scarlett, I have never seen anything quite like this before. This new CNN Center is more exciting than Tara in julep season. The tours of the CNN and Headline News studios gave me a fascinating look behind the scenes of the 24 hr. news networks . . . and all of this excitement has left me famished.

Fiddle-dee-dee, Rhett. As God is my witness we'll never go hungry here. Not with the sumptuous feats served at Bugatti and the Cafe of the Omni Hotel, not to mention all the tempting delights of the food court. Why, Rhett, promise me tonight we'll dine, dance and romance the night away at the Lion's Den Restaurant.[20]

Thus is fiction co-opted in the service of commerce and myth mingles with reality.

Britain abounds in literary landscapes. the 'Lorna Doone Country' of Somerset; 'Daphne du Maurier Country' in Cornwall; 'Brontë Country' and 'James Herriot Country' in Yorkshire; 'Land O'Burns' in Scotland; 'Dylan Thomas Country' in Carmarthen Bay and Teifi Valley; 'Catherine Cookson Country' in South Tyneside; 'Shakespeare Country' in the Midlands; 'D.H. Lawrence Country' in West

Nottinghamshire; 'The Lake District Country' immortalized by Wordsworth and the lakes poets; 'Hardy Country' in Dorset; and the 'London' of Johnson, Keats, Dickens, the Bloomsbury Group, etc. These 'countries' may be formally described as landscapes of imaginative reflection. Their authors certainly drew from the local geography, folklore and people to create fictional representations in their novels. But if this is correct it is just as true that these imaginary landscapes reflect back upon the physical spaces and folk traditions which they sprang from. For example, the 'Casterbridge' of Hardy's 'Wessex' is so real to many people that they experience a sense of anti-climax when they visit the town of Dorchester which was Hardy's model for his imaginary town. However, their sense of being in a place in which the image of Hardy's fiction is reflected is supported by numerous features in the 'real' town. Thus, Dorchester's town planners have permitted certain streets to be called after the names of characters in Hardy's novels. Similarly, a blue plaque has been authorised on the wall of a building in the town centre (now a bank), which proclaims that the building was where Michael Henchard, the eponymous hero of Hardy's *The Mayor of Casterbridge* 'lived'.

The interweaving of fiction and reality is so strong in some landscapes that local leisure services departments have organized physical space into themed literary 'trails'. Tourists are asked to follow literary landmarks which relate to the fiction of the local novelist. For example, the Medway leisure services department issues a complimentary leaflet for 'The Dickens Trail'. It begins by asserting that Rochester, Chatham and the surrounding countryside is 'synonymous' with the novels of Charles Dickens. Local reference points are defined and their landmark status in Dickens' fiction is revealed. For example, Restoration House in Crow Lane, Rochester, is revealed as the model of Miss Havisham's Satis House in *Great Expectations*; the Royal Victoria and Bull Hotel in the High Street is said to be the model for the The Bull in *Pickwick Papers* and The Blue Boar in *Great Expectations*; John Jasper, one of the main characters in *The Mystery of Edwin Drood*, is said to have lived on top of Chertsey's Gate, at the junction of the High Street and Boley Hill.

Similarly, in 1985 South Tyneside launched the 'Catherine Cookson Trail'. As with the 'Dickens Trail', physical space is organized around fictional landmark sites. For example, Gambling Man Gallery, in Wapping Street, South Shields is identified as the setting for Cookson's

Physical reference point	*Literary Landmark*
Castle	*Pickwick Papers* / *Great Expectations*
Cathedral	*Great Expectations* / *Pickwick Papers*
Chertsey's Gate	Home of John Jasper *(Edwin Drood)*
Mr Topes	Lodging of Mr Datchery *(Edwin Drood)*
Minor Canon Row	Minor Canon Corner *(Edwin Drood)*
150–54 High Street	Uncle Pumblechook's Shop *(Great Expectations)*
The Vines	Priory Garden *(Great Expectations)* Monks' Vineyward *(Edward Drood)*
Restoration House	Satis House *(Great Expectations)*
Eastgate House	Westgate House *(Pickwick Papers)* Nun's House *(Edwin Drood)*
Watts Charity	The Seven Poor Travellers *(Christmas Tale 1854)*
Old Corn Exchange	Moonfaced Clock *(The Uncommercial Traveller)*
Guildhall	*Great Expectations*
Royal Victoria & Bull Hotel	*Pickwick Papers* (The Bull) *Great Expectations* (The Blue Boar)
Fort Pitt Fields	Scene of duel between Mr Winkle and Dr Slammer *(Pickwick Papers)*
Conservative Club, Star Hill	The Theatre *(Edwin Drood* and *The Uncommercial Traveller)*

Figure 4a: 'The Dickens Trail', Rochester

Physical Reference Point	Literary Landmark
Gambling Man Gallery	Setting for *The Gambling Man*
Sir William Fox Hotel, Westhoe Village	Setting for *Katie Mulholland*
Mill Dam Bank	Setting for *Colour Blind*
Corstophine Town, South Shields	Setting for *The Blind Miller*
Marsden Bay	Setting for *Mrs Flannigan's Trumpet*
Seafront, Sandhaven	Setting for *The Tide of Life*
South Shields Museum	Catherine Cookson memorabilia to be housed here.

Figure 4b: 'The Catherine Cookson Trail', South Shields

novel, *The Gambling Man*; the Sir William Fox Hotel, Westoe village is revealed as the setting for the events and characters in *Katie Mulholland*; and Marsden Bay, South Shields is identified as the setting for *Mrs Flannigan's Trumpet*. Figure 4 compares the two trails in terms of physical reference points and literary landscapes. Literary landscapes do not just focus on the fictional characters and settings of novelists, they also address features of the novelist's 'real' life. Tour operators are increasingly using this as a theme in the organization of literary landscapes. For example, in Sun Valley, Idaho, you can eat at Ernest Hemingway's favourite restaurant and sit at the table where he ate his last meal; you can drink at the Ram and Duchin, the Tram Bar and the Alpine (now the Whiskey Jacques) in Ketchum, which were all drinking haunts of Hemingway; you can also drive to Trail Creek Cabin, a Sun Valley Resort Party Cabin, where Hemingway, Gary Cooper and Ingrid Bergman spent New Year's Eve in 1947.[21] Similarly, in cities with strong literary associations like London, Paris, Vienna, San Francisco and New York, guided literary walks are fixed features of the local leisure and tourist industry. For example, The Streets of London Company offers weekly tours of 'The London of Sherlock Holmes', 'The London of Charles

Dickens' and 'Literary London' which covers places associated with Orwell, Shaw, Pepys, Johnson, Sheridan, Goldsmith and Shakespeare. The status of 'reality' is, of course, the crux of postmodernism. Frankfurt Marxism proposed that advanced industrial society is a world of drastically reduced meaning. Manipulation, conformity and repression dominate; dissent, diversity and irregularity are not tolerated. Postmodernism takes the opposite view. It proposes that contemporary society is now so overloaded with meaning that our received methods and criteria of determining fact from fiction and ultimately, the real from the imaginary, have exploded. 'We are gorged with meaning,' complains Baudrillard (1987: 63), 'and it is killing us'.

One corollary of this is that the legitimacy of the authorities charged with maintaining order comes under intense attack. Competing groups issue authority claims which not only challenge the legitimacy of the official power structure, but also call into question the 'order' which supports this legitimacy. Literary landscapes illustrate the point very clearly. We may cite three examples from recent British experience.

In the autumn of 1986, the Ramblers Association held a rally in Brontë Country. The issue was the lack of free access to Stanbury Moor, an area owned by the Yorkshire Water Authority. The Authority operated a policy of barring people from roaming freely over the land which has strong associations with the Brontë novels. The Ramblers Association alleged that the Authority was being negligent in its public responsibility to manage the space for recreational use as opposed to merely public utility use. The rally was one of thirty-five protests in the Ramblers 'Forbidden Britain' campaign.[22]

Another example of competing authority claims in respect of the management of a literary landscape refers to D.H. Lawrence Country in Nottinghamshire. In 1988, British Coal announced plans to develop 180 acres surrounding Lawrence's birthplace of Eastwood in Nottinghamshire for opencast mining. The announcement provoked fierce criticism. The Moorgreen and District Action Group launched a protest campaign with Lady Chatterly, the heroine of Lawrence's novel, as the spearhead of the campaign. They argued that to destroy the landscape where Lady Connie 'strolled', and where much of *Women in Love* is also set, would be an act of vandalism. British Coal is presented as an unprincipled marauder attacking an immortal order of things. Which is something of an irony, because similar criticisms were made by contemporaries of Lawrence in respect of the sexual frankness and libertarianism of his fiction. The unavailing local hostility was one factor behind Lawrence's decision to quit Britain for a more equable moral climate.[23] It was not until the 1970s that Lawrence's memory was officially rehabilitated and the local council and private leisure interests began to develop 'Lawrence Country' as a regional tourist resource.

The third example refers to Thomas Hardy Country. Hardy, we know, actively supported the transmogrification of his imaginary landscapes and characters into the 'history' of 'Wessex'. For example, he participated in Hermann Lea's *Guides to Thomas Hardy's Wessex* (first published in 1913), which included directions to, and photographs of, the 'real' places in Hardy's fiction.[24] Lea's *Guides* enable the intrepid tourist to walk in the footsteps of Jude Fawley *(Jude the Obscure)*, Clym Yeobright *(The Return of the Native)*, Tess *(Tess of the D'Urbervilles)*, Gabriel Oak *(Far From the Maddening Crowd)*, Henchard *(The Mayor of Casterbridge)* and Giles Winterbourne *(The Woodlanders)* (see Figure 5). A recurring theme in Hardy's fiction is the annihilation of the countryside and traditional ways of life by the onslaught of modernity. Today, Thomas Hardy's literary landscape is besieged by the same threat. In 1987 and 1990 property developers attempted to reshape Hardy's Wessex by announcing major developments around Stinsford churchyard, which is literally the heart of Hardy Country.[25] In 1987 the landscape was threatened by plans to build 560 houses and a business park half a mile from the churchyard. The plans were resisted by protest groups who accused the planners of attempting to commit an act of sacrilege. In 1990 commercial developers proposed plans to construct a 100-bed motel and conference centre, a fast-food restaurant and an on-site sewage treatment plant in Stinsford. The proposed development coincided with plans from another property developer to build motorway-style services and heritage centres on the site. Protesters argue that the main service station development would obliterate the landscape which is at the centre of Hardy's novel, *Under the Greenwood Tree*.[26]

What these examples show is that literary landscapes have a political significance in our culture.[27] In a society in which the commodification of physical space is the order of the day, literary landscapes are presented as escape areas which cannot be tampered with. At least, this is the position which is familiar to us in modernist discourse: that troubled discourse which sought to lay down an

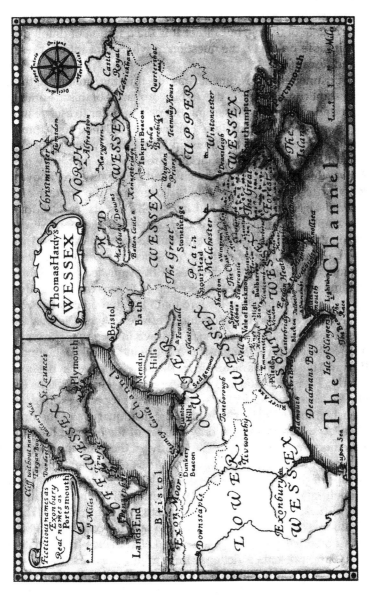

Figure 5: Thomas Hardy Country

immortal order of things while, at the same time, recognizing the necessity of progress. However, from a postmodernist standpoint, the fundamental question is not the contradictions inherent in this troubled state of things, but rather it is the question of ontology or, to put it more precisely, the question of what is meant by 'preserving' and 'escaping'.

The postmodernist argument runs like this: the mobility of things is a constant condition. The inevitable corollaries of this are ambiguity and undecidability. Preserving the past in order to escape into it is therefore seen as impossible. For merely to define something as unchangeable alters our relationship to it. Literary landscapes and, for that matter, heritage sites, do not preserve the past, they represent it. If this is correct, authenticity and originality are, above all, matters of technique. The staging, design and the context of the preserved object become crucial in establishing its 'reality' for us. For example, in the Catherine Cookson Trail the homes where Cookson was born and raised were demolished some time ago in the name of progress. However, their 'presence' is represented by steel street markers which locate the sites of the vanished original buildings. Similarly, the impact of the Streets of Dickens tour in London is diminished by the fact that his two main London houses have been demolished. Number 1 Devonshire Terrace, where Dickens lived between 1839 and 1851, was knocked down in 1959 to make way for an office block. All that remains is a frieze in *bas relief* depicting the author and the chief characters from the novels written in the house. Similarly, Tavistock House, Tavistock Square, where Dickens lived after the lease on the Devonshire Terrace property expired, was demolished in 1901. The site is now the headquarters of the British Medical Association and the only marker of the original house is a commemorative blue plaque. The 'reality' of these absent properties depends upon context. It is a conjuring trick of the tour guide using the props of the marker and the immediate locale to spellbind us.

What implications does the postmodern position have for understanding the political significance of literary landscapes? From a postmodern standpoint, the campaign to save the countryside where Lady Connie 'strolled' or Tess of the D'Urbevilles 'roamed' with Angel Clare, presents a fictional Britain and presents it as reality. The politics of preservation, on this reading, simply confirm the postmodern tenet that we live in a society in which the 'completely real' is identified with the 'completely fake' (Eco 1986: 7).

THEME PARKS

The attractions developed in the theme parks of the 1970s and '80s were very varied. The two main factors causing variation were locale and the product portfolio of the managing company. Take the subject of locale first: Thorpe Park in Surrey is a water-based leisure park. It was developed from a series of disused gravel pits. Such sites are often shunned by property developers because the natural water table is exposed on excavation and often restricts building. By treating the water as an asset, the developers of Thorpe Park were able to exploit the characteristics of locale as themes for a range of attractions: the 'Thunder River' water ride; the 'Magic Mill' ride; reconstructions of a Roman port, a full-size Roman fighting galley, signal towers, baths, temple and forum. The Cedar Park, Ohio; Adventure Island, Florida; and the Worlds of Fun Park, Missouri, make similar use of natural physical features to organize attractions. As for the subject of the product portfolios, the managing companies of theme parks organize attractions around their corporate products as and when it is viable. For example, the Walt Disney Company ensures that its attractions at Disneyland, California, and Disney World, Florida, feature the main Disney cartoon characters. Similarly, the Universal Studios theme park in Hollywood organizes its attractions around movie hits like *Jaws*, *E.T.* and *Back to the Future*'.[28] In both cases, the attractions not only reinforce the corporate images of the companies, they also underwrite the market in on-site commodity memorabilia such as T-shirts, watches, pens, bags, stationery, key-rings, slides, etc.[29]

Although there are as many themes as there are theme parks, certain meta-themes recur. In what follows I want to concentrate on the two paramount ones: velocity and time-space compression.

(i) Velocity

I could feel my brain mushing against the top of my head. I've always wanted to know how it felt to jump from an eighth-story window.

The Orient Express tosses you around a lot, but the Timber Wolf creaks and groans. Makes an old codger feel like a kid again.

These are two verbatim responses reported by the *New York Times* in August 1989 from participants rating the 'thrill factor' in, respectively, the Texas Cyclone (roller coaster) and Sky Screamer (free fall) rides at the Texas Astroworld theme park, and the Orient Express and Timber Wolf (roller coasters) and Typhoon (water slide) rides at the *Missouri Worlds of Fun/Oceans of Fun* theme park.[30] They illustrate an obvious and prominent fact about theme park attractions: rides propelling bodies through great speed are a frontline attraction. The Great Adventure theme park at Jackson, Missouri, is centred on the 'Great American Scream Machine', a 17-storey-tall ride billed as 'the tallest and fastest looping roller-coaster in the world'; the Six Flags Magic Mountain theme park in California is organized around a series of 'white-knuckle' rides, such as 'Tidal Wave', a 20-foot wall of water that creates a 'monstrous' 40-foot splash, the 'Colossus' billed as 'the largest dual-track wooden roller-coaster in the entire world, the 'Log Jammer', billed as 'the longest water flume ride in the entire country. It creates the feeling of being up a creek . . . without a paddle', 'Ninja' which propels you at speeds of up to 55 miles per hour while careening at angles of up to 180 degrees, and 'Condor', 'it raises you 112 feet in the air, spins you around and send you spiralling back to the ground at a rate of 26 feet per second. No wonder they call it the wildest ride in captivity'.[31] European theme parks have not left themselves out of the picture. Phantasialand in Germany features the 'Mountain Railway' and 'Waterfall' rides. Alton Towers in England offers the 'Alton Beast' roller-coaster and 'Cork-screw' attractions. De Efteling in Holland, described in *The Economist* as 'the doyen of European Parks',[32] offers a variety of family rides, including water-based attractions.

Can we not see the preoccupation with 'endless motion' which Kroker and Cook (1986: 249) list as an identifying characteristic of postmodernism, expressed in a vivid and concentrated form in these 'white knuckle' attractions? Is there not in the desire to invert the body, to defy gravity, a parallel to be drawn with the inversion and sliding of signs which is at the heart of postmodernist vision? At least one author has thought so. Bennett (1983: 148), writing on the persistence of velocity in theme park attractions, describes the rides as 'inverting the usual relations between the body and machinery and generally inscribing the body in relations different from those in which it is caught and held in everyday life'. Here mere difference and speed are identified as sources of pleasure. No functionalist or grand evolutionary narrative is attributed to them.[33] The fascination with difference for its own sake is also evident in the time-space compression attractions featured in contemporary theme parks. It is to this subject that I now wish to turn.

(ii) Time-Space Compression

'This year,' declares the Busch Gardens, Williamsburg, tourist leaflet for 1986, 'you can visit England, France, Germany, Italy without leaving the USA.' How is this miraculous feat accomplished? The theme park contains four reconstructions of 'typical' English, French, German and Italian villages. The tour leaflet description of the English village can serve as an example of the general characteristics of the scheme:

> Enter *Banbury Cross* and find yourself surrounded by all the sights and sounds of Merrie Old England. Taste English treats, shop for fine gifts, and thrill to the Olympic style ice show in the Globe Theatre. Visit Heather Downs to see our world famous Clydesdales. Cross the castle drawbridge into Hastings and join in the fun and games of Threadneedle Faire, an authentic Renaissance Carnival.

What strikes the British reader most forcefully about this description is the reckless eclecticism which it displays. Space and time are dissolved. One crosses a drawbridge into 'Hastings' and finds oneself in the midst of a 'Renaissance' Carnival called 'Threadneedle Faire'. Signs and attractions obey the necessity of impact and sensation rather than nature or history. 'Merrie Old England' pulsates on the floor of the Globe Theatre in the form of an 'Olympic style ice show'.

The Busch Gardens park attempts to annihilate temporal and spatial barriers by bringing the old country of Europe into the heart of modern America. As such it reflects a common meta-theme in the organization of modern theme park attractions. For example, the 'World Showcase' pavilion in Disneyland boasts reconstructions of no less than ten countries: Canada, the UK, France, Morocco, Germany, Italy, Norway, China, Mexico and Japan. The Alpine Village is a Bavarian village offering 'classic old world fares' such as Wienerschnitzel, Sauerbraton and German beer, served by staff dressed in native Bavarian costumes, and the buildings, sights and sounds of old Bavaria. The Alpine Village is located off Torrance Boulevard, Torrance, California. A full-scale settlement is designed and operates as a simulation of reality.[34] Phantasialand in Germany offers the 'Chinatown', 'Alt-Berlin' and 'Mexico' attractions. In Britain the Chessington World of Adventures includes 'The Mystic East' attraction, boasting the sights and sounds of the Orient. As the tourist leaflet puts it, 'climb aboard the boat which takes you on a magical voyage up and down Dragon River – pass beneath a gigantic Japanese Buddha, through beautiful temples and pagodas, and the magnificent Golden Palace of Bangkok. Meanwhile, just off the M1, between Derby and Nottingham, is The Great American Theme Park. It showcases simulations of the Niagara Falls, Mississippi paddleboat life, the Santa Fe Railroad, Silver City ('a real Western town') and the El Paso arena.[35]

From the standpoint of postmodernism, the development of time-space compression attractions for amusement does not anticipate a fundamental change in everyday life, it reflects it. For simultaneity and sensation are at the heart of postmodern experience. In the words of Harvey:

> Through the experience of everything from food, to culinary habits, music, television, entertainment, and cinema, it is now possible to experience the world's geography vicariously, as a simulacrum. The interweaving of simulacra in daily life brings together different worlds (of commodities) in the same space and time. (1989: 300)

Time-space compression attractions give the consumer the 'experience' of stepping across continents in seconds or shedding centuries in minutes. However, as exciting as this may be for us, it could not be accomplished so easily, unless the same principles of compression were operating the outside world. Psychologically speaking, our resistance to the notion that we 'arrive' in Europe when we enter Busch Gardens, Williamsburg, is disarmed by the circulation of disjointed signs representing remote objects which bombard us as part of the small change of daily life.

I shall return to the implications of the last observation in the closing pages of the next section. However, before doing so I want to try to draw some of the themes in this chapter together by considering the question of the novelty of the attractions considered in the foregoing pages. I want to start with what may, at first sight, seem to be an unusual resource: the sociology of Erving Goffman.

CONCLUSION: EMIGRATING FROM THE PRESENT

Goffman's sociology is essentially concerned with the problem of boundaries. It explores the spatial and cultural settings, the 'frames of interaction', in which social routines, ground rules, excusable infractions, bypassings and tolerated violations are exploited and developed. Goffman (1967) argued that modern society includes institutionalized 'action places' in which the individual can let off steam and engage in licensed revelry. Examples include casinos, cinemas, sport arenas, strip clubs, amusement parks, race tracks and pool halls. Goffman viewed action places as frames of controlled excitement.[36] They are described as escape centres in which the rules of everyday life are relaxed and the boundaries of social behaviour are rolled back. For example, touching, shouting and frank observing, which are restricted at work and in other places, are tolerated and even encouraged in action places. Goffman writes as if action places offered the individual the opportunity to become a momentary *emigré* from the pressures of work and the prescriptions of 'Society'.

Goffman's concept of action places would *appear* to fit the four leisure forms described in this chapter. For example, theme parks and heritage sites are certainly places in which the rules of everyday life are relaxed and the rules of 'normality' are bypassed in tolerated ways. One sees this not only in the rides and time-space compression attractions, but also the re-enactments of the past using costumed actors or tableau. Similarly, one of the common denominators behind all four leisure forms is that they seem to offer the experience of momentary escape from the encumbrances and pressures of everyday life.

On the other hand, it is important not to lose a sense of historical perspective. One of the criticisms regularly made of Goffman's sociology is that it is over-absorbed with the present. Because of this it mistakenly implies that social practices and institutions are new, whereas in fact they have a long history behind them. The point is certainly also applicable to the leisure forms described in this chapter. For example, 'white knuckle' rides were a common attraction in nineteenth-century fairs and amusement parks. So were time-space compression attractions and simulations of impossible journeys.[37] Kasson (1978: 61–71), in his useful history of attractions in the amusement parks of *fin de siècle* America, provides a number of useful examples: Luna Park in Coney Island featured reconstructions of a Venetian city complete with gondoliers; an Irish village; Indian palaces and the streets of Delhi; it also boasted a series of simulations of the Fall of Pompeii; the eruptions of Mount Vesuvius; the devastation of Martinique; Pennsylvania's Johnstown's Flood (1889); and Texas's Galveston Flood (1900). Steeplechase Park offered visitors 'A Trip to the Moon'. The attraction involved visitors boarding a rocket with port-holes which displayed a series of shifting images designed to simulate movement through space. After supposedly landing on the moon, the passengers left the space-craft to explore the caves and grottoes, where they were met by giants and midgets in moonman costumes. Passengers also met the Man in the Moon seated upon his throne, and moonmaidens presented them with green cheese as a souvenir of their journey. Similarly, Bogdan's (1988) history of the freak-show leaves the reader in no doubt that techniques of simulation and staged authenticity were widely used in American circuses and side-shows from at least the 1840s. While Saxon's (1978) biography of the circus performer, Andrew Ducrow, suggests that similar techniques were being used in Astley's Amphitheatre, London, as early as 1825.[38]

A similar general point can be made about the social criticism of the attractions described in this chapter. Contemporary critics fume that history has been replaced with simulations of the past (Horne 1984; Samuel 1988). Neil MacGregor, the Director of the National Gallery in London, bemoaned the introduction of themes in heritage sites on the grounds that they imply that 'the exploration of the past need not be a serious endeavour, requiring time and commitment, but should be in essence undemanding and diverting'.[39] While Hewison (1987), in a widely read study, lamented the development of an amusement industry which, he submits, is intent upon turning the British Isles into an enormous theme park. Is there not a parallel to be drawn here with the argument used by rational recreationists that many popular 'amusements today are inane . . . stupid or aimless' (Cutten 1926: 75)? And can we not find here an echo of Kracauer's (1975: 67) scornful dismissal of the 'undemanding' and 'diverting' entertainments staged by the capitalist 'distraction factories'?[40] Here then, it might be argued, is evidence of palpable and irrefutable continuity. The popular action places of today are condemned in the same terms as the popular action places of Modernity. That is, they reproduce mere distraction; they fail to elevate the people; they are not serious enough. In Kracauer's critical commentary there is also the argument that the distraction factories represent a distinct order of things, that is, they exert a determinate ideological effect. The argument is mirrored in the work of contemporary critics like Marin (1977: 54), who castigates the Disneyland theme park on the grounds that it is

> a fantasmatic projection of the history of the American nation, of the way in which this history was conceived with regard to other peoples and the natural world. Disneyland is an immense and displaced metaphor of the system of representations and values unique to American society.

From a postmodernist standpoint such criticism betrays a disabling sense of nostalgia. Two points must be made. In the first place, such criticism assumes that society and action places can be managed to produce moral elevation and improvement. The assumption recalls the moral economy of bourgeois society which fetishized the principle of 'a necessary balance' between work and leisure, action and rest, private and public life. For postmodernists the economic, aesthetic, technological and cultural forces unleashed by Modernity have changed our life-world unutterably. The principle of 'a necessary balance' in life has been swept away, like a bridge before a flood, leaving behind a residue of disjointed fragments. The second point is that social criticism of the type at issue, is permeated by the belief that a viable distinction can be made between high and low culture. In refuting this belief, postmodern authors maintain that a series of related modernist beliefs have also collapsed, e.g. progress vs reaction, present vs past, left vs right, modernism vs realism, abstraction vs representation (Huyssen 1986: 217).

Goffman (1974: 560) criticized William James and Alfred Schutz for holding on to a notion of 'paramount reality' against which the 'multiple lifeworlds' which they drew attention to, can 'finally' be measured. In Goffman's view, 'paramount reality' is simply a contrast term. 'When we decide that something is unreal,' he remarked, 'the reality it isn't need not itself be very real' (1974: 560). Although he exploited this observation to explore specific strips of activity, his sociology stopped well short of claiming that the 'primary frameworks' which society has evolved to help us make sense of 'what is going on' have disintegrated. But this is precisely the claim made by postmodernist authors. For example, Baudrillard, writing on Disneyland, contends:

Disneyland is presented as imaginary in order to make us believe that the rest is real, when in fact all of Los Angeles and America surrounding it are no longer real, but of the order of the hyperreal and of simulation. It is no longer a question of a false representation (ideology), but of concealing the fact that the real is no longer real. (1983: 25)

Under postmodernity, it might be said, everyone is a permanent *émigré* from the present. For the present is acknowledged to be a sign system in which images and stereotypes from the past and the future, from the locale and the globe, are impacably intermingled, admitting no principle of determinacy.

One implication of this is that attractions which simply rely on spectacle eventually generate a sense of anticlimax. Why visit a leisure attraction in search of momentary thrills, when the daily life of the metropolis is so rich in the changing, organized spectacles orchestrated by the advertising industry, television, cinema and other branches of the mass media? Is this not one reason for the relative decline of traditional amusement resorts like Coney Island and Blackpool, and working-class holiday camps like Butlin's, since the 1960s? At any rate, the four leisure developments described in this chapter cannot be understood simply as action places or escape centres. The reproduction of attractions designed to stimulate excitement as an end in itself, is balanced with attractions that aim to provide education and opportunities for sociation. Black Spots, Heritage Sites and Literary Landscapes are designed not merely to distract us, but also to inform us. What they inform us about may be open to a large number of objections regarding accuracy and relevance. However, there is no mistaking the objective of making these attractions learning experiences and opportunities for wholesome interaction. Theme parks exhibit similar characteristics. They emphasize the importance of high standards of cleanliness; a pleasant landscaped environment; the courteous uniformed staff (Gray 1986: 17). Similarly, the philosophy behind the construction of Disneyland, articulated in a Disney Productions Investment pamphlet in the 1950s, stressed the educational role of theme parks:

The idea of Disneyland is a simple one. It will be a place for people to find happiness and knowledge. It will be a place for parents and children to share pleasent times in one anothers company: a place for teachers and pupils to discover greater ways of understanding and education. Here the older generation can recapture the nostalgia of days gone by, and the younger generation can savour the challenge of the future. Here will be the wonders of Nature and Man for all to see and understand. (Quoted in Mosley 1985: 221)

In 'Tomorrowland', 'Frontierland', 'Main Street USA', Disneyland has attempted to realize this mission to educate and enlighten the people. The 'Epcot Center' in Disneyworld, Florida, claims to have taken this mission one stage further in the construction of Epcot 'World'. This styles itself as 'an experimental prototypical community of tomorrow that takes its cue from the new ideas and new technologies that are emerging from the creative centers in American industry' (Birnbaum 1988: 103).[41] The Epcot Center claims to educate people by showing them the future world which is at the fingertips of modern science and technology. The design and marketing of theme parks as learning experiences is by no means confined to the Disney parks. For example, Stone Mountain in Georgia displays an Antebellum Plantation and Antique Auto and Music Museums; Beaulieu Manor in Hampshire offers a collection of over 200 historic motor vehicles; and the Dombwalls Theme Park near Liskeard, Cornwall, presents the 'Edwardian Experience' which claims to recreate that time.

Although it would be unwise to be cynical about the idealistic motive of staging themes in leisure attractions as learning experiences, it would also be rash to ignore the commercial appeal of this strategy for businesses intent on maximizing revenue. For learning is predicated in the idea of development, the idea of adding to one's knowledge and understanding. It involves building on learning experiences, and repeating specific experiences is a necessary part of the process. By developing the theme of attractions as learning experiences, leisure managers and marketing staff create the basis for return visits. In the two Disney parks return visits are estimated to account for 80 per cent of attendance.[42]

The leisure forms described in this chapter support the general proposition that the distinctions between work and leisure, the distinctions between the world of duty and the world of freedom, have lost much of their force experientially, and are therefore of dubious analytic value.[43] In a society in which personal prosperity and security depend so much upon an openness to new channels of communication and receptivity to new information, rather than obedient loyalty to caste or community, it is obvious that leisure forms must change. The ways in which they are changing points to the de-differentiation of spaces and signs – an observation which connects with Lash's argument that 'the fundamental structuring trait' of postmodernism is 'de-differentiation' (1990: 11). Bourgeois culture invested certain spaces and signs with an 'auratic' quality. The individual was required to relate to them with gravity, respect and sobriety. If the cemetery provides us with the ideal example it is because of its physical size in the landscape of modernity and its elective affinity with the sacred in bourgeois culture. Who, in bourgeois society, would have dreamt of allowing the cemetery to become a tourist attraction? Yet today, Jim Morrison's grave in Père Lachaise is the fourth biggest tourist attraction in Paris.[44] Who, in bourgeois society, would have suggested that the cemetery should be classified as a spectacle or exhibition? Yet today, the National Federation of Cemetery Friends in Britain, ask us to regard cemeteries as 'outdoor museums'.[45] The gravity and solemnity of Black Spots have been reduced by moves to make them more colourful and more spectacular than other sights on the tourist trail. For example, in 1987 the government of Thailand unveiled plans to restore the famous Death Railway as part of a programme of investment in tourism. An estimated 16 000 allied prisoners of war and 100 000 Asian labourers died in the process of laying the track connecting Burma to Thailand. Suggested accessories in the investment programme included hotels, eating areas, gift shops and display areas. 'It is as if', protested a spokesman for Burma Reunion, a Death Railway veteran's association, 'Auschwitz was to be reopened as an amusement park'.[46]

Black Spots, then, provide a powerful example of the relabelling of signs to convey a more 'leisurely' significance and the redeployment of land use for the purposes of recreation. But one might just as easily refer to the development of heritage sites to illustrate the same principle of de-differentiation. For example, in post-industrial Pittsburgh, redundant steel mills are being renovated as museums and heritage centres;[47] Albert Dock in Liverpool, a former working dock, has been redeveloped as a recreation resource for the north-west, featuring 'The Tate Gallery of the North', 'The Merseyside Maritime Museum' and a variety of shopping malls; in Lothian, near Edinburgh, the Prestongrange and Lady Victoria mining collieries have been closed and repackaged as 'The Scottish Mining Museum'. In the general context of the deindustrialization of the American and

British economies, and the switch towards investment in services and the new technology, old work sites are being transformed into centres of leisure and recreation.

De-differentiation refers to the context of contemporary leisure experience. It does not refer to an event of apocalyptic, complete transformation. On the contrary, it is possible to draw upon several recent studies to show that traditional leisure activities based in community participation and privatized hobbies are quite compatible with the new leisure forms described here (see, for example, Roberts 1983; Bishop and Hoggett 1987; Glyptis *et al* (1987). However, the altered context is hardly of negligible significance. Briefly, it is one in which qualities of leisureliness have become more pronounced in the organization of work and public life. The most obvious effect of this is that our sense of place has been coloured by the leisure amenities that we have on our doorsteps. Job advertisements now include a reference to local leisure amenities as part of the standard job description: Glasgow, for example, is often described as 'the European capital of culture', 'a city of over 70 parks and open spaces', with Loch Lomond 'a short car drive away';[48] similarly, jobs in the industrial cities of north-west England are often sold to potential job applicants as being on 'the edge of the scenic Lake District'. Spaces of leisure, recreation and heritage are part of our daydreams of a better life. People dream of moving, or actually relocate, to Dorset or 'Old Carmarthenshire' to live in Thomas Hardy's 'Wessex', or 'Dylan Thomas Country'. Fictions constructed by the leisure industry blend with local and civic history to establish our immediate sense of reality. For example, in Manchester a specially commissioned mural depicts 'The Manchester Story'. It begins with images of the original Roman settlement, through to the invention of steam power and the development of science, industry and the arts in the city. It ends with portraits of the famous television characters Albert Tatlock and Hilda Ogden,[49] simulacra which underwrite this history with a very typical form of contemporary 'authority'.

These examples may appear to be trivial, fragmentary and superficial features of life. They are certainly features which have tended to be overlooked in most 'serious' studies of contemporary leisure experience.[50] However, they are also perhaps, the items which most powerfully contribute to our sense of place and normality. What they show is that leisureliness is now a generalized quality of our social order. Our lives may be burdened by responsibilities, and we may sweat and hurry to fulfil our daily obligations, but, despite all of this, our existence is surrounded by images of lives of pleasure and lives of charm. The tourist industry is undoubtedly one of the principal conductors of these images. Hoardings, advertisements, television commercials and holiday brochures remind us in arresting, and sometimes in aggressive ways, of a life of contrast which is just an airline ticket or railway journey away. If much leisure practice can be criticized for capitulating to the chained activities of everyday life, can we not see the holiday as a genuine form of escape, an example of real emigration, from the obligations of the present in a totally different world?

The next chapter explores this question by way of an examination of the structuring and experience of tourism in the present day. It begins where many criticisms of tourism begin, with the image of a shrinking world, sinking irremediably into a permanent state of disrepair.

5

Wonderful World

Disintegration. The 'Cookites' triumphant, and the ancient and arcadian tourist retreats polluted. This, in essence, was the aristocratic response to the rise of mass tourism in the late nineteenth century. Never again would the cultivated class of northern Europe be able to savour the joys of Rome and the marvels of Athens free from the sullied ranks of their ill-born countrymen. By the end of the *Belle Époque*, the mien of the aristocracy on the question of tourism was set: the Mediterranean colonies of refuge had been lost, and paradise was destroyed (Pemble 1987: 168–82).

And what of the self-made plutocrats and artisans who inherited 'paradise'? What was their view of mass tourism? After an initial burst of enthusiasm which celebrated mass tourism as one of the benefits of the march of progress, there was the same lapse into sullen resentment and gloomy introspection that had characterized the response of their aristocratic forebears. By 1955 Lévi-Strauss, no less, was lamenting that,

> journeys, those magic caskets full of dreamlike promises, will never again yield up their treasures uncontaminated. A proliferating and overexcited civilization has broken the silence of the seas once and for all. The perfumes of the tropics and the pristine freshness of human beings have been corrupted by a busyness with dubious implications, which mortifies our desires and dooms us to acquire only contaminated memories. (1955: 43)

'Proliferating', 'overexcited' and 'contaminated' – were these not the same epithets used by rational recreationists in the nineteenth century to describe the moral turpitude of the residuum? In complaining of the dangers of open access to tourist spaces, is not something negative also being implied about the character of the tourist? Certainly, in casting himself (1955: 51) in the role of 'a modern traveller' chasing after the 'vestiges' of 'a vanished reality', Lévi-Strauss gives reason to suggest that he views the real enemy of the traveller to be the tourist.

If the contrast between travellers and tourists in Lévi-Strauss's commentary hints at a structural division it is no accident. High culture, the culture of the traveller, saw itself as the polar opposite of low culture, the culture attributed to the tourist. This polarization is evident in the late nineteenth-century and twentieth-century travel literature. The first section of this chapter examines the structural characteristics of the division between travellers and tourists. It also explores the category of 'the post tourist', which some commentators maintain is growing in influence. There are three remaining sections. The second section examines the symbolic construction of tourist sights. Travel brochure blurbs and newspaper reports are examined to consider the uses of bracketing and misinformation in presenting sights. Bracketing refers to the elimination of sight features which are deemed to be 'unsightly'. The third section explores the subject of the organization of tourist escape areas: the beach, the hotel, monuments and the wilderness. The claims of managers who administer these escape areas to transport you into a different world or to take you outside yourself are critically examined. It is argued that these claims are only capable of realization in illusion. It does not follow from this that tourists should be viewed as passive victims of the manipulations of the tourist industry. Participation in these illusions brings its own rewards and a tentative attempt is made to suggest the form and content of these rewards. The final section of the chapter asks the pertinent question, why be a tourist? The question is pertinent because postmodernism suggests that the distinctions between reality and fantasy, interior and exterior, personal and political have collapsed. If this is correct, the status of the holiday as an escape route from the reality-chains of everyday life is open to question. Let me work through the four sections in the order listed above.

WHAT IS A TOURIST?

Lévi-Strauss's hostility to the tourist is echoed in several quarters. 'The modern tourist,' declares Carroll, 'is so without any capacity to sublimate, to release himself to the unknown, to dare to open his ears to the treacherous Sirens, that he surrounds himself in a material package, in which every minute is preplanned' (1980: 183). Barker (1990), like Lévi-Strauss, argues that mass tourism is a blight, and documents its evils. 'Tourism,' he asserts, 'sucks cities dry. Far from livening them up, it ends by sending them to sleep – a kind of urban valium' (1990: 7).

What image of the tourist is being invoked here? The tourist is associated with the gross values of the welfare state.[1] Tourists are presented as lacking initiative and discrimination. They are unadventurous, unimaginative and insipid. For them, travel experience is akin to grazing – they mechanically consume whatever the tour operator feeds them. Their presence coarsens the quality of tourist sights. Mass tourism is often likened to a plague, which destroys the beauty and serenity of civilization.[2] The polar opposite of the tourist is the traveller. The traveller is associated with refined values of discernment, respect and taste. Travel is seen as pursuing the ageless aristocratic principle of broadening the mind. It is posited as an exclusive confrontation between self and Nature and self and Culture. Society is elided from the equation. Instead travel experience is presented as a resource in the task of self-making. Travel is required to yield an intensified, heightened experience of oneself. It shakes you up in order to make you a more mature, complete person. Fussell, commenting on the contrasts between travel and tourism, writes:

> If travel is mysterious, even miraculous, and often lonely and frightening, tourism is commercial, utilitarian, safe and social . . . Not self directed but externally enticed, as a tourist you go not where your own experience beckons but where the industry has decreed you shall go. Tourism soothes, shielding you from the shocks of novelty and menace, confirming your view of the world rather than shaking it up. (1990: 21)

What evidence is there that tourist experience is unadventurous, unimaginative and insipid? Critics point to the itineraries of package tours which are often very intensive. For example, in 1990 TWA offered US tourists a four-day tour of 'London plus Countryside'. Day 1 consisted of driving into 'the lush Thames Valley'; a visit to Hampton Court Palace; a drive to Oxford 'where we take a look at the venerable colleges'; a visit to Blenheim Palace and 'stern Warwick Castle' before heading north to Solihull for dinner; day 2 commenced with a visit to Coventry Cathedral; then on to Stratford-upon-Avon and 'Shakespeare Country'; then a drive through 'England's most picturesque hills and dales, the Cotswolds', and 'the wilder Wye valley', before ending in Cardiff; day 3 began with the 'amazing Roman complex' in Bath; then on to Stonehenge, 'was it an ancient observatory, or a place of pagan ritual?'; then on to Winchester and ending in Portsmouth for dinner and 'a stroll along the Esplanade'; day 4, commenced with a visit to Nelson's flagship the 'Victory'; then on to Arundel Castle in Sussex where you can 'pause below the battlements for photos'; then on to Brighton; ending in Rye, before heading back to London and the flight home. Similarly, Swissair in 1990 offered American tourists 'The William Tell Experience'. This is an eight-day tour through William Tell Country. Day 1 consisted of the flight from the USA to Zurich; day 2 included the arrival at Zurich and an overnight stay in a hotel; days 3 and 4 were spent in Lucerne, described as a place of 'night firework displays, folk festivals, nostalgic lake cruises and the famous painted Chapel Bridge'; day 5 consisted of a trip from Lucerne to Lugano via the William Tell Express; days 6 and 7 were spent in Lugano, described as a place of 'concerts and lakeside gardens', and lake cruises past picturesque fishing villages; day 8 consisted of an 'early breakfast' and departure by train to Zurich Airport and 'same day arrival in North America'.

It is relatively easy for critics to pour derision upon tourist experience when package tour itineraries are this intensive. For example, Carroll (1980) pictures the package tour as a chain of appointments which obstruct tourist experience of 'abroad'. 'The tourist,' he submits, 'might as well be confined to a repeating series of jumbo jet flights, international airport interludes, air-conditioned taxi rides and International Hilton stops' (1980: 144). But how accurate is this acerbic comment? Two points must be made. In the first place, Carroll's statement ignores the salient fact that tourists are raised in cultures which present the host national values as 'obviously' and 'naturally' superior and unsurpassable.[3] The British or American tourist that steps onto foreign soil for the first time does so with a sense – and it would be wrong to claim that it is more than a sense – of entering Babylon. Different language, different customs, different media, different climates, are initially disturbing. One does not know what to do if something goes wrong. One is in the midst of unfamiliar surroundings and practices. On these circumstances, if tourists choose to surround themselves with some of the accoutrements of home, it need not be despised as evidence of an unadventurous, unimaginative cast of mind. Secondly, Carroll appears to treat the tourist as a passive consumer of staged experiences. This ignores the rather obvious fact that no matter how planned and packaged a tour may be there is always room for tourist bypassings and deviations from the tourist script. Not least because tourists have the capacity to be ironic about what the tour operators throw at them. 'Tourists', remark Cohen and Taylor, 'even when searching for authenticity are capable of ironically commenting on their disappointment in not finding it: they see through the staged authenticity of the tourist setting and laugh about it' (1976: 118).

Although Cohen and Taylor do not use the term 'post-tourist', the ironic consciousness which they describe is now called by that name (see Feifer 1985: 257–71; Urry 1990: 100–2). Three features identify the post-tourist. To begin with, the post-tourist is aware of the commodification of tourist experience. Instead of abhorring it in the manner of the tourist, the post-tourist treats it playfully. 'The post tourist', remarks Urry, 'knows that they are a tourist and that tourism is a game, or rather a whole series of games with multiple texts and no single, authentic tourist experience' (1990: 100).[4]

The second feature of the post-tourist is the denial of progress in tourist experience. This contrasts with the mental attitudes of both the traveller and the tourist. As we have seen, the traveller views travel experience as a resource in the quest for self-realization. Travel experience is required to evolve into 'maturity' – a condition which is marked by 'wisdom', 'insight' and 'taste'. As for the tourist, touring is motivated by the desire to consume authentic experiences (MacCannell 1976: 91–108). Hence the preoccupation with witnessing and recording sights – the camera-clicking which critics of mass tourist culture castigate with such sententiousness. The post-tourist, by comparison, is attracted by experience as an end in itself and not by what the experience teaches about one's inner resources, or whether the attraction is authentic. Axiomatic to this mental attitude is the recognition that the tourist experience may not, and often does not, add up to very much.

The third feature of the post-tourist is positive identification with intertextuality. The post-tourist is stimulated by the interpenetration or collision between different facets and representations of the tourist sight. The accessories of the sight – the gift shops, the eating places, the tourist coaches and other tourists – are celebrated for being as much a key part of the tourist experience as the sight itself. This again contrasts sharply with the outlook of both the traveller and the tourist. The traveller goes abroad or visits a sight for a reason: to gain experience which will reveal some truth about his or her relationship to the world which is obscured in the routine hustle and bustle of daily life. Travel experience is required to be focused and meaningful. Similarly, the tourist goes touring with the objective of witnessing something and having a record of the fact. It is, of course, no accident that the organization of package tours highlights attractions which offer photo opportunities. Being recorded in the same frame as the sight is exactly the sort of posterity which the tourist values most highly. Despite the many particulars which divide them, both travellers and tourists are alike in pursuing focused experience when they go abroad. It follows that anything which conflicts with this focus is valued negatively. For this reason, the traveller abominates other tourists *per se*, since they threaten the solitude which ultimately validates the travel experience. Likewise, the tourist is hostile to any obstacle which obstructs his or her witnessing and recording the sight, for this soils the consumption experience.

Traveller, tourist and post-tourist – it would be unwise for the reader to view these forms as links in an evolutionary chain. Travellers and tourists have obviously not been replaced by post-tourists. The most that can be claimed is that post-tourist sensibilities are currently evident and growing. This much, at any rate, is clear from the business strategy of tour operators in the 1970s and '80s. There has been an upsurge in 'fantasy' holidays which offer 'out-of-the-ordinary' experience. Examples include 'Murder Mystery Week-Ends' in which the tourist is involved in solving a murder staged by actors; the three-day US Space Camp holidays held at the US Rocket Center, Alabama, where tourists are trained to do a space shuttle mission from launch to landing; and Sox Exchange, Montpelier, Vermont, a seven-night fantasy baseball camp which offers tourists the chance to train and play with former baseball greats.[5] The influence of television in underwriting the appeal of 'out-of-the-ordinary' experience is, of course, considerable. For example, in 1988, three-day 'Granada TV Weekends' were on offer to British tourists. These consisted of tours around the lots of the Granada television studios in Manchester. 'On our fantastic weekends,' advised the sales material, 'you'll be escorted on a fascinating tour behind the camera, strolling down the most famous cobbled street in England, Coronation Street – you might even have a pint at the Rovers.'[6] Other on-site attractions include reconstructions of the Edwardian Baker Street home of Sherlock Holmes, Berlin's 'Checkpoint Charlie' and the House of Commons. The week-end also takes in a tour of the countryside featured in the popular television series, 'Last of the Summer

Wine'. Tourists are also offered simulated 'worlds' in which 'impossible landscapes' offer the trigger for out of the ordinary experience. For example, in Billund, Denmark, an entire Lilliputian environment has been created. Legoland consists of 35 million bricks which reproduce miniatures of famous buildings and landscapes from around the world. Other specific attractions include an African safari with lifelike wildlife, the Statue of Liberty, Mount Rushmore, 'Legoredo,' and 'Fabuland' playtown. The 'Adventureland', 'Fantasyland' and 'Main Street USA' attractions in Disneyland and Disneyworld provide other examples.

Perhaps in these developments we find the essence of Lévi-Strauss's troubled vision of the 'vanished reality' of escape in today's world. For they brazenly present themselves as simulations. The attraction derives from ironically confronting them as 'real'. One can experience 'competing' with legendary, retired baseball greats at the Sox Exchange; or entering the world of 'Coronation Street' in the Granada Studios week-end tour; but in both cases one is aware that the experience refers to a simulation. In this, cannot we see the lineaments of the post-tourist? 'The post tourist,' writes Feifer, 'knows that he is a tourist: not a time traveller when he goes somewhere historic; not an instant noble savage when he stays on a tropical beach; not an invisible observer when he visits a nature compound. Resolutely "realistic", he cannot evade his condition of outsider' (1986: 271).

One of the most important themes in postmodern literature is that our orientation to things is fatally compromised by the glut of data which clogs our channels of communication. We are so drenched in signs and meanings that we find it difficult to make judgements and commitments about how we should live and what we should do.[7] The database in the tourist industry is certainly wide. To name but a few obvious channels of communication, it takes in travel brochures, posters, anecdote, cinema, television, fine art and advertising. Indeed, as Barthes (1979: 3–22) noted of the Eiffel Tower, some sights function as universal symbols in global culture. Other examples might include the Pyramids, the Taj Mahal, Big Ben, the Parthenon, the Great Wall of China, the Statue of Liberty, and Red Square. We 'know' about these sights before visiting them *in situ*. How does the tourist industry present sights? What methods are used to key tourists into travel attractions? These questions form the backdrop for the discussion in the next section.

L'INVITATION AU VOYAGE

'You know,' wrote Baudelaire, 'that nostalgia for countries we have never known, that anguish of curiosity? There is a country . . . where everything is beautiful, rich, honest and calm . . . where order is luxury's mirror; where life . . . is sweet to breathe; where disorder, tumult and the unexpected are shut out' (1962: 32). Bourgeois culture maintained a sense of order through the evocation of central dichotomies which were adduced as 'natural', 'obvious' and 'inviolate'. Baudelaire, in general a disaffected critic of bourgeois society, shows in the passage cited above, continuity with the culture that nurtured him. He defines the 'foreign' country as the opposite of the immediate conditions of 'home': the exact contrary of 'disorder', 'tumult' and the 'unexpected'. Until recently the tourist industry which, after all, was also nurtured in the womb of bourgeois society, observed the same example. Even today most travel brochures seek to entice tourists with evocations of countries and 'worlds' which are presented as the opposite of the immediate conditions of 'home'. For example, the 'Tradeways Faraway Holidays Brochure' for 1985/6 described Brazil as 'a reverse image of monochrome Britain. Latin exuberance and colour are the order of the day . . . The horizons are infinite. The history dramatic. The people vivacious. The traditions flamboyant. The mood extravagant'. In the same vein, the 'Air New Zealand' campaign for 1986 presented New Zealand to Europeans as the opposite of the immediate conditions of 'home'. 'In a world where holidays have become almost as pressurized as the lifestyle you leave behind,' trilled the advertisement, 'it's refreshing to find a spot like New Zealand. From alps to fiords to white Pacific beaches, forests and vineyards to tranquil lakes, New Zealand is blessed with an easier pace.' The Scottish Tourist Industry has adopted the same marketing strategy. It presents Scotland as a land out of time. In contrast to the haste and impersonality which apparently dominates the rest of the world, the visitor to Scotland is promised 'A real Scottish welcome'. Scotland's history is vigorously championed to the point where historical personalities are presented as living presences. For example, the Scottish Tourist Board's brochure to Scotland for 1987, maintained that the tourist will 'meet many of Scotland's historical figures – writers like Sir Walter Scott, Robert Burns, Robert Louis Stevenson. You'll hear about likeable rogues such as Rob Roy Macgregor; as well as great names who made their mark beyond Scotland – David Livingstone or Mungo Park – and rebels with a cause such as Bonnie Prince Charlie'. Scotland is presented as an enchanted fortress in a disenchanted world. Brochures for Denmark, Germany, Sweden and Australia take this tendency to its logical extreme by presenting holidays in these countries as the embodiment of myth. For example, the Longship Holiday Campaign for vacations to Denmark, Germany and Sweden launched its 1986 campaign with the question: 'Do you believe in Fairy Tales?' The advertising blurb continued:

> If you thought that Fairy Tales only existed in books a trip to historic Copenhagen with Longship Holidays will make you think again. Because we can take you to the actual statue of the Little Mermaid, immortalized by the great Danish storyteller, Hans Christian Andersen. We can also take you to Germany, to the Sleeping Beauty castle or the historic town of Hamelin. In Sweden you can see the descendants of the geese that flew little Nils across the country on their backs.

Similarly, the Australian Tourist Commission in their 1988 'Travellers Guide' to the Australian Bicentennial celebrations, presented Australia as 'Land of the Dreamtime'. The Aboriginal legends are used as a marketing tool to depict Australia as a land of ancient magic and enchantment.

In marketing enticement, the tourist industry must necessarily bracket out disenchanting aspects of nation and locale. For example, in presenting Australia in an ahistorical fashion as the land of 'Dreamtime', the Australian Tourist Commission brackets out the racial, political, and economic tensions that exist between the 'host' Aboriginal population and the white settlers. Similarly, in presenting Scotland as a land out of time, the Scottish tourist Board brackets out the less enchanting features of Scots life, such as urban deprivation, industrial pollution and crime.[8]

Bracketing and stereotyping are not, of course, only matters of accentuating the positive mythical or material properties of a nation or locale. Most advanced cultures have a pronounced range of associations with 'foreign' countries, not all of which are flattering or beckoning. For example, the popular British view of Australia is of an empty, wild continent, sparsely populated with a naive and boisterous population. The deep associations of convict life and banishment die hard, even in the British culture of the 1980s where the Australian soap opera 'Neighbours' reigned supreme. Similarly, as late as 1964, a British guidebook to Europe could describe the French male as 'passionate, practical and preoccupied with money-making, love-making, his belly and the subtler evasions of the law'.[9] The same guidebook describes the Spanish as 'passionate', 'splendid', 'sometimes cruel', 'haughty' and 'formal'. The guidebook goes on to claim that the *métier* of the Spanish male is 'lounging against street corners and commenting in some detail upon the physical attributes or disabilities of the women who pass him by'.[10] It is extremely difficult to estimate or calibrate the generality of these negative associations. Yet to anyone who resides in Britain it is an obvious fact that they rise up boiling with potency at times of international conflict, whether it be sporting fixtures like the World Cup and the Ashes, or a military war like the battle for the Falklands when the 'bash the Argies' mentality materialized with undeniable celerity.[11]

Definitions in terms of difference and opposition are, of course, typical of bourgeois culture. Their persistence in the tourist industry is a measure of the influence of that culture in present-day consciousness and practice. However, it would be a mistake to limit bracketing to the received mental maps of populations. Bracketing in the leisure industry is far more tangible, calculated and deliberate. For example, in 1987 the Dorset leisure and recreation committee responsible for producing the 'Dramatic Portland' tourist guide was criticized for presenting a fabricated view of the sight. The picture in the guide showed the Isle of Portland set in a blue sea, calm and alluring as a Mediterranean lagoon with the 'majestic' Chesil beach linking the Isle to the mainland. What the picture did not show was 17 enormous tanks of the Navy fuel base which dominate the beach. These had been retouched from the photograph. 'It's not unusual to try to hide eyesores', claimed the Council general manager. However, a spokesperson for the English Tourist Board pointed out that 'deception only leads to disappointment'.[12] Another example of calculated, deliberate bracketing was supplied by a Consumer's Association report published in 1988. The Consumer's Association in Britain studied 27 brochures from companies offering holidays in the Algarve, Portugal. They found that the centre of Quarteria was presented in the brochure as consisting of whitewashed cottages and narrow, cobbled streets. In fact, the Consumer's Association discovered 'one of the least attractive resorts on the Algarve almost entirely taken over by ugly modern development. We did find a couple of cobbled streets, but they're very much the exception'. One hotel is described in one brochure as being '150 yards from the nearest beach'. However, the Consumer's Association investigation found that an apartment block had been built between the hotel and the sea.[13]

Bracketing techniques are not confined to manipulating the physical appearance of sights. They also cover the manipulation of the sounds of sights (through noise pollution legislation), and even the smells of sights. For example, in 1987 the Tory council of Great Yarmouth received a record number of complaints about the offensive smell of dung deposited by the 20 horses that pull landau carriages along the seafront. The Council responded by ordering the owners of the horses to put nappies on the animals. 'We are going all out to attract new tourists,' explained a tourist official, 'and we don't want them put off by having dung littered along the road'.[14]

Bracketing, fabrication and misinformation are also practised regularly in the scripts of tour guides. For example, Goldberger (1990) examines the tour scripts used by tour guides in Manhattan. Goldberger points out that bus and boat tours are often the first introduction that visitors to the city receive. He describes two popular bus tours of the city: 'Lower New York' and 'Upper New York and Harlem'. The tour of 'Lower New York' lasts for 150 minutes, although 20 minutes are spent in a *de rigueur* stop at a souvenir shop *en route*. Goldberger argues that the tour presents a view of lower New York which is becalmed in the 1950s. Neighbourhoods which now consist of renovated lofts, restaurants and advertising agencies were described by the tour guide as 'the garment district', 'the toy district' and 'the insurance district'. The conversion of these manufacturing spaces to residential uses which occurred in the 1970s (Zukin 1988) was simply ignored. New neighbourhoods which had grown up in the last 30–35 years like TriBeCa, were not even recognized. Instead the spatial configuration of the downtown area was mapped out to conform to the patter of the tour guide rather than to any factual basis.

The tour of 'Upper New York and Harlem' is described by Goldberger (1990: 22) as 'a festival of enthusiastically presented misinformation'. For example, the Hotel Arsonia on 73rd Street was described by the tour guide as being one hundred years old, whereas in fact it was built in 1904; at the Dakota Building at 72nd Street and Central Park West, the home of Yoko Ono was described as being on the second floor: actually her apartment is in the same building but several floors up. Moving down Central Park West, Madonna and Richard Dreyfuss were erroneously described as living in the San

Remo apartments; brownstones were described as being built by
Dutch settlers in the 1800s, which is not the case; Columbia was
described as one of four Ivy League universities, which is inaccurate;
and Woody Allen was described as living at 960 Fifth Avenue, which
is not the case. The tour guide reinforced negative stereotypes.
'Spanish Harlem,' she declared, 'is very dangerous. You have to be
careful everywhere. It's still a great town to be a tourist in, but most
other people are leaving New York' (Goldberger 1990: 22). Similarly,
the barbed wire surrounding the renovation scaffolding at the Knick-
erbocker Club at 62nd Street (which the tour guide erroneously
referred to as the 'Republican Club') was described as being there 'to
keep the riff raff out'. The result was a decidedly one-sided view
of New York as a place drenched with menace and danger – a view
indeed which is, in some ways, reminiscent of the view of the exterior presented to bourgeois women and children in the 1820s, 30s
and 40s.[14]

Polarization through stereotypical dichotomies was, as we have
seen, typical of bourgeois culture. For example, it is evident in the
bourgeois divisions between work and leisure, the interior and the
exterior, capital and labour, male roles and female roles. The division between 'home' and 'abroad' should be regarded as part of the
same set-up. If it is correct to maintain that bourgeois culture was *the*
culture of Modernity and, further Modernity is giving way, or has
given way, to Postmodernity, it follows that many of the divisions
consecrated by bourgeois culture are now redundant. This, after all,
was the burden of the analysis of male and female roles, the interior
and the exterior, and work and leisure contained in chapter 2 and 3.
Certainly the division between home and abroad, and the battery of
stereotypes which accompany it, have been challenged from within
the tourist industry. For example, the 'Encounter Overland' holiday
group which began in 1963, developed a tourist philosophy which is
highly critical of conventional practice in the industry. It attacks the
tourist industry infrastructure which, it alleges, insulates the tourist
'from the very things he has travelled half way around the world to
see'.[15] The 'Encounter Overland' philosophy is based on six selling
points:

(1) To allow the tourist to absorb the atmosphere and appreciate
some of the complex influences that have shaped the country.

(2) To become acquainted with the social and political conditions
and 'to sense the price paid for progress'.[16]

(3) To appreciate the ecology, beliefs, values and taboos of the country.

(4) To follow the natural rhythm of life in the country.

(5) 'To start to feel that . . . you belong and have a part to play – if only the part of the wayfarer, of the traveller who combines a dependence on the daily life around with his own mobility and self-sufficiency.'[17]

(6) To become more knowledgeable and to increase one's awareness.

The emphasis here is on involvement and consciousness-raising. Like the culture of the traveller, the philosophy exhibits unconcealed distaste for the contrivances of mass tourism. However, unlike the culture of the traveller which focuses on auratic objects, the philosophy shows enthusiasm for meeting ordinary people and sharing their daily experiences. 'Enjoy their countries,' enjoined the 'Encounter Overland' advertising blurb for 1990, 'learn the differences and enjoy the similarities.'[18] The de-differentiation of space and culture is palpable here. Different countries are seen not as 'foreign' or 'alien' as was the case under Modernity. On the contrary, they are seen as both continuous and discontinuous, both similar and different, with and from our domestic spatial and cultural conditions. The result is that the originality, uniqueness and singularity of our own culture is called into question. We no longer see ourselves as confronting other cultures with all to teach and nothing to learn. Rather the 'reality' of our own received conventions, beliefs and practices becomes problematic.

Tourism is not simply a matter of arriving at a destination, it also involves the experience of travelling. The latter has been somewhat neglected in the literature on leisure and travel.[19] This is a pity because here some of the most revealing transformations in the phenomenology of travel can be detected. For example, Schivelbusch (1980: 52–69) compares the eighteenth-century experience of travelling in a railway compartment. In the former, the range and quality of external stimuli are relatively well defined; the passenger can perceive details of the landscape and even take in the sounds and smells of the exterior. With railway travel the experience is transformed. Increased velocity correlates with a diminution in the quality and range of perceptions; details in the exterior become blurred and indistinct; smells become neutralized and sounds become muffled. Nineteenth-century passengers often likened rail travel to a dreamlike state. It provided an exact parallel indeed, with the 'phant-asmagoria' of discontinuous and rapidly changing stimuli and sensations which writers like Simmel identified in the modern me-tropolis. The experience was not necessarily offensive or disturbing. To be sure, the design features introduced into first class train com-partments after the 1850s, sought to privatize the experience. The interior space of the compartment was designed to be as comfortable and reassuring as the interior space of the home. The passenger, usually untrammelled with the inconvenience of strangers in the same compartment, was to be in a position to contemplate the exter-nal panorama of the landscape in serene surroundings. The design aim was to reduce distractions and to minimize contact with strangers. The same characteristic was evident in the organization of space on ocean liners. On early ships there were two classes: First Class and Steerage.[20] Each was designed as a self-contained area with its own complement of cabin facilities and standards of furnish-ings. Ocean liners require large areas of public space in which pas-sengers can be distracted from boredom. The early ships were equipped with a Dining Salon, Smoking Room, Ladies' Parlour, Verandah Cafe, Promenade Deck, Gymnasium and Swimming Pool. In these communal areas it was theoretically possible for First Class and Steerage to mingle. However, in practice a variety of formal and informal restrictions, such as dress codes, reserved sec-tions and admission charges, militated against interaction. In 1921 the American Quota Act raised barriers to immigration. Liners which had been designed to bear emigrants across the Atlantic at rock-bottom prices were redesigned for tourist use. Space in Steerage was upgraded to create second and third class accommodation. Areas of recreation were extended to include squash courts, swimming pools, Turkish baths, and, after the 1930s, a Sports Deck. However, ex-panded facilities did not mean expanded class participation. The dominant users of the new recreation areas were first class travellers. At the same time, first class accommodation was improved. For example, the *Bremen* (1929) offered first class passengers ten rooms; second class passengers six rooms; tourist class and third class three each. The *Queen Mary* (1936) offered twelve rooms in first class; eight in tourist class, and five in third class (Oliver 1980).

First class travel was associated with exclusivity and luxury. This is still the case today. Cruise companies like Swan Hellenic, Royal Viking and Royal Cruise continue to attract a large monied market in search of glamour. For example, the 1989 Royal Viking travel programme offered 'shipboard activities' which included 'experts in sports, arts and world affairs to share their knowledge and experience with you'.[21] Passengers were promised instruction by Gary Player and other professionals; guest appearances by Omar Sharif in the liner's bridge programme; and guest lectures by 'ambassadors and prime ministers, celebrated authors and actors, renowned authorities in every area of human interest and endeavour'.[22] The intention is to continue associations with the *grand luxe* conditions of ocean liners in their heyday, when aristocrats, wealthy heiresses and show business stars could be seen on the promenade deck of ships like the *Mauritania* (1907), *Aquitania* (1914), *Île de France* (1927), *Normandie* (1935) and *Queen Mary* (1936) (Brinnin and Gaulin 1988).

Attempts to match the high culture of the great days of first class rail travel also exist. For example, in the late 1980s the Venice–Simplon Orient Express, which had been discontinued in 1977, was revived. The advertising blurb bills it as 'The World's Most Romantic Adventure'. The emphasis is upon luxury, relaxation and pleasure. However, the revised programme is also self-consciously ironic in tone. For example, the restored compartments, brass lamps and charcoal fires are described as 'redolent of a nobler age'. The simulated character of the experience is openly acknowledged. For example, some journeys in the 1988 programme included a 'Departure into Intrigue' entertainment in which 'the Edwardian skullduggery of the McIntrigue family' is staged between London and Venice. As with an orthodox 'Murder Mystery' week-end, actors stage a murder, mysteries unfold, clues are revealed, and passengers are encouraged to discover 'who done it'![23]

However, these forms of luxury travel are treated with disdain by many tour operators who emphasize the frivolity and inauthenticity of luxury travel. They associate exclusivity with the diminution of experience rather than the heightening of experience. By missing low culture and the mechanics of tourism, the luxury passenger is criticized for impoverishing his or her travel experience. For example, companies like Encounter Overland make social mixing within the tourist group and between the tourist group and the host culture a selling point of the holiday.[24] Project work is used as a basis of team-building. The 1988/89 brochure quoted one holidaymaker as describing his trip as 'the best six weeks of my life . . . the bogging down, bridge building and truck repairs were all part of the fun'.[25]

Here 'the trip of a lifetime' is associated not with exclusivity and luxury but group experience and work. 'Activity', in this holiday programme does not mean watching others getting their hands dirty, it means getting your own hands dirty. Another example is provided by the 1987 'First Fleet Re-Enactment Voyage' from England to Australia offered by the Twickers World holiday company. The journey consisted of a convoy of square-rigged sailing ships which aimed 'to follow the route of the original voyage of the First Fleet bound for Australia from England in 1787'. Tourists were only accepted as crew members. The travel brochure blurb gives a clear idea of what was to be expected of participants:

> They will be taught crew duties, such as going out on the rigging, and will be expected to work as part of a disciplined team, for life and limb depend upon it. Accept the discipline, the dangers and discomfort and this will be an expedition to exceed your wildest dreams.[26]

The journey of 235 days was sub-divided into seven legs, each with its own price.[27] The trip from London to Sydney, taking in all stops, was advertised as costing £18,238.

As we have seen, the de-differentiation of spaces and functions is identified by commentators as a key characteristic of postmodernity. Is there not something in the notion of 'the trip of a lifetime' equalling disciplined crew-work, which points to a radical change in our concepts of 'work' and 'leisure'? Can we not see in the marketing of work activity as 'liberating', 'free' experience evidence of de-differrentiation? It is not necessary to invoke the idea of a world turned upside down to support these propositions. De-differentiation is nothing but the pursuit of the contradictions of modernity. Postmodernism, it might be said, is the acceptance of these contradictions – not as necessities or impediments, but as conditions to work with. The proposition that some forms of work are now valued as 'leisurely' experience is only strange if we continue to ignore the historical effect of Modernity. The role of Modernity, as we saw in chapters 2 and 3, was to mobilize continuous innovation in all social and economic conditions. The effect of this was to test established roles and socio-economic divisions to the point at which they ceased to be sustainable.

The next section moves on from the question of the invitation to the voyage, to the subject of the organization of tourist escape areas. These may be formally defined as lifeworlds which offer tourists loopholes of freedom, in which they may drop 'out of the continuity of life' (Simmel 1971: 187). Here the tourist expects to find adventure, excitement and release. A whole book could be written on the topography and phenomenology of these spaces. They include parks, cafes, promenades, metropolitan squares, airport lounges, railway stations, oceanliners and shopping centres.[28] However, since my purpose here is to indicate their significance for modern tourism and not to provide a comprehensive guide to them, I will confine myself to four examples: the beach, the hotel, monuments and the wilderness.

TOURIST ESCAPE AREAS

(i) *The beach*: the ambiguity of the beach has been noted by several commentators. 'The beach,' writes Fiske, 'is an anomalous category, overflowing with meaning because it is neither land nor sea, nature nor culture, but partakes of both' (1989: 56). Bennett (1983) and Shields (1990), drawing on the work of Bakhtin (1968), argue that the beach is marked by 'the carnivalesque elision of rules of everyday life' (Shields 1990: 63). These writers maintain that the beach is a site of transgression, a place of licence, bodily disclosures and excess. This much is culturally coded in the style of beach architecture. Beach houses, esplanades, promenades and pier entertainments are typically more exuberant, colourful and vulgar than inland architectural styles (Banham 1971: (37–55). Other cultural signs signify that the beach is different: postcards, candyfloss shops, beach entertainers, palmreaders and novelty shops.

Tourists associate the beach with relaxation and rest. Sunbathing is perhaps the most obvious manifestation of this. However, the beach is also valued as a place of adventure and sexual possibility. A strong theme in the postcards is female nudity and sexual encounters. If the beach is a place of bodily disclosure, women are called upon to go further than men. In this sense, beach culture might be said to represent male triumphalism, for women are incontrovertibly the paramount objects of display. On the other hand, there is also a strong populist tendency in beach culture. The shedding of clothing, within the licensed limits of public nudity, is seen as a right of everyone. Similarly, Banham (1971: 39) refers to 'the freemasonry of the beaches' which permit 'a man in beach trunks and a girl in a bikini to go to almost any beach unmolested – even private ones if they can muster the nerve to walk in'. This reading of the beach as a common possession is a pronounced feature of beach culture (Walton 1983: 206–8).

These remarks pertain to the suburban beach. They do not necessarily apply to the non-suburban beach. Indeed here different forces of attraction apply. In the case of the suburban beach adventure derives from cultural stimuli: the propinquity of other bodies, partially unclothed, the variety of beachside attractions, the joyful vulgarity of beach architecture. As for the non-suburban beach, adventure derives from 'natural' stimuli: the first footprint in the sand, deserted vistas, the lack of litter and the absence of a sense of haste. Although these 'natural' stimuli are culturally defined, it is the stark minimalism of this 'pre-social', 'pre-human' order which is attractive. With the suburban beach the opposite applies: the fecundity of cultural stimuli is the magnet upon our resources.

In many respects the beach is the apodictic instance of postmodernism. In the eighteenth century and the first half of the twentieth it was a site associated with health (Walton 1983; Shields 1990). In the second half of the nineteenth century, the suburban beach became de-differentiated as a place of adventure and seduction. In the second half of the twentieth century it has gradually become an axis of consumption and transformation. The cult of the sun-tan exemplifies this. Successful tanning requires the consumption of sun-tan lotion and the abandonment of work. It is quintessentially, a transformative activity. Often, the process literally involves the shedding of skin to acquire a new look. Display and appearance determine tanning activity. If, as Baudrillard (1985: 126–34; 1988) intimates, postmodernism is a social consciousness organized around an economy of signs rather than an economy of commodities, the tan is one of the most accessible and universal signs. It instantly conveys health, leisure, vigour and sophistication.

Beach culture is also highly eclectic. For example, Blackpool Pleasure Beach, once the archetypal working-class seaside resort, now offers time-space compression attractions (the Edwardian 'Gaslight' Bar, 'Diamond Lil's Saloon' and 'River Caves' attractions), and the experience of popular narrative universes (the Starship Enterprise' attraction) (Bennett 1983: 151). These co-exist in equivalence with traditional beach attractions: fish and chip shops, seashell stalls, souvenir shops, candyfloss shops, and the like. In some cases, eclecticism is so strident that it supports the image of the beach as a self-contained world from which we need never stray. For example,

Redondo Beach in Los Angeles, presents itself as a landscape so rich in culture and diversity that the rest of America is reduced to a desert and Europe and Africa dwindle into remote foothills of insignificance (see Figure 6).

(ii) *The hotel:*[29]

'The service business is very rewarding. It makes a big contribution to society. A good meal away from home, a good bed, friendly treatment from those who come in contact with our customers – these are all so important. It's important to make people away from home feel at home and feel that they're among friends and are really wanted. When they come to our restaurants and hotels, we try to treat them well enough that they'll come back, and I think most of them do' – J. Willard Marriott founder of Marriott Corporation and Marriott Hotels. (quoted in O'Brien 1987: 320)

'I decided there and then that the trick in packing a box is to pack a full box. This had nothing to do with crushing or overcrowding, only the intelligent use of what is available. I have never had reason to change my mind. Truthfully, the manner in which waste space is unearthed and utilized can mean the difference between a plus and a minus in an operation. And a very exciting part of the game' – Conrad Hilton founder of Hilton Hotels on the renovation plans for his first hotel, *The Mobley*, Cisco. (Hilton 1957: 114)

The hotel is a serviced space in which the basic requirements of life – food, drink, warmth, shelter and security – are supplied by others. It is reminiscent of the domestic bourgeois interior in defining itself in opposition to the tumult and disorder of the exterior. However, whereas the domestic bourgeois interior consisted of privatized, particularistic space, the hotel reduces everything to a state of equivalence (Kracauer 1975).

The hotel lobby is the key transitional area. It is often decorated in a style of baroque splendour with marble pillars, lavish ornamental panelling and frescos depicting classical scenes or tourist sights in the locale. The use of potted plants and, in some cases, fishponds, reinforces the sense of Nature being controlled by Culture. The lobby is like the gateway of an ancient walled city. It signifies the entry point between the inhospitable exterior and the sanctuary of civilization. Certain markers reinforce this sense of transition. The cleanliness of the hotel lobby signifies an efficient, healthy environment which contrasts with the disorder and dirt of the streets. The shoe-shine boy provides a ritual cleaning which removes the random deposits of the exterior from the person. The lobby is a place of chance meetings and assignations. Everyone is unattached from their work and family habitats. They seem open to connections.

Although the lobby is a public space it offers plenty of retreats into privacy. Signs to the escalators which bear guests to the seclusion of their private rooms are prominently displayed. Telephone cubicles provide easy and immediate contact with the outside world. Easy chairs, often with their own side-lights, allow guests to sink into contemplative isolation. These features reinforce the sense of the hotel as quintessentially a transitional area between the public and the private, the exterior and the interior.

The hospitality which the staff show to guests is often offset by a palpable sense of role distance. In fact the display of hospitality in hotels is generally very stylized. This reflects the money connection which is the pre-eminent link between the hotel staff and the guest. Tipping may be referred to as an example. Guests who ask hotel staff for advice are aware of the obligation to pay for it. In the exterior asking for advice or requesting assistance is regarded to be part of the code of civility. In the hotel it is transformed into the code of commerce. This ethos is emphasized in the lobby by the presence of souvenir shops and display areas offering guests elegant perfumes and jewellery.[31] Perhaps this accounts for the attitude of indifference which many guests who visit hotels regularly or live in them continually exhibit. As long ago as 1928, Hayner (1928: 793) used the term 'the blasé attitude' to describe this state of affairs.[32] Where hospitality is conditioned by money relations it is bound to seem superficial, unfelt and insincere. Indifference or a blasé attitude are plausible responses to long-term exposure to these social conditions.

The globilization of the hotel has led to the standardization of architecture and services. The design of the building, the lay-out of the front desk, the design of the bar and recreation areas, the lay-out of the rooms and the range of 'gifts' in the bathroom are bureaucratically applied so that guests can feel at home wherever the building is located. The universalization of hotel culture was a goal in the business strategies of many major hotel chains. 'Each of our hotels,'

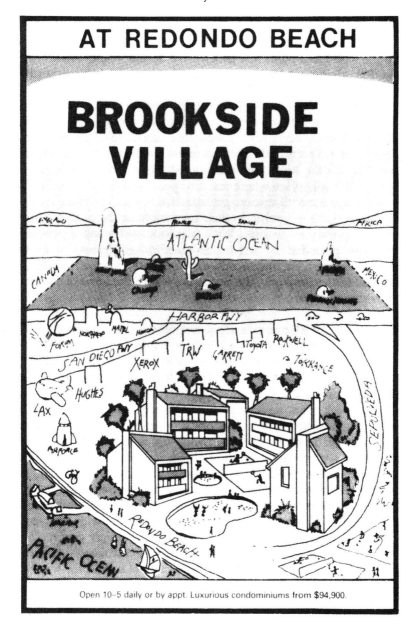

Figure 6: The view of the world from Redondo Beach
Source: Soja 1985: 232

declared Conrad Hilton, 'is a little America' (quoted in Crick 1989: 307). Indeed, Hilton regarded the spread of the Hilton chain throughout the world as a politically progressive development. 'We are,' he asserted, 'doing our bit to spread world peace and fight socialism' (quoted in O'Grady 1982: 50).

Hotels are presented to guests as transcending the flat, colourless, unglamorous, habitual world. However, they do not sever the link with the money economy. Indeed this link is their *raison d'être*. Hence many aspects of the flat, colourless, habitual world are reproduced inside the hotel. The transitional area of the hotel lobby is perhaps the only place where one can speak genuinely of a sense of personal openness. Elsewhere privatization rules. Even in the escalator guests think of getting to their own room or the next appointment as quickly as possible. With television, radio and a personal telephone provided as part of the standard equipment of every room, the guest has the means to re-enter the familiar world of habitual connections and, through this, weaken the sense of being in a transitional area.

(iii) *Monuments*: Monuments share a number of characteristics with black spots, heritage sites and literary landscapes. All appeal to collective consciousness and aim to focus on a tangible object. All seek to memoralize the past and try to represent its 'presence'. However, monuments are crucially different from the rest in one respect: black spots, heritage sites and literary landscapes mark the verifiable location where an historical event occurred; monuments have a looser relationship with history because they are generally concerned with merely *representing* historical events.

Monuments are seductive. They draw us in by making a bold or overpowering visual statement. Correlative with this boldness and intensity there is an inevitable diminution of historical subtlety and complexity. The monument attempts to impress us with one view, even if we come to it aware of the partiality of every perspective. Where might such an exercise in mythology be calculated to have its most seductive effect? In that most seductive of myths, the 'capital' city in which the nation's soul is said to reside. In Washington DC one finds the Vietnam Veterans' Memorial. This construction, set in polished black granite, commemorates the names of 58 022 Americans who died in the Vietnam war. How ironic to encounter this tragic monument in the seat of American power where the orders authorizing and ratifying the manoeuvres which led to the loss of so many American lives were signed, sealed and delivered. Similarly, in London one finds a number of monuments which are designed to symbolize national solidarity and the collective consciousness of the past. One thinks of Nelson's column, erected in the 1840s to celebrate the victory of Nelson at the Battle of Trafalgar, and the Cenotaph which is a national memorial to the British dead of two world wars.

Monuments are designed to have a timeless quality. The Taj Mahal in India was constructed between 1632 and 1653 by the Emperor Shah Jahan in memory of his wife Mumtaz Mahal. Twenty thousand people were involved in the building process. Similarly, the neo-classical Lincoln Memorial in Washington was intended to be an everlasting monument to the defender of the Union. Engraved in the wall above the white marble statue of Lincoln are these words:

IN THIS TEMPLE
AS IN THE HEARTS OF THE PEOPLE
FOR WHOM HE SAVED THE UNION
THE MEMORY OF ABRAHAM LINCOLN
IS ENSHRINED FOREVER

The desire to achieve eternity, to last forever, is one of the symptoms of megalomania. And anyone who has visited the temples built in the names of the rulers of Ancient Egypt at Luxor, the Taj Mahal and the Lincoln Memorial is surely aware of the megalomaniac quality they share in common with their grandeur and beauty.

It is in connection with monuments that one reads Benjamin's essay on art and mechanical reproduction with a sense of recognition. Doubtless auratic objects were always subject to exaggeration and hyperbole.[33] Anyone who troubles to consult the engravings of the Seven Wonders of the World by the sixteenth-century Dutch artist Maerten van Heemskerck (1458–1574) can find evidence of this. The reproductions of the Colossus of Rhodes and the Pyramids (see Figures 7 and 8), reflect a mixture of traveller's tales and imaginative flight.[34] The Pyramids simply do not look like the Pyramids,[35] and the bestriding figure of the Colossus of Rhodes would have been technically impossible in terms of ancient bronze casting methods (Clayton and Price 1988: 11). Benjamin's essay argues that manual methods of reproduction preserve the authenticity of the auratic object. Because one can compare the reproduction with the original or, if the original has vanished, with historical facts relating to the original and its context. The relationship of preservation is necessary to protect the shared notion of paramount reality since without it reality becomes indeterminate, a question of values, all things to all men and women. It is precisely this spectre which Benjamin raises in his argument that mechanical reproduction has violated our relationship to the originality or authenticity of the object, so that aura, in general, has declined. The reproduction is more mobile, available and accessible than the original.[36] In mass culture, argues Benjamin (1955: 225), the reproduction is 'closer' to the masses. Indeed it stands in for reality. The new technical forces signal a move from 'uniqueness and permanence' to 'transitoriness and reproducibility' in cultural life. And this has evident consequences for the relationship between artists and audiences, performers and spectators. Benjamin writes of the growth of the 'sense of the universal equality of things' (225).

Can we not see in the massive circulation and commodification processes surrounding monuments of global importance evidence of the tendency to reduce sights to a state of equivalence? The welter of photographic reproductions in travel brochures, badges, postcards, T-shirt images, transfers, videos, key-rings, pendants, souvenir pens and other tourist trinkets, certainly bring the monument, the auratic object, 'closer' to the masses. The divide between high and low culture is softened. The privileged status of the monument in relation to its audience is no longer automatic. Hence, the sense of anticlimax which often accompanies the visit to a monument. We see it; but have we not seen it before in countless artefacts, images, dramatic treatments and other reproductions? And for most of us, is it not more accessible, mobile and meaningful in these forms?

Monuments cannot be detached from history. There is no correlation between what they were designed to signify and what they signify to us today. Like all escape areas, they are culturally mediated and their meaning is negotiable. Not the least irony in the marketing practices of the tourist industry is that the labour in print and pictures which is meant to isolate the uniqueness of a given monument has the opposite effect. We flick from reproductions of the Parthenon to the Lincoln Memorial, from the Eiffel Tower to Big Ben, with Benjamin's 'sense of the universal equality of things' at the back of our minds.

(iv) *Wilderness*: Bourgeois culture equated progress with the cultural domination of Nature. One of the strongest appeals of the wilder-

Figure 7: Maerten van Heemskerck's sixteenth-century representation of the Pyramids in Egypt. *Source:* Clayton and Price (1988: 6)

Figure 8: Maerten van Heemskerck's representation of the Colossus.

ness as a leisure resource is that it appears to reverse this order. In the wilderness nature appears to dominate culture. The mountains, the forests, the lakes, the moors, the deserts and the national parks seem to have resisted the juggernaut of modernity. Free from the wreckage of the metropolis these places seem to be oases of serenity. Certainly they are widely celebrated as the quintessential escape areas in contemporary society. 'Going to the wilderness,' remarks Wright, 'is not just another way of occupying leisure time, it is a special way, which satisfies deep emotional and intellectual needs as well as providing a change of environment and activity' (1975: 189). Drawing on the anthropological research of Radcliffe-Brown and Lévi-Strauss, Wright argues that in our culture the wilderness is associated with strength, independence and freedom. The 'deep emotional and intellectual needs' which the wilderness satisfies are needs of self-renewal and collective remaking: 'While other societies,' concludes Wright, 'reaffirm themselves through religious rituals and traditional observances, we seem to accomplish this, at least in part, through a return to faith in the land' (189).

This is certainly a plausible analysis. And Wright is careful to underline that our faith in the strength, freedom and independence of the land is a myth (191–4). However, what also needs to be emphasized is that the mythical status of the wilderness does not pass unnoticed by the tourists and travellers who flock to it with such devotion. In calling the major national parks 'museumized nature', MacCannell (1990: 25) aims to draw attention to their simulated character. From the first – Yellowstone, USA (1872); Abisko, Stora Sjofallet and Peljekaise, Sweden (1909); Zernez, Switzerland (1914) and Covadonga and the Ordesa Canyon, Spain (1918)[37] – national parks were defined by legislation which designated the activities which were compatible and incompatible with their status. This legislation eventually provided for an infrastructure of park services which executed a policing function over this 'natural' space. Far from offering us experience of pre-social nature, unscarred by history, class or politics, the parks are, in fact, social constructs, man-made environments in which Nature is required to conform to certain social ideals. For example, it must radiate cleanliness, vastness, emptiness, silence and peace. In other words it must be the exact opposite of the metropolis. The parks are stage representations of nature. Far from signifying the triumph of nature over culture, 'they quietly affirm the power of industrial civilization to stage, situate, limit and control nature' (MacCannell 1990: 25). MacCannell's critique suggests that we can demystify the meaning of national parks. He argues that they are tokens of our guilt at having annihilated the rest of nature in the name of progress. 'We destroy on an unprecedented scale,' he remarks, 'then in response create parks that can replay the nature – society opposition on a stage entirely framed by society' (ibid). Implicit here is the notion that the wilderness has a real meaning and that it can be revealed by decoding the set of forms, usages and relationships in contemporary culture through which the category of 'the wilderness' is represented.

Interestingly, Baudrillard, who also examines the category of the wilderness in his work, produces an entirely different line of analysis. Confronting the Californian desert he is struck by its 'brilliant, mobile, superficial neutrality, a challenge to meaning and profundity, a challenge to nature and culture, an outer hyperspace, with no origin, no reference points' (1988: 124). Baudrillard does not see the desert as polarized with culture. On the contrary, he sees no difference between the two. Commenting on life in the cities of California, he writes, 'culture itself is a desert there, and culture has to be a desert so that everything can be equal and shine out in the same supernatural form' (126). Postmodernism bathes everything in the same depthless, indifferent light.

WHY BE A TOURIST?

Curiosity was one of the strongest motives behind travel for pleasure. The traveller sought to leave the drab particulars of *locale* behind and enter a more colourful, intoxicating world. The contrast of conditions between 'home' and 'broad', the attractions of discontinuity, was at the crux of travel culture. The rise of mass tourism appeared to weaken this contrast. The tourist in collusion with the vacation official and the transport chief seemed to regiment and rationalize travel experience. The agents and structures of the tourist industry seemed to reduce the experience of travel from home and abroad to a state of equivalence. The tourist leaves the airport terminal in one capital city and arrives in its replica three thousand miles away. He or she is searched and questioned by one set of customs officials upon departure, and is searched and questioned again by their doubles on arrival. The tourist takes a cab from the hotel to the airport terminal in one continent, and takes a cab from the airport terminal to the hotel in another continent. The depthlessness and transparency of travel experience matches the depthlessness and transparency of the surrounding culture.

The critical literature on tourism sees these conditions as a cause for lamenting the reduction of travel experience. Lévi-Strauss (1955), Carroll (1985) and Fussell (1990), criticize mass tourism as a viral agent conspiring in the disenchantment of the world. Against this, the emerging literature on post-tourism recognizes these conditions as a fact of life, rather than the excuse for an elegy on the decline of life (Feifer 1986; Urry 1990). De-differentiation *has* weakened the contrast between home and abroad. One only has to walk along the shopping and amusement areas of any metropolis to find evidence of this: Korean and Indian restaurants in London; Chinese film theatres and Indian fashion shops in Los Angeles; African music clubs and Latin-American galleries in Paris. In some complexes de-differentiation is formally incorporated as a design feature. For example, Chaney (1990) refers to the Metroland Centre in Gateshead which is advertised as the biggest shopping centre in Europe. Various sections of the centre have been built to incorporate simulations of 'foreign' locales and different times. Examples include the 'Antiques Village', the 'Forum' and the 'Mediterranean Village'. Time and space compression techniques which earlier, in the discussion of Busch Gardens and the 'World Showcase' pavilion in *Disneyland* (pp. 163–5) I mentioned as attractions in amusement parks, are here presented as part of the normal facts of daily life.

The backdrop to all of this is television culture. As a cultural form its relationship to differences in time and space is entirely promiscuous. News bulletins are mixed with costume dramas, which in turn are mixed with travel programmes, films, documentaries of movie stars and rock performers and current affairs discussions. Television gives us a window on the world without incurring the risks and inconveniences that beset the traveller and the tourist. Indeed it is openly celebrated as providing a more penetrating, uncluttered view of events than direct personal experience.

A good example of this is provided by David Beresford (1990). Beresford is a newsman who covered the release of Nelson Mandela. He describes the folklore among Western journalists that grew up at the prospect of witnessing this event:

> Being there, or at least the fear of not being there – at the gates of Victor Verster as Nelson Mandela completed his long road to freedom – was a notion which haunted foreign correspondents in

South Africa for years, until the moment itself arrived to relieve them from the nightmare. But it was replaced by another, if lesser nightmare, of being there and not being there.

Beresford goes on to recount his frustration at being at the scene of Nelson Mandela's release from prison, but having his view blotted out by the throng of journalists and cameramen covering the event. He contrasts his lack of clear vision with the situation of television viewers at home who witnessed the event in close-up, courtesy of the TV cameras on board circling helicopters working for American television. Beresford later had the unnerving experience of attending the Mandela Concert at Wembley Stadium. Here, in common with other concertgoers, he arrived to 'find two gigantic television screens on either side of the distant platforms to ensure that fee paying patrons got what they were accustomed to in their living rooms' (Beresford 1990).

Television bestows the sense of privileged perception upon the viewer. This may be ill founded for, as a variety of commentators have remarked, television constructs 'reality' rather than reflects it.[38] But it is also seductive. Through television and other media the post-tourist can realize the ultimate experience of de-differentiation in travel: he or she can 'calmly go travelling' without leaving the home. As Feifer puts it:

> The passive functions of tourism (i.e. seeing) can be performed right at home with video, books, records, and TV. Now there is even the Sony Walkman, the portable tapedeck: with headphones to enable the anti-tourist to remain in a place of his choice mentally while is physically travelling around. (Emphasis in original) (1986: 269)

McLuhan (1973) in a famous analogy argued that electronic media are creating a 'global village'. With hindsight, the analogy of a refugee camp might be deemed to be more appropriate. For, far from reinforcing a sense of place, the electronic media heighten the sense of displacement. For example, private areas of life are made public; the boundaries between social groups disappear; 'dead' events are replayed as 'live' happenings (Meyrowitz 1985; Poster 1990: 44–5). Being there and not being there is the condition of the television viewer and this is one reason why Baudrillard uses the example of television to demonstrate hyperreality.

At the same time one must not imagine that the displacement associated with de-differentiation is a one-sided process. The dissociation of the viewer from the event which television normalizes, is paralleled by the sense of anticlimax which the tourist often experiences upon being in the tourist sight. The transference of exotic values to the mundane world of the metropolis which complexes like the Metroland centre exhibit, is mirrored by the transference of mundane values to the sacred soil of the tourist sight. Consider one of the most potent tourist symbols in Western civilization: Manger Square, Bethlehem, where Christ is said to have been born. 'Manger Square,' writes one travel writer, 'has become a raucous smelly car park, lined on one side by the new Tourist Shopping Centre, on another by the police station.'[39] The gift shops, stocked with souvenirs like plastic camels; crucifixes in wood or mother of pearl, small, medium or large; Virgin Marys with or without Child; manger scenes; holy water from the River Jordan and earth from the Holy Land, are abhorred as degrading the site. Bracketing out these features in the tourist travel brochures serves to intensify the sense of anticlimax. Tourists feel doubly cheated: the sight which is imagined to be pure, clean and tranquil is perceived as de-sacralized by the commercial requirements of the tourist industry; and the tourist feels deceived by the tourist literature which 'prepares' him or her for the visit. Manger Square is hardly unique in this respect. Auratic tourist space is not immune to commercial blight. Even the approach to the Sphinx in Cairo is dotted with car parks for tourist coaches, T-shirt shops, soft drinks bars and souvenir shops selling papyrus and replicas of the Sphinx and the Pyramids.

De-differentiation is also evident in the repackaging of many inner-city areas and tourist rights in the 1970s and '80s. Cities which had been traditionally associated with industrial grime and roughness, such as Pittsburgh and Glasgow, have been redefined as places of leisure and tourism. In 1990 Glasgow occupied the position of European city of culture – an honour which would have been unimaginable even as late as the end of the 1960s and early '70s. The redefinition of cities with a reputation for roughness as exciting tourist venues reached a landmark in the 1991 Northern Ireland Tourist Board campaign. For over twenty years the region has been devastated by bombings and assassinations. By the 1980s the Province was getting barely 150 000 visitors a year, the majority of whom were fishermen and golfers. The 1991 campaign aimed to dust off the region's rough image. The marketing slogan was 'Belfast – A Hibernian Rio'.[40]

The redefinition of Belfast as an 'Hibernian Rio' is a calculated attempt to replace a negative set of cultural associations with a positive set. Together with the campaigns in Pittsburgh and Glasgow,[41] it shows how far de-differentiation is now accepted as a normal and ordinary part of popular culture. The de-differentiation of interior space which, for example, enables us to simulate tourist experience within the home, is paralleled in the de-differentiation of the exterior which includes intimate, personalized space in the vast, anonymous expanse of metropolis. It was perhaps always an illusion to believe in hard and fast lines between home and abroad, work and leisure, private and public. But now these categories seem to be entangled and harder and harder to separate in satisfactory ways.

These 'normal' and 'ordinary' conditions have left their mark on our dreams of escaping. The dreamworld of the metropolis offers experiences of the remote in space and in time which are a mere bus-ride away. We move from a visit to the Chinese quarter of town, to a reconstruction of a nineteenth-century industrial centre and have tea in a Mediterranean village located in the town shopping centre. Similarly when we fly to a resort in the tropics, in search of 'a world which is the perfect antithesis of our own' we drive to the Hilton hotel in a Ford taxi, we lunch in a McDonald's restaurant, check-in to a Sheraton hotel, watch CNN on the in-house cable channel and round off the day with a visit to the cinema to catch the latest thriller from Hollywood. The globalization of culture tinges our experience of escape with the shadow of familiarity. And yet our dreams of escape continue to entrance us and we are nagged by the feeling that our lives will be catapulted into a completely different realm by the activity of travel. In the next chapter I will return to the question of why leisure and travel continue to intoxicate us. But before coming to that point I want to take up again the topic of the artificiality of our escape experience.

6

Conclusion

We drive to Zion National Park in Utah. This is where you come for the Zion experience. We are directed to the drive-in area at the edge of the Park. A gigantic cinema screen starts to flicker, amplifiers hiss into life. We watch a drama documentary of park life. We see vistas of the terrain, close-ups of rare fauna, studies of wildlife. We do not have to leave the car. There is no risk of bad weather disturbing our enjoyment of the park. We are free from the nuisance of being with other people. When the movie is over we drive out to the freeway which takes us home. We have had enough of Nature for today. Ten years ago all of this would have seemed like science fiction. But in 1991 the World Odyssey group announced a plan to 'extend' the wilderness experience of Zion Park by building the cinema screen. A spokesperson commented:

> There's a market for this. The one and a half million people who visit Zion each year won't have to sweat or get their heart rate above wheel-chair level. Whole busloads can come to Springdale, have the Zion experience and be in Las Vegas that night.[1]

Convenient, accessible and clean – the Zion project symbolizes our absolute estrangement from Nature. We no longer distinguish between the sign of escape and its signifier. Both are equally relaxing and equally real.

From Zion Park we move on to Bali. This is where we come to gain 'the exotic South Seas experience'. We bring with us romantic notions of primitive life.They are reinforced by the colour photographs and copy in the travel brochure and the 'Introduction to Paradise' video that we see on the in-flight travel service. In Bali we expect to find authentic natives following simpler ways of life. The Balinese cater for our expectations by mounting a variety of staged performances. One of the most popular is 'the Batuan Frog Dance'. Tourists see this as an example of timeless Balinese ritual. But the dance is not an indigenous part of Balinese culture. It was invented by tour operators in response to the desires of the tourists. Most of the 'primitives' who perform the spectacle are law and dance students. Our expectations are fulfilled by this staged event; but we do not notice that our expectations are counterfeit.[2]

THE RECURRENCE OF REASSURANCE

The Zion Park cinema screen and the Batuan frog dance are stereotypes of modern popular leisure and tourist forms. They offer passive, relatively unchallenging consumption experience in a clean and secure environment. They can be relied upon to start and end on time. The consumer can slot the experience into his or her free-time schedule. Essentially these leisure attractions cater for our desire to be reassured by our escape experience.

Many popular leisure and tourist attractions are based upon idealized roles and stereotypical situations which are calculated to deliver the feeling of reassurance. For example, we visit the Old Tucson Wild West town in Arizona and the Sheriff always kills the bandits for us; we go to the Disney island where the pirates threaten to attack us but we always avoid their clutches; Freddie terrorizes us on Elm Street but he is always repulsed. In these leisure attractions good triumphs over evil with mathematical precision. They constantly reinforce the message that everything is fundamentally all right. Eco (1986) in his travels in hyperreality noted the onslaught of the nostalgia industry in the US leisure sector. America is being dotted with ghost towns, reconstructions of pioneer villages and waxworks museums displaying models of dead movie stars. They are collective representations of an idealized, purified past which contrasts pointedly with the anonymous and anomic conditions of Modernity. Our lives seem to be fraught with complex and ambivalent implications. Against this the nostalgia industry offers a gallery of coherent stories and satisfying resolutions.

FROM POPULAR CULTURE TO HYPERREALITY

The cultural studies approach in the sociology of leisure encourages us to see 'struggle' and 'resistance' in the sinews of consumer capitalism. We are asked to be conscious of the inventiveness and power of actors in challenging and subverting the capitalist codes of consumption. Popular culture is portrayed as a forcing ground for consciousness raising. Struggle and resistance are seen as yielding an authentic orientation to reality which will act as the springboard for revolutionary change.

It is worth trying to unpack the theoretical mechanism powering this line of analysis. The cultural studies approach posits a universal ontology on the premises of the universal necessity to labour. To put it differently, the necessity of work is conceived of as furnishing us with common experience. Under capitalism of course, this necessity is mediated through the structural inequality between the owners/managers of capital and the majority who only have their labour power to sell. Exponents of the cultural studies approach rightly claim that this structural inequality exposes the claim of capitalists to deliver 'freedom' and 'choice' to all as mere ideology. The workers are not 'free' to dispose 'voluntarily' of their labour power. On the contrary, they are caught up in the immense universe of the capitalist market. In order to survive they must sell their labour power to the capital-owning class and in their 'free' time they are surrounded with objects and commodified experiences which are calculated to perpetuate their enslavement.

This is pretty much the standard Marxist line. Where exponents of the cultural studies approach try to go beyond it is by showing the real vitality of workers' resistance to capitalist values. The workplace, the community, the commodity and even the commodified experience (drinking in the pub, watching football, following a band) are all conceived of as stations of resistance in which capitalist codes of production and consumption can be challenged and resisted. Clarke and Critcher (1985: 216) in their book on leisure approvingly quote Raymond Williams's concept of 'the long revolution'. Their argument reiterates the centrality of class inequality in explaining social development. They hold out the prospect of a rainbow coalition between the various oppressed groups against the rule of capital.

The debate with the cultural studies approach turns on the proposition that there is a universal necessity to labour. Following Marx, it is certainly plausible to argue that the will to labour, the will to act to shape the physical and social world, is an integral part of human nature. As such the necessity to labour is a characteristic of the species (Geras 1983). But the proposition of universal ontology which derives from this argument is not very interesting: all of us want to act upon the physical and social world, to expend our labour power. So what? More interesting matters are raised by asking 'what are the socio-economic conditions in which the want to labour is expressed'? This is precisely the point at issue between exponents of the cultural studies approach and their critics. As we have seen, the cultural studies approach holds that under capitalism labour power is not voluntarily expended by the worker but is forcibly extracted by the capitalist. Consequently the 'freedom' and 'choice' which the worker elects to exercise in leisure activity under capitalism is inevitably problematic. For the worker is choosing 'freedom' from the limited range of choices available to him or her under the system of structural class inequality.

But how accurate is it to claim that the worker is any longer tied to the market by the iron necessity to make a present of his or her labour power to the capitalist? Economists speak of the trend from Fordism towards flexible accumulation in the last twenty years of capitalism. That is, flexibility has replaced rigidity in the planning and organization of labour processes, labour markets, products and patterns of consumption (Harvey 1989: 141–72). It would be naive to imagine that this flexibility has failed to translate into the experience of work. Workers who choose to interrupt work patterns and take early retirement are now common. In addition insurance schemes and welfare state provision has modified the naked cash nexus of Marx's day.[3]

This is not an apology for capitalism – the system remains rooted in structural inequality. However, it is at odds with the picture of work which is developed in the cultural studies literature. This picture foregrounds the compulsion to work. Furthermore it presents work as a prison of self-denial, anguish and alienation. Moorhouse (1989: 26) has rightly questioned whether this picture of work orientations and work experience corresponds with known patterns. He notes that many workers depart from cultural studies protocol and actually enjoy work. They see it as an activity which is a source of pride and companionship as well as economic reward. Moorhouse (ibid.) also questions the cultural studies proposition that a thread of resistance runs through popular culture. When it comes to hard evidence, he asserts, the cultural studies position is somewhat insubstantial. 'They are forced to stress the informal, street, spontaneous elements in leisure,' writes Moorhouse, 'as opposed to people's experiences of participation in the commercial mode . . . [Their position] displays a real lack of detail about what most people actually do or feel in their "free time". (ibid).' This is bluntly expressed; indeed, it is probably expressed too bluntly, for cultural studies writers may reasonably respond that their work has always been steeped in history. While one may quibble with the perspective that they use to explore history, it is quite clear that they make a serious attempt to enter into the history of people's feelings and actions concerning 'free time' relations. All the same, Moorhouse is on firm ground to suggest that there is a paucity of evidence regarding examples of resistance through leisure in the cultural studies account of the present day.

Another, rather basic, point needs to be made about the cultural studies tradition. This concerns its prime unit of analysis: popular culture. For exponents of the cultural studies popular culture is the culture of the working class. Their work is concerned with 'the double moment of creativity and constraint' between popular culture and the commodity world of capitalism. They regard leisure as 'never wholly free nor totally determined activity. It is always potentially an arena for cultural contestation between dominant and subordinate groups' (Clarke and Critcher 1985: 227). There are strong evolutionary overtones in the argument of class 'contestation'. The working class is conceived of as learning through struggle. The climax of this struggle is described in conventional Marxist terms. For example, Tomlinson (1989: 106) maintains that struggle 'mobilizes collectivist strategies and ideals cast in aspirantly transformational form'.

Embedded in these notions is the rather familiar bourgeois principle that leisure experience is geared to self-realization. Granted, for exponents of the cultural studies approach the self in question is theorized in collectivist terms as 'the working class' and not as 'the isolated individual' beloved in bourgeois thought. Nonetheless, there is an identical emphasis upon leisure experience raising consciousness and promoting maturity. But does what we know about the action of Modernity support the view that history should be seen only as a pattern of evolution? The projects of bourgeois individuation and working-class revolutionary consciousness both confronted a market economy in which circulation and exchange processes present an ever-changing play of commodities and spectacles. Modern market conditions give continuity to some forms of experience, but they also promote fragmentation elsewhere. For example, the personal

and stable conditions of the community are replaced by the anonymous and episodic conditions of the global market. The velocity of
exchange and circulation processes accentuate the sense of contin-
gency in social life. Earlier chapters have shown how the bourgeois
project of individuation which sought to educate the senses through
leisure experience was undermined by the action of modern market
processes which produce the bombardment of the senses. Has not
working-class consciousness succumbed to the same process of internal fragmentation? The workplace and work community now
compete with the mass communications industry in the organization of working-class association and practice. Objective conditions
of restricted income, cramped housing and low geographical and
social mobility do not necessarily translate into the subjective realization of class identity. The constant play of cultural commodities
and commodified experience produces a mix of continuities and
discontinuities rather than an enduring evolutionary pattern of progressive class consciousness. It also produces a restless questioning
of 'reality'. Mass reproduction, the imitation and 'extension' of nature and history and the procession of dramatized mass spectacle
organized by the mass communication industry, produce a social
environment in which calculated myth and simulation structure the
contours of daily life. Duplications of auratic objects are venerated as
being more real because they are more 'personal' than 'the original'.
Extensions of nature and history are celebrated for being more user-
friendly than 'the real thing'. Under conditions of mass reproduction, standardization and hyperreality, the sign of authority
possesses no originality or finality.[4]

For exponents of the cultural studies approach the denial of authority is an act of consciousness-raising. It exposes the rule of
hegemony. It is but a short step from this to positing the inevitability
of collectivist action. As we have seen, students of cultural studies
take this step with sober enthusiasm. But how plausible is it to
maintain that consciousness-raising and radicalization are the only,
or even the principal responses to mass reproduction and standardization? According to students of the cultural studies approach the
imprimatur of hegemony is like a splinter in the eye. In the end we
won't tolerate it. We will pluck it out. We will destroy it in order
to satisfy our repressed will to see more clearly again. However, do
some of the masses, and perhaps the majority at that, not also
embrace it? Do they not prefer 'the glamour of distraction'[5] to revolutionary objects?

MONTAGE

'The Big Apple. New York! New York! What a City! Thanks to television and movies, visitors often feel they've been there, but nothing beats the experience . . . From the razzle-dazzle of Broadway to the sober skyscrapers of the financial district, from the opulence of some of the world's finest hotels to the tranquility of Central Park, from the UN Headquarters to Radio City Music Hall, New York has it all.'[6]

'The characters you love – and hate – are waiting to meet you at the Charles Dickens Centre . . . Here's Mr Pickwick – kind hearted, jovial, lover of good food and wine. There's poor Nancy who tried to help Oliver and was murdered by the evil Bill Sikes. Witness Scrooge's horror as he meets the ghost of Marley, and beware Quilp, the sinister dwarf from the Old Curiosity Shop. Watch out for the crafty rogue Fagin and enjoy many more scenes and characters that bring the Victorian world alive.'[7]

'See the Greatest Rock Show in the world. Experience the Greats of Rock and Pop. The skills and artistry of Madame Tussaud's combine with the technology of the future. Audiomatronic techniques bring the great rock starts to life in a unique performance. All recordings come from Compact Disc for highest quality sound.'[8]

'Experience a by-gone age at old Calico Ghost Town. Here you can relive the dreams of long-ago prospectors as you roam the Tunnels of Maggie's mine or climb aboard a railroad car destined for old workings to the north . . . This is but a brief glimpse of our silver mining town . . . discover it for yourself, and you'll agree that even in 1881, she's still "pretty as a gal's Calico skirt".'[9]

'Pittsburgh . . . offers something for everyone from historic sites and museums to include rides, riverboat cruises, a submarine and a new science center. Of course, if you prefer cultural performances, galleries and major league sports, Pittsburgh is the place to visit. Families enjoy and water parks, hay or slough rides and numerous fairs and festivals . . . Have a wonderful time in Pittsburgh.'[10]

'Glasgow': Miles Better.'[11]

'The year is 1093 AD and you are the guests of the royal family. As you wine and dine and make merry at a sumptuous medieval feast, you'll see spectacular pageantry, dramatic horsemanship, dangerous swordplay, falconry, sorcery, romance – and to crown it all – an authentic jousting tournament . . . Medieval Times. It's a show that's become a legend.[12]

'In the dark autumn of 1888 Londoners were terrorised by a sense of brutal murders committed by a man who became known as Jack the Ripper. Nobody has ever discovered who Jack The Ripper was, although numerous fascinating theories have been put forward. We visit the dark alleyways where the murders took place, and discover how Jack the Ripper killed his victims and mutilated their bodies. The tour takes the form of a 'whodunnit', as the guide tells you about some of the leading theories, but also gives you clues to enable you to work out for yourself who the murderer was. At the end we reveal the secret that has remained hidden for 100 years – the identity of Jack the Ripper. We also visit the 'Jack the Ripper' pub.'[13]

'We believe that fun and entertainment are elements that make the difference between a good tour and a great tour. To help you make the most of every minute of your vacation, we have scheduled an impressive array of special highlights: dazzling song and dance shows, fascinating slide trips, gourmet dinners and exciting rides. Each has the flavour of the region – and sharing them with new friends can add that extra touch to your European trip that makes it unforgettable.'[14]

'Eden Camp, Malton . . . Experience the sights, the sounds, the fire and smoke of: The Blitz – U boat attacks on Atlantic Convoys – The Rise of the Nazi Party – The Home Guard – Evacuation – The Black Out – Rationing – The Sound of the 40's – plus, on a lighter note: Fashions of the 40's – a complete window shopping Street of Shops – Worker's Playtime . . . Our special living museum is constructed, appropriately, in the huts of a genuine prisoner of war camp. This fascinating display holds, and reveals to you, the vital spirit which triumphed in 1945.'[15]

'Legoland may best be described as a children's kingdom in the heart of Jutland's green and wooded countryside . . . Copenhagen's harbour district has been copied in detail and there are many towns and sights from all over the world.'[16]

'Forbidden Paris: An 'X' certificate tour should ensure that the clients enjoy both security and quality. We have solved this problem. Firstly we offer you a show that is more than just 'sexy', and then in one of the most renowned places of this sort a show that is strictly for an audience that has been forewarned. The truth and eroticism of these live sex shows will be sure to surprise you.'[17]

'It's something that will never be finished, something I can keep developing, keep 'plussing' and adding to. It's alive. It will be a live breathing thing that will need changes. When you wrap up a picture

and turn it over to Technicolor you're through. Snow White is a dead
issue with me . . . I want something live, something that would grow.
The park is that. Not only can I add things to it, but even the trees
will keep growing. The thing will get more beautiful year after year.
And it will get more beautiful as I find out what the public likes.' –
Walt Disney on the plans for the original Disneyland.[18]

'Take a stroll down High Street 1920. Take your family and friends
to Beamish: simply acres of nostalgia.'[19]

NO ESCAPE?

The thorough artificiality of modern life creates constant anxieties
about the nature of our real feelings. The person today who constantly worries about who he or she is, or how he or she should act
to do good in the world is seen as being too serious. Intensity
betokens introspection and this can be unattractive to others. Consumer culture encourages a positive, feel-good, keep-fit, acquisitive
attitude which marginalizes the traditional question of what life is
for. Even death is something that happens to other people.

In such circumstances our inner life becomes characterized by a
certain numbness. We shrink from deep commitments and cast our
energies in leisure out toward reassuring, consumerist experience
which requires passive involvement or transitory relationships which
avoid putting ourselves on the line. Our blatant interest in the distant in space and in time is a symptom of our growing distance from
inner relationships.

For most people the quest for escape is seen in terms of a projection out of the values of immediate society. We long for things which
are far away from routine existence. We are drawn to the exotic in
fashion and amusement. However, we confront these attractions as
members of a particular class, race, nation and civilization. And
were we able truly to abandon these identity values we could not
function. Our escape attempts are therefore themselves artificial.
They are encoded activities with structural parameters. There is no
escape.

What then accounts for the obvious popularity of leisure and
travel as ways of escape? The proposition that I wish to put forward
is that leisure and travel enable us to experience the rapid, hectic
contrasts of Modernity in concentrated form. The package tour of

the British Isles which takes in London on day one, moves to the West Country the following day, stopping off in Wales in the evening; tours the Midlands on day three, with supper in Brontë country; and ends on day four with a six-hour tour of Edinburgh, is a caricature of the fragmentary, jarring, rapidly-changing conditions which characterized Modernity. Movies, rock shows and many forms of sport also offer us experience of pressurized change, intense contrasts and rapid movement. Although it is no doubt possible to cite many counter-examples, popular leisure activity seems to thrive on fragmentary, contrasting and fleeting experience. Far from demonstrating a reaction to the routines of life as some commentators allege,[20] leisure often involves the intensification and extension of these routines. Thus the fragmentary, disjointed and ever changing conditions of the metropolis are reproduced in dramatized or sensational form in the sports arena or the cinema screen. Thus, too, the sense of disappointment that many of experience when we visit some long-desired tourist spot or take up a leisure pursuit which we think will deliver us from the mundanity of everyday life. Leisure, one might say, is not the antithesis of daily life but the continuation of it in dramatized or spectacular form. And whereas most of what happens to us in ordinary life is ambiguous and inconclusive, popular leisure forms typically provide us with a satisfying, reassuring sense of resolution. We participate, we get carried along, with the furious and energetic to-and-fro of a tennis match or a soccer game, but we know that the contest must eventually come to an end; similarly, our nerves may jangle and our senses may peel as we watch a movie chiller or a violent piece of theatre, but at the back of our minds is the sure knowledge that the performance is only a performance which, moreover, must end on time. Whereas the anxieties of ordinary life may nag away at us for days or months and even years, the heightened sensations that we experience through participating in popular leisure activities are over in a few minutes or hours.

LEISURE SOCIETY / 'EIGHT HOURS OF RECREATION'

'The leisure society', that optimistic gift of imagination, has coruscated through Western social thought, especially from the moment of the Enlightenment. We have scrabbled around for routes to get there, devised machineries of transport and invented beautiful vistas of a future near at hand but elsewhere. The communist road in Eastern Europe sought to follow the star of freedom but only crashed into the rocks of economic and political 'necessity'. As the materials of Eastern European communism plummet down above our heads we in the West have comforted ourselves with our 'prescience'. But it is perhaps no exaggeration to say that prescience is always more persuasive in the mind's eye than in actuality. In the West as we drink a draught to the end of communism perhaps we should reflect upon our own adventures in escape. For example, Le Corbusier's (1929) radical manifesto of town planning, *The City of Tomorrow*, envisaged the day made up three components: eight hours of work, eight hours of recreation and eight hours of sleep. With that love of purity and rational form which we (105–24) have suggested were the hallmarks of bourgeois culture, Le Corbusier advocated the creation of 'garden cities'. Life in them would follow the principle of 'freedom through order' (Le Corbusier 1929: 211). They were to be models of rational planning. For example, Le Corbusier's 'Voisin' scheme for Paris envisaged the annihilation of existing buildings and transport routes and their replacement with functional, grid-like street patterns and skyscrapers. Workers were to be conveyed by fast-track trains and multi-lane highways from their homes to shopping centres, workplaces, recreation spaces, sport stadiums and back to their home. Housing space was to be constructed in high-rise cellular dwellings. Each dwelling was to be two storey high, with a hanging flower garden for ornamentation and 'set-backs' which would operate as private play and recreation areas. At the foot of each building Le Corbusier planned communal recreation areas. The emphasis was on convenience and ease of movement. As he put it: 'You come home, you change, you can take your exercise *just outside your home*' (1929: 205); emphasis in the original). For Le Corbusier, vertical cities would be bathed in light and air and they would liberate the spaces below for rest and recreation. He regarded 'exhibition sports' and popular leisure forms as degraded activities. Recreation in garden cities would provide 'healthier' more 'uplifting' experience (1929: 202).

Le Corbusier never succeeded in piloting his 'Voisin' scheme through the thicket of planning laws and cash limits in Parisian government. However, he did achieve a small-scale trial-run in his *Unité d' habitation* scheme (1946–52), a high-rise, mass housing development in Marseilles. It is an eighteen-storey block, 185 feet high,

420 feet long and 60 feet wide. The building rests on concrete legs with 12 acres of surrounding parkland. Hughes (1991: 188–90) describes the development as an experiment which failed disastrously:

> Corbusier meant it to contain a gymnasium, a paddling pool for children, a palaestra for exercise and a bicycle track. Today the pool is cracked, the gymnasium closed and the track littered with broken concrete and tangles of rusting scaffolding . . . There is little privacy in this nobly articulated beehive of raw concrete . . . None of the Marseillais who lived there could stand Corbusier's plain, morally elevating interiors, so they restored the *machine a habiter* to the true style of suburban France. The flats of the *Unité* are crammed with plastic chandeliers, imitation Louis XVI bergéres, and Monoprix ormulu – just the furniture Corbusier struggled against all his life.

While Le Corbusier was not directly responsible for the postwar high-rise workers' housing developments elsewhere in Europe and the Americas his ideas were an unquestionable influence. With a depressingly small number of exceptions, Hughes's account of the fate of the *Unité* scheme applies equally to them.

FALSE ENDING

If any motto sums up the story of Modernity it is 'Beware Triumphalism'. The end of communism, the end of poverty, the end of ethnic conflict, the end of ignorance, the end or racism, the end of the work, the end of war, the end of capitalism – have all been proclaimed in the last hundred years; all have proved to be false dawns. One task of sociology is to account for why these hopes are unrealized. We do so by examining the specific conjunction of social, economic and political forces which enable some types of human will to prevail and others to be frustrated. But in examining the relations between specific classes, interest groups and the changing balance of power between the sexes, it is perhaps all too easy to lose sight of the context in which these relations occur. As Baudelaire, one of the first writers to take Modernity seriously, wrote:

(The) transitory, fugitive element, whose metamorphoses are so
rapid, must on no account be despised or dispensed with. By
neglecting it, you cannot fail to tumble into the abyss of abstract
. . . beauty. (1962: 13)

The process of exchange, circulation and commodification which
characterize modern market society carry strong tendencies towards
fragmentation because they only require fragments of the individual
personality to be involved. This is an obvious fact about many
forms of contemporary leisure activity. For example, we watch the
evening TV news with one eye on a magazine and half a mind on
an office meeting scheduled for tomorrow. We stroll through the
countryside with a Walkman playing classical music through our
headphones and a camera in our hand. Dedicated leisure activity is
quite rare, which is why the compulsive hill-walker, the serious
amateur musician, or even the serious reader of fiction, stand out so
starkly. Most of us are content to flit from activity to activity. We
neither seek nor claim expertise in anything. We follow the latest
movie or musical recording, we read the latest novel or attend the
weekly sporting fixture. But our engagement is partial and episodic.
Passions and interests quickly roused are just as quickly forgotten.
Most of us have difficulty in remembering fully the plot of the
novel we read last summer or the story of the Hollywood block-
buster which we watched a year ago. Our leisure allows us to
enter a different rhythm of life and provides us with momentary
distraction.

However, modern life is made-up of contrast and distraction. We
do not escape the gravitational pull of Modernity by launching into
leisure and travel activity as ways of escape. On the contrary, the
restless dissatisfaction and desire for contrast which often colours
our leisure and travel experience reflects modern values. We are
never convinced that we have experienced things in our 'free' time
fully enough; we are always dully aware that our experiences could
be better; no sooner do we enter 'escape' activities than we feel
nagging urges to escape from them. In these conditions it seems folly
to see leisure experience as paving the way towards self-realization
or consciousness-raising. For the subjects of 'the self' and 'consciousness-raising' are open to contrasting and changing interpretations
and debate. The ephemeral, the fugitive and the contingent describe
our experience of leisure just as they are at the heart of the phenomenology of Modernity.

Notes

1 THE MANAGEMENT OF PLEASURE

1. See especially Locke (1689).
2. A fact which implicitly strengthens the plausibility of Elias's thesis of state formation, the development of monopoly mechanisms in taxation and the legitimate use of physical force and the transformation of the personality structure.
3. Burton's learning was encyclopaedic. Although the accuracy of his knowledge may be faulted with hindsight, it was a marvel for his own times.
4. For a chilling visual comment on this see Francisco de Goya, 'The Sleep of Reason Produces Monsters', in the 'Caprichos'.
5. See Rousseau (1974).
6. By 1820 it had risen to 11.5 million (Porter 1982: 333).
7. Weber (1923: 223): 'We know that in Bengal, for example, the English garrison cost five times as much as the money value of all goods carried thither. It follows that the markets for domestic industry furnished by the colonies under the conditions of the time were relatively unimportant, and that the main profit was derived from the transport business.' As I have already noted in the main text this view is contradicted by Hobsbawm (1969: 53) who puts greater significance on the economic importance of colonialism.
8. See Paine (1792) *Rights of Man*, Part 2, especially 'Of the Old and New Systems of Government' and 'Of Constitutions' (pp. 193–206 and 207–31.
9. Combination has been outlawed in specific industries prior to the 1799 and 1800 Acts, e.g. the tailors in 1721 and 1767, the woollen trade in 1726, the hatters in 1777, the papermakers in 1797. By the time of the 1799 and 1800 Acts over 40 Acts were on the statute books forbidding combinations to raise wages.
10. See, for example, Corrigan and Sayer (1985: 3–11) for their discussion of Marx, Durkheim and Weber.
11. See, for example, Dingle (1980); Berridge and Edwards (1987); and Mort (1987).
12. All of these writers stress the role of the state in 'organizing the subject'. However, they do so from very different and, arguably, irreconcilable, sociological perspectives.
13. They also suggest that a fourth 'moment' began in the mid 1970s with the beginning of the open attack on the welfare state and the reassertion of unfettered market forces.
14. See, for example Huizinga (1924); Pirenne (1936); Bloch (1962); Burke (1978); and Ariès (1981).

15. *Sir Walter Raleigh's Letters of Patent for Virginia 1584*, in Haklyut (1986: 63–4).
16. Vale's (1977) account of the principal aristocratic recreations in the sixteenth and seventeenth centuries is a useful resource here.
17. Smith, Ferguson, Millar, Rousseau and Hume produced the original and essential formulations of the argument.
18. Simmel (1907) should also be referred to as a classic, albeit strongly contrasting, statement of this argument.
19. Report of Dr Sutherland 'General Board of Health', in Russell (1895).
20. Lamb (anon.) 'The Manufacturing Poor', *Fraser's Magazine* XXXVII, 1848.
21. See Mort (1987: 63–147).
22. Borzello (1987) attributes this phrase to Lord Rosebery.
23. Samuel Barnett was a leading figure in Victorian philanthropic reform. He helped Octavia Hill found the Charity Organisation Society in the 1860s. Between 1884–1906 he was warden of Toynbee Hall, Whitechapel — Britain's first settlement house.
24. See Borzello (1987: 51–2). The success of the exhibitions eventually led to the founding of the Whitechapel Art Gallery in 1901.
25. From Barnett and Barnett (1888: 113); cited in Borzello (1987: 62).
26. For more on the bourgeois world of leisure see Rojek (1989: 95–104).
27. The elasticity of the concepts has perhaps been illustrated most terribly in this century in the cases of Auschwitz, Buchenwald and Dachau under the Nazi terror.
28. *Scouting for Boys* was originally published in 1908. The passage cited is quoted by Springhall (1977: 59).
29. Quoted by Mangan (1985: 22).
30. See, for example, Gathorne Hardy (1979); Dunning and Sheard (1979) and Mangan (1981).
31. Wardle (1970) quotes from the 1889 Nottingham School Board report which stated that secondary education should aim to produce 'quieter streets, more self respect and more respect for others'.
32. From the 1968 edition of Marx and Engels.
33. See, for example, Berger *et al* (1974); Connerton (1976).

2   THOROUGHLY MODERN WOMAN

1. The acts applied to a number of naval ports and army garrison towns in England and Wales. They empowered the police and medical practitioners to notify justices of the peace if they suspected a women of being a prostitute. The suspect would then be forcibly taken to a certified hospital and subjected to compulsory medical examination. The acts allowed women to be detained for up to three months. The acts were compatible with many abuses. They were opposed by middle-class women's organizations such as the Ladies National Association founded by Josephine Butler.

2. The activities of conservative moralists like Mary Whitehouse, Victoria Gillick and Margaret Thatcher in the UK, and the Republican demonstrator Phyllis Shalafly in the US are often mentioned in this regard.

3. For an interesting discussion of the incompatibility between Marxism and feminism see Anderson (1983). Anderson argues:

> Universal though the cause of women's emancipation may be, one so radical that men too will be freed from their existing selves by it, it is insufficiently operational as a collective agency, actual or potential, ever to be able to uproot the economy or polity of capital. For that, a social force endowed with another strategic leverage is necessary. Only the modern 'collective labourer', the workers who constitute the immediate producers of any industrial society possess that leverage. (1983: 92–3)

4. Some of them were half-brothers and -sisters.

5. For a discussion of the Victorian myths woven around the idea of Ancient Greece see Jenkyns 1980.

6. See pp. (80–2).

7. One only has to think of the fiction of Jane Austen to review models of female manipulators of male power.

8. For example, on the variety of individual needs, *The Marriage Book* confides:

> The sex needs of all are not the same. Individuality enters here rather more than it does even in diet, and any of us who have had the experience knows how irksome eating by formula becomes if no recognition is made of one's own particular tastes and habits. (nd: 31)

And on adjustment *The Marriage Book* states: 'The relationship must be reciprocal. There must be mutual adaptation, and it is this that makes the experience a process of mutual adjustment (ibid.).

9. The theoretical inspiration for Wouters's thesis of informalization is, of course, Norbert Elias's theory of the civilizing process.

10. On the crowded Victorian bourgeois interior of this period, Dutton writes:

> The quantity of furniture in the average drawing room was no less astonishing than the poorness of its quality. In many rooms, obviously in large houses and belonging to wealthy owners, there would be nothing to be seen which would now be worth more than few pounds, if subjected to the cold test of the auctioneer's hammer; but even where some finer furniture from a happier period survived it would be mixed in complete insouciance, with worthless *bric à brac*. (1954: 115)

11. Catherine Beecher co-authored her book with her sister, the novelist, Harriet Beecher-Stowe.

12. Co-authored with Ogden Codmen Jr.

13. For a review of these positions see Rojek (1985: 85–139).
14. As we have seen (70–1), improvements in the technology of publishing and retail distribution facilitated this process.
15. Lady Troubridge makes the point after regaling her readers with salutory tales of women who had resisted 'the new spirit'. As she elaborates:

> It is up to all of us to cast aside our stiffer and more outworn notions of what is and is not correct, and to steer a course nicely blended between old-fashioned courtesy and new-fashioned informality. (1926: 9)

16. Speculation on the origins of this association is a bottomless pit. However, there can be little doubt that the stereotyping and scapegoating of 'the infidel' by the Christian church at the time of the Crusades was a significant influence.
17. The reference is from the 1968 edition of Marx and Engels.
18. According to Thompson, middle-class men were attracted to prostitutes for two main reasons. First, they were prey to received ideas of the 'unrestrained' sexual drives of lower-class working girls. Second, the male practice of postponing marriage until the late twenties or early thirties for economic reasons, 'made these outlets peculiarly necessary for middle class men' (1988: 257–8).
19. His relationship with a maid, Hannah Cullwick, required her to alternate between the roles of lady and servant as part of an extended cycle of elevation and degradation ceremonies. Munby, a London barrister, eventually married Hannah in 1873. However, he insisted that the marriage be kept secret and the cycle of elevation and degradation continued.
20. The main reason for increased contact was the growth of employment opportunities for middle-class women, the development of voluntary welfare work, the improvement of street safety through concrete pavements, electric street-lighting and more street patrols, changes in retail distribution, notably the rise of the department store, and the increased circulation in news and information through the mass media.
21. For a commentary and critique of the formalist position in leisure studies, see Rojek (1985: 85–105).
22. 1874 was the year when Harrod's Stores was first used for trading purposes. The business started as a wholesale grocer and tea dealer in 1849. The development of the shop into a department store was an organic process. For a description of the process, see Dale 1981: 15–19.
23. For example, employees at *Bon Marché* numbered 1,788 in 1877; 3,173 in 1887 and 4,500 in 1906 (Chaney 1983: 23). By 1914 *Whiteley's* had a staff of 4000 and *Harrod's* 6000 (Hamish Fraser 1981: 132).
24. In a telling but speculative passage Schivelbusch (1980: 189) compares the experience of the circulation of customers in the department store to the experience of circulation felt by the rail traveller.:

The department store put an end to sales conversation, as travel by rail put an end to verbal exchanges among travellers. The latter were replaced by travel reading; the former, by a mute price tag. This change resulted from the increased turnover of goods; the increase in quantity required new forms of distribution and behaviour in travel space as well as in commercial space. Not only did the department store change the relationship between seller and buyer, it also changed the buyer's attitude towards the goods sold. In the transition from the traditional retail shop to the department store, the customer's perception of the goods changed in a manner analogous to the traveller's perception during the transition from coach to train.

25. This remark is not meant to imply that department stores surrendered their sense of spectacle. In fact, Selfridge's opened to a fanfare of publicity which billed it as the most spectacular emporium in the world. 'Never before,' wrote Pound, 'as shoppers had they been treated as guests or flattered with the illusion that they are connoisseurs of their surroundings as well as what they wished to buy' (1960: 67).

26. Garfinkel's extraordinary attention to detail and concern to decipher the full dynamics of face-to-face relationships and social contacts remains the best counter to the vanities of 'realist' sociology.

27. Showalter (1981: 330) in noting that nymphomania, puerperal mania and ovarian madness have also virtually disappeared, remarks that new 'female' diseases like anorexia nervosa and agoraphobia have taken their place.

28. Fixed programmes of activity for work, leisure, prayer and sleep were much the fashion in the bourgeois class. For example, see my discussion of Benjamin Franklin's 'scheme of employment' (Rojek 1989: 95–7).

29. Carroll is not alone in raising doubts about the rise of female participation in public life. For example, see Nisbet (1975: 81, 111).

30. One of the most outstanding critics of the view of society as a collection of relatively independent variables was Adorno. He wrote: 'To the isolated, isolation seems an indubitable certainty; they are bewitched, on pain of losing their existence, not to perceive how mediated their isolation is. (1973: 313)' For an important critique of the position that leisure should be viewed as 'free time' see his recently translated articles, 'The schema of mass culture' and 'Free time' in Adorno (1991).

31. The use of the term 'central planning and regulation' is not intended to make a political point. These critics may be sceptical of the idea of state planning on the grounds that it is always authoritarian and inflexible. On the other hand, they are just as dismissive of non-socialist totalizing concepts such as 'the invisible hand of the market' or 'rational choice' which they would dismiss as metaphysics.

3 DISORGANIZED LEISURE?

1. See Smiles (1894: 88).
2. For example, writing on the elective affinity between capitalism and protestantism Weber (1930: 67, 157) wrote, 'leisureliness was suddenly destroyed . . . not leisure and enjoyment, but only activity [which] serves to increase the glory of God' is encouraged.
3. For an important analysis of Simmel's view on leisure see Frisby (1989: 75–91).
4. Cohen and Taylor (1976) attempt an inventory of contemporary 'escape attempts'.
5. Simmel's discussion suggests that any attempt to escape from ceaseless hurry and contradictions of modernity through leisure will achieve only a 'momentary' effect.
6. McLuhan in the 1960s used the term 'the global village' to express this phenomenon.
7. Charles Dickens was a noted amateur mesmerist. See Kaplan (1988: 182–3; 235–6; 246–7).
8. For a discussion of the Commission's Report see, Wiener (1988: 17–18).
9. By Flaubert's day, of course, the Ancient world of Rome and Athens was already being impinged upon by members of the plutocracy and the artisan class. The trend for those with a Romantic disposition was to journey to the Orient. Nerval visited the Orient in 1844 and Flaubert followed in 1849.
10. A permanence which was visibly under threat with the rise of mass tourism in the 1880s. The paradise of the aristocracy and the high bourgeoisie became clouded with the shadow of destruction from this date (see Pemble 1987: 167–81).
11. Nerval's *Voyage en Orient* (1851) and Du Camp's *Souvenirs et paysages d'Orient* (which was in part dedicated to Flaubert) were instrumental in spreading the popularity of the Orient as a place of 'real feelings', seduction and escape.
12. Epitaphs like this are pretty common in the great Victorian cemeteries, e.g. Highgate, Norwood, Kensal Green (London), Necropolis (Glasgow).
13. Reading Victorian and Edwardian fiction, biography and autobiography, it is striking how much spare time is taken up with strenuous activity: charades, card games, amateur dramatics, bible readings, games, walking, doing good works and fund raising for charities (see Hardyment 1973: 139–55; Hobsbawm 1975; Kaplan 1988: 273–6, 319–20, 363–6, 496).
14. Barnum took over the museum in 1841. His self-appointed brief was 'to present to the American public such a variety, quantity and quality of amusement, blended with instruction, "all for 25 cents, children half price", that my attractions would be irresistible, and my fortune certain' (1869: 115). Barnum's attractions in the 1840s and '50s in-

cluded, in his own words, 'educated dogs, industrious fleas, auto-matons, jugglers, ventriloquists, living statuary, tableaux, gipsies, Albinoes, fat boys, giants, dwarfs, rope dancers, live 'Yankees'', pan-tomime, instrumental music, singing and dancing in great variety, dioramas, panoramas, models of Niagara, Dublin, Paris, and Jerusa-lem; Hannington's dioramas of Creation, the Deluge, Fairy Grotto, Storm at Sea; the first English Punch and Judy in this country, Italian Fantoccini, mechanical figures, fancy glass blowing, knitting machines and other triumphs in the mechanical arts; dissolving views, Amer-ican Indians, who enact their warlike and religious ceremonies on the stage' (ibid: 103).

15. Other 'live' 'transient novelties', as Barnum calls them, were 'rhino-ceros, giraffes, grizzly bears, ourang-outangs, great serpents, and what-ever else of the kind money would buy or enterprise secure' (ibid: 107).

16. The significance of travel experience added, to what Bourdieu (1986) referred to as 'the cultural capital' of the bourgeois class. It conferred upon them the mark of distinction which reinforced their property ties.

17. Modernity consistently posed the question of negation. So it is no surprise that the bourgeois stratification of the interior as the focus of reality should receive its negation in the form of J.K. Huysmans (1884) novel *A Rebours*. Here Huysmans creates a fictional interior for his neurotic hero, Duc Jean Floressas des Essientes, which, in being a palace of calculated artifice is celebrated as being more real than the reality outside.

18. Schivelbusch's analysis of the opening up of new public spaces through the technology of electric lighting may be contrasted with Sennett's (1977) account of the shrivelling up of public life.

19. Again a pointed contrast can be drawn here between Schievelbusch's position and that of Sennett.

20. The consistency of 'post industrial' writers should not be assumed here. For example, Bell (1973) describes leisure in post-industrial soci-ety as a harried quality of life. He remarks, '"Free time" becomes more and more precious . . . Man, in his leisure time, has become *homo economicus*' (1973: 474).

21. This was paralleled by the exhaustion of the debate on the transition from capitalism to communism – an exhaustion precipitated by the collapse of the East European 'experiments' in communism.

22. Wittgenstein is clearly a major influence here.

23. The work of Nietzsche is perhaps the key parallel.

24. The situationists in the 1960s also drew attention to the replacement of reality with representation.

25. This was also, of course, observed by Veblen (1925) in his critique of the 'leisure class'.

26. Douglas Hurd, the Home Secretary of the time, quoted in the *Daily Telegraph* 4.6.1986. See also Rojek (1988).

4   FATAL ATTRACTIONS

1. *Daily Mirror* 22.12.1988; *Guardian* 24.12.1988.
2. *Guardian* 9.3.1987.
3. *Guardian* 11.4.1988.
4. I took the tour in August of 1989. Tourists are issued with a photocopy of Marilyn Monroe's death certificate and maps of Hollywood Memorial Park Cemetery and Westwood Memorial Park Cemetery where many of the Hollywood famous are buried. The tour soundtrack features funeral music, interspersed with relevant snippets (radio bulletins from the time, interviews, theme tunes) relating to the deceased when the funeral hearse pulls up to the Black Spot. Among the Black Spots featured on the tour are the hotel where Janis Joplin died of a drug overdose; the hotel where Divine died of a heart attack; the Chateau Marmont, off Sunset Boulevard where John Belushi died of a drug overdose; the house where Bugsy Siegel was assassinated in 1947; the bedroom where Lana Turner's daughter stabbed her mother's lover, Johnny Stampato; the restaurant where James Dean ate his last meal; the apartment where Aunt Em of *Wizard of Oz* fame committed suicide; the apartment where Mae West died; and the Knickerboker Hotel where MGM's chief dress-designer, Irene Gibbons, slashed her wrists and jumped out of a fourteenth-floor window in 1962.
5. Mystery still surrounds his death. The official version maintains that he died of a heart attack in his apartment. Another version submits that he died of a drug overdose in a club called 'The Rock 'n' Roll Circus' on Rue de Seine. Inevitably, there are also rumours that he never died at all. He just retreated from the glare of the media spotlight to write poetry on a secret island hideaway.
6. Sean O'Hagan: 'With the Pilgrims at Rock's Stinking Shrine', *Sunday Correspondent* 1.7.1990.
7. When I first visited the site in 1984 the bust was still *in situ*. Someone had placed an imitation joint in its mouth.
8. See 'From the Grave', Editorial, *Evening Standard* 15.2.1989; and Martin Walker, 'The King is Dead, or Long Live the King', *Guardian* 21.1.1990.
9. In 1989, 600 000 people visited *Graceland*. 400 miles away in Pilgrim Forge, near Knoxville, Tennesse, there is 'The Elvis Presley Museum'. This boasts a collection of authentic Elvis memorabilia – the first dollar bill Elvis ever gave to God (authenticated by the pastor, who sold it for £4700); the last sunglasses he ever wore; his pyjamas; his nasal spray applicator; his Flexamatic razor; his bathroom scales; a few pairs of his underpants; and X-rays of his left hand and sinuses.
10. However, even Bellamy recognizes that the exploits of Robin Hood were embellished by balladeers, troubadours and story tellers. The existence of secondary figures in the legend, such as Friar Tuck, Little John and Maid Marian, almost certainly owes more to the imagination of romancers than to any factual basis in history.

11. Both quotes are from the *Nottingham Trader* 16.3.1988 and 30.3.1988.
12. The leaflet is produced by the Plymouth County Development Council in cooperation with the Massachusetts Division of Tourism.
13. Similar heritage schemes which use 'interpreters' to recreate the days when America was young (i.e. unpoliticized, unracialized) can be found at the Sleepy Hollow Restoration in the Hudson Valley; and the Village of Waterloo in New Jersey. Waterloo's tourist brochure invites you to 'watch village artisans demonstrate early cloth-making at the Weaving Barn, follow every turn of pottery making at the Pottery Shed; Go Back to the days of herbal cures and country sachets at the village Apothecary; and 'thrill to historical reenactments throughout the village'.
14. 'Possible Dreams', Anne Troksoff, *TWA Ambassador*, August 1990, 15–21.
15. The use of invented characters like Lija Wedge, to personalize the display is a common feature of heritage centres.
16. Lincoln's speech is composed from several fragments from his collected works.
17. The remark recalls Lyotard's observation on the eclecticism of postmodern style (see p. 129).
18. All quotations come from the complimentary tourist leaflet supplied at the site.
19. All quotations from C. Thatcher, 'Dear Sherlock Holmes', British Airways *High Life* Magazine, May 1986.
20. The advertisement was printed in the *Atlanta and Georgia Visitors Guide*, Spring/Summer 1988, published by the Atlanta Convention and Visitors Bureau.
21. *New York Post* 'Travel', 25.8.1987.
22. *Guardian* 6.10.1986.
23. Other important factors were, of course, his health and the public disapproval of his relationship with Frieda.
24. The *Guides* were repackaged by Penguin in 1986.
25. Hardy's heart was buried in Stinsford Churchyard; his ashes are interred in Westminster Abbey.
26. The plans were reported in the *Guardian* 30.4. 1987 and 14.4.1990; and the *Observer* colour magazine 17.12.1989.
27. And this is a useful corrective to those fallacious views in leisure studies which invite us to view leisure as an 'escape' from the 'paramount reality' of the real world.
28. See Schmalz, J. 'Move Theme Park Fight: Nastiness is Not A Fantasy', *New York Times* 13.8.1989.
29. It is estimated that each visitor to Disneyland spends $25.30, including admission. 47 shops and 31 restaurants and snack bars sell Disney-related products (Gray 1986: 18).
30. 'Coasting and Sliding at 12 of America's Amusement Parks', *New York Times* 13.8.1989 pp 14–17.
31. All quotes come from 'Six Flags Magic Mountain' flyer 1989.
32. 'Theme Parks in Europe ,' *The Economist* February 1987.

33. However, elsewhere in his discussion Bennett (1983: 148) changes tack and maintains that 'in releasing the body for pleasure rather than harnessing it for work, part of their [the rides'] appeal may be that they invert the normal relations between people and machinery prevailing in an industrial context'. This makes a distinctly functionalist proposition and carries with it all of the old false dichotomies which have bedevilled thought and research in the study of leisure and culture: the dichotomy between leisure and work, normality and abnormality, private and public life, etc.

34. It is not the only full-scale example of a purpose built village-size simulation on US soil. In Georgia lies the town of Helen, 'Georgia's Alpine Village'. In the words of the Atlanta and Georgia Visitor's Guide', Spring/Summer 1988: 'Nestled alongside a sparkling stream in the mountains of Northeast Georgia, Helen offers the best of the Old and New Worlds'. The whole village is designed in Swiss chalet style.

35. There is no gainsaying the popularity of theme parks as leisure attractions. The *New York Times* (13.8.1989) reported that 400 million people per year visit the US Theme Parks. In Europe the most popular theme parks are De Efteling (Netherlands – 2.5 million visitors per year); Alton Towers (UK – 2.3 million); and Phantasialand (Germany – 2 million). In the UK, the most popular theme parks after Alton Towers are Thorpe Park (1.3 million); Chessington World of Adventures (1.2 million). Sources: Company Reports, *Leisure Management*, 1987 7(5): 29; 1987 7(9): 29; 1990 10(10): 52.

36. Although the approach of Elias and Dunning to the study of leisure contrasts sharply with that of Goffman, there is a parallel here, i.e. their concept of 'mimetic leisure' indicates that many contemporary leisure forms let off aggressive emotions through mock combat and controlled contests.

37. As Kasson (1978: 18–27) points out, the inspiration for many of these pioneering time-space attractions came from the great nineteenth-century expositions of Science, Industry, Culture and the Arts. The World's Columbian Exposition in 1893 in Chicago featured exhibitions of Italian Renaissance Art; a reconstruction of Venice called 'The White City'; reconstructions of Viennese streets, Turkish bazaars, Irish and German castles, Persian palaces and South Sea Island huts. The dominant monument of the Exposition was the gigantic steel wheel designed by George W.G. Ferris. The Exposition aimed to combine fun with the instruction and edification of the people. However, the moral attitude that the Expositions should never be permitted to become too much fun was never far from the surface. For example, 'Ogden's Penny Guide to the International Exhibition in Glasgow (1901) solemnly observed that leisure and recreation have 'no place in the ordinary scope of the Exhibition'. Similarly, MacLeod's (1903) report on the financial accounts of the 1881 and 1901 Exhibitions in Glasgow included the po-faced conclusion that:

It is to be earnestly hoped that the financial success attending our two exhibitions in Glasgow will not cause cities to seize upon the idea of imitating them as a means of mere money raising, otherwise it will have exhibitions becoming as great a nuisance as the modern bazaar' (quoted in Goldsmith 1985).

Evidently, the project of moral regulation was dear to the hearts of the Glasgow city fathers at this time. Yet even they could not resist the demand for popular, exciting amusements at the exhibitions. As the Glasgow magazine 'The Bailie' (1.11.1911) noted in respect of the 1911 Exhibition:

Clearly, the Joy Wheel, the illuminated Fountains, the Mysterious River Rides, the Aerial Railway, and even the Rattlesnake Pit, had more of a drawing power than lectures on bee-keeping and domestic upholstery.

38. Of course, optical illusions for the purposes of amusement had a longer history than this. The shadow show originated in the East. It became fashionable in Europe in the 1770s when Ambroise brought his shadow show to London. Goethe organized a famous shadow show in Trefurt in the 1780s, and Dominique Seraphin, in 1784, opened her highly successful shadow show in France. Likewise, in 1787 the Edinburgh portrait painter, Robert Barker, patented his invention of the 'Panorama'. This was a gigantic cylindrical painting depicting a monumental scene such as 'The Battle of Waterloo'. The painting surrounded the spectator and each panel was expertly lighted in order to give the illusion of reality. Finally, in 1781, Phillipe Jacques de Loutherbourg opened in London his *Eidophusikon*. This was an entertainment which used a three-dimensional painting and lighting effects to produce 'a reality effect'. De Loutherborg's invention was the basis for the Diorama. Louis Jacques Mande Daguerre and Claude-Marie Bouton opened the first Diorama in Paris in 1822. It was followed by the second Diorama in Regent's Park London one year later. The Diorama was a partially translucent picture, illuminated before and behind by an intricate system of lamps and shutters to produce effects of changing light and transformations (see Robinson 1973: 1–5).

39. MacGregor, N. 'Museums for their own sake', the *Guardian* 12.10.1990.

40. Kracauer writes:

Everyone goes through the necessary motions at the conveyor belt, performing a partial function without knowing the entirety. Similar to the pattern in the stadium, the organization hovers above the masses as a monstrous figure whose originator withdraws it from the eyes of its bearers, and who himself hardly reflects upon it. It is conceived according to the rational principles which the Taylor system takes to its final conclusion. The hands in the factory correspond to the legs of the Tiller Girls. (1975: 70)

Advanced capitalism hides the owner of capital from the view of the workers behind managerial representatives so that the monotony of the production system seems depersonalized and unalterable. In much the same way, distraction factories are here alleged to present the masses with synchronized shows in which the authorship of the audience is neutralized and responses are calculated by the manipulation of spectacle and melodrama. Adorno and Horkheimer (1944) develop the same general line of argument in their ferocious indictment of 'the culture industry' and its role in 'mass deception'.

41. These are, in fact, the words of Walt Disney himself who uttered them in 1966.
42. Gray (1986: 19).
43. Given the degree to which a taken-for-granted assumption in the field (rarely examined and rarely questioned) is that there is a dichotomy between work and leisure, this point needs to be emphasized.
44. See Jones (1990: 23).
45. *Guardian* 19.11.1986.
46. *Guardian* 25.2.1987.
47. 'Changed City is Trying to Save Steel Heritage', *New York Times* 22.8.1989.
48. Glasgow was, of course, the European 'City of Culture' in 1990.
49. For the benefit of non-British readers, these are two fictional characters from the long-running Granada Television twice-weekly series *Coronation Street*.
50. No doubt exponents of the cultural studies approach, and some variants of the feminist approach to leisure, will object to this observation. For example, Tomlinson (1989: 104–5) asserts that cultural studies uses ethnographic principles to explore the 'familiar' in everyday life. The problem is that the cultural studies approach in practice invariably pulverizes the meaning of the fragmentary by subsuming it under preconceived analytical grounding concepts – notably the neo-Marxist concepts of class struggle and ideology. For a critique of the cultural studies approach to the study of leisure and culture, see Rojek (1992).

5.   WONDERFUL WORLD

1. This is particularly clear in Carroll's (1985) book where the welfare state is one-sidedly presented as the author of the dependency culture.
2. This view is, of course, prefigured in the late-nineteenth-century bourgeois horror directed against the mass tourist (see Pemble 1987).
3. As the *Sun* newspaper blared on the occasion of the meeting of the British and French bore-holds for the Channel Tunnel:

> This week the tunnels from Britain and France meet under the Channel. For the first time in millions of years the Europeans are no longer cut off from merry England. Welcome back to civilization. (*Sun* 30.10.1990)

4. Urry here, of course, paraphrases Barthes. The latter (1977: 146) wrote of the necessity for the postmodern critic to view the text not as 'a line of words releasing a single "theological" meaning but a multi-dimensional space in which a variety of [meanings], none of them original, blend and clash'.

5. For more on the US Rocket Center and Sox Exchange holidays see A. Troskoff: 'Possible Dreams' *TWA Ambassador* August 1990 15–21. Troskoff reports that most tourists at the Sox Exchange are in their fifties.

6. Granada TV tour brochure.

7. Weber makes the same point, see Weber (1970: 152–3).

8. This is not, of course, to imply that urban deprivation, industrial pollution and crime are more intense in Scotland than elsewhere. Rather the point is that these contrary aspects of Scots life need to be suppressed to maintain the sentimental vision of 'the enchanted fortress'.

9. Craddock and Craddock (1964: 20).

10. Ibid. (32).

11. This is not to imply that the British are unique in this regard. The mobilization of prejudice is a feature of the media and daily life at times of crisis in all of the advanced societies.

12. *Guardian* 18.12.1987.

13. *Holiday 'Which?' Report* (March 1988), featured in *Guardian* 4.3.1988.

14 *Daily Mirror* 7.11.1987.

15. *Encounter Overland Brochure* 1988/89: 8.

16. Ibid.

17. Ibid.

18. Ibid.

19. Schivelbusch's (1980) wonderful book on the railway journey is a notable exception.

20. To give some idea of the numbers of passengers carried: the *Luciana* (1893) carried 450 in First Class and 1000 in Steerage. With the growth in the size of liners, technical improvements and interior design transformations, the numbers increased. For example *The Majestic* (1921) carried 5000 passengers (Oliver 1980: 13).

21. *Royal Viking Line Cruise Atlas* 1989.

22. *Royal Viking Line Cruise Atlas* 1989.

23. The escape into this world of luxury and romance is not cheap. The 1988 travel leaflet quoted the price of the trip from London to Venice at £620.

24. Social mixing is however, limited by age. *Encounter Overland* only accept travellers in the 18–40 age group.

25. *Encounter Overland Brochure* 1988/89: 7.

26. *Twickers World Brochure*: Wildlife, Cultural and Wilderness Journeys 1987–88.
27. The sub-divisions were as follows:
    London–Portsmouth (5 days) £798
    Portsmouth–Tenerife (21 days) £2425
    Tenerife–Rio de Janeiro (53 days) £3150
    Rio de Janeiro–Cape Town (42 days) £2695
    Cape Town–Mauritius (30 days) £2255
    Mauritius–Fremantle (49 days) £3150
    Fremantle–Sydney (35 days) £3765.
28. Benjamin's 'Arcades' Project is a seminal influence in this regard (see Buck-Morss 1989).
29. To some degree this section is based on fieldwork notes taken in the Atlanta Marriott Marquis, the New York Algonquin, the New York Plaza, the Edison Hotel, New York, the Hiyatt on Sunset Boulevard, the Chicago Hilton, the Washington Hilton, the San Francisco Hilton, the Cairo Sheraton, the Central Hotel, Glasgow, the Park Lane Hilton, London, the Inter-Continental Hotel London, the Russell Hotel, London, and the Waldorf, London.
30. Kracauer's untranslated works on the hotel lobby and the detective novel are pathbreaking works in this regard.
31. In his Autobiography Conrad Hilton gives a good example of the capitalist tendency to colonize all space and turn it over to profit-making purposes. He writes:

    > The manner in which waste space is unearthed and utilized can mean the difference between a plus and a minus in an operation . . . Why, I found waste space even in "the greatest (hotel) of them all." The four giant columns in the Waldorf-Astoria's beautiful New York lobby were phonies, decorator's items, completely hollow and contributing nothing to the support of the building or the stock-holders either. When we had *vitrines*, shiny gold plate and sparkling glass display cases built into those columns, discriminating per-fumers and jewelers fought for the privilege of displaying their wares there. (1957: 114)

32. The phrase, of course, recalls Simmel's work (for a discussion of Simmel's view of the blasé attitude and its relation to leisure see Frisby 1989: 80–1). However, Hayner appears to have been more influenced by the Chicago School, especially Louis Wirth.
33. Certainly there is evidence that travellers' tales created exaggerated and mythological images of foreign sights – for the most authoritative inventory of the history of travel myths and travel fictions, see Adams (1962).
34. The seven wonders of the ancient world were, The Great Pyramid of Giza; The Hanging Gardens of Babylon; the Statue of Zeus at Olympia; the temple of Artemis at Ephesos; The Mausoleum at Halicarnassus; the Colossus of Rhodes; the Pharos at Alexandria (see Clayton and Price 1988).

35. The engravings of Fischer von Erlach in 1721 are more accurate.
36. Baudrillard also makes the point in connection with his discussion of the Orders of Production and Simulation (see pp. 130–1).
37. See Waycott (1983) for a useful guide to the history and attractions in National Parks in Western Europe.
38. See, for example, Meyrowitz (1985), Fiske (1987).
39. Parr, M. 'Away in a Manger', *Observer* Colour Magazine 21.12.1986.
40. Quoted in the *Guardian* 3.1.1991.
41. The 'Glasgow's Miles Better' campaign of the early 1980s is often seen as a model in this regard.

6. CONCLUSION

1. *Guardian* 19.2.1991.
2. 'Tourist Trappings', *Chicago Tribune* 22.8.1991.
3. Computer technologies raise the question, 'Is the human body the most efficient means of achieving modern production goals?' Increasingly, computers and cyborgs supplement the body in economics and warfare.
4. Interestingly, Freud also concludes that Modernity involves the constant questioning of reality. However, his method of reasoning is entirely different. For example, in an open letter written on the occasion of his seventieth birthday, he refers (1984: 44–56) to an instance which relates directly to leisure and travel experience. Freud recalls that over 30 years earlier he visited the Acropolis for the first time. In typical bourgeois fashion, Freud associated travel with self-realization. 'When one first catches sight of the sea,' he wrote, 'crosses the ocean and experiences as realities cities and lands which for so long had been distant, unattainable things of desire – one feels oneself like a hero who has performed deeds of improbable greatness. (455)' However, upon seeing the Acropolis for the first time Freud was struck with an absurd and disturbing thought. 'So all this really *does* exist,' he observed, 'just as we learnt at school' (449; emphasis in the original). Why Freud reasoned, should the Acropolis have ever been an object of doubt in his mind? He found his answer in orthodox Oedipal terms. Freud's father would have considered a visit to the Acropolis to be impossible. He was too poor to contemplate the trip. Therefore, Freud reasoned, it was as if in standing before the Acropolis he was standing against his father. In affirming the reality of the external object he was denying the reality of his father. Now, whether one agrees with Freud or not, his train of reasoning does suggest an alternative line of questioning reality – a line which privileges infantile experience.
5. This phrase is associated with the writings of Kracauer.
6. Amex/TWA travel flyer for New York 1986 extract.
7. From the Charles Dickens Centre, Rochester, flyer 1989.

8. From the 'Rock Circus', London Pavilion flyer 1990.
9. Calico Ghost Town flyer 1990 extract.
10. 1991–92 *Greater Pittsburgh Official Visitor's Guide*, extract.
11. This is the slogan of the successful Glasgow City tourist campaign of the 1980s.
12. 'Medieval Times' flyer, California.
13. Guided Walks of London flyer 1989, extract.
14. Pan Am/Globus Gateway Europe Guide 1987/8, extract.
15. From 'Rydeale: The Quest' flyer.
16. From the Denmark and Legoland Scanscape Holidays 1988 brochure.
17. From the Paris Vision Tour brochure 1989.
18. Quoted in Mosley (1985: 220).
19. Beamish Flyer 1990, extract.
20. See, for example, Elias and Dunning (1986).

Bibliography

Abercrombie, N., Hill, S. and Turner, B.S. (1980) *The Dominant Ideology Thesis*, London, Allen & Unwin.

Abse, J. (1980) *John Ruskin*, London, Quartet.

Adams, P. (1962) *Travelers and Travel Liars 1660–1800*, New York, Dover.

Adorno, T. (1973) *Negative Dialectics*, London, Routledge & Kegan Paul.

Adorno, T. (1991) 'Free time' pp. 162–170, in Adorno, T., *The Culture Industry: Selected Essays* (Introduction by J.M. Bernstein) London, Routledge.

Adorno, T. and Horkheimer, M. (1944) *Dialectic of Enlightenment*, London, Verso.

Anderson, P. (1983) *In The Tracks of Historical Materialism*, London, Verso.

Andrew, E. (1981) *Closing the Iron Cage*, Montreal, Black Rose Books.

Anger, K. (1975) *Hollywood Babylon*, New York, Dell.

Anger, K. (1984) *Hollywood Babylon 2*, London, Arrow.

Appleyard, B. (1986) *Richard Rogers*, London, Faber.

Ariès, P. (1981) *The Hour of Our Death*, London, Allen Lane.

Bachelard, G. (1938) *The Psychoanalysis of Fire*, Boston, Beacon.

Bachelard, G. (1964) *The Poetics of Space*, Boston, Beacon.

Bailey, P. (1987) *Leisure and Class in Victorian England*, London, Methuen.

Bakhtin, M. (1968) *Rabelais and his World*, Cambridge, Mass., MIT Press.

Banham, R. (1969) *The Architecture of the Well-Tempered Environment*, London, Architectural Press.

Banham, R. (1971) *Los Angeles*, Harmondsworth, Penguin.

Barker, P. (1990) 'Time to Turn Back the Coach People' *Evening Standard* 18.6.1990.

Barnett, S. and Barnett, H. (1888) *Practicable Socialism*, London, Warne.

Barnum, P.T. (1869) *Struggles and Triumphs*, Harmondsworth, Penguin.

Barthes, R. (1977) *Image-Music-Text*, Glasgow, Fontana.

Barthes, R. (1979) *The Eiffel Tower and Other Essays* New York, Hill & Wang.

Bassuk, E. (1986) 'The Rest Cure' pp. 139–51, in Suleiman, S.R. (ed.) *The Female Body In Western Culture*, Cambridge, Mass., Harvard University Press.

Bataille, G. (1962) *Eroticism*, London, Marion Boyars.

Baudelaire, C. (1962) 'The Painter of Modern Life', London, Phaidon Press.

Baudrillard, J. (1981) *For A Critique of the Political Economy of the Sign*, St Louis, Telos Press.

Baudrillard, J. (1983) *Simulations*, New York, Semiotext.

Baudrillard, J. (1985) 'The Ecstasy of Communication' pp. 126–34 (in Foster, H. (ed.) *Postmodern Culture*, London, Pluto.

Baudrillard, J. (1987) *The Ecstasy of Communication*, New York, Semiotext.

Baudrillard, J. (1988) *America*, London, Verso.

Baudrillard, J. (1988) *The Evil Demon of Images*, Sydney, The Power Institute.

Baudrillard, J. (1990) *Fatal Strategies*, New York, Semiotext.

Beath, N.H. (1986) *The Death of James Dean*, London, New England Library.

Beeton, I. (1861) *Book of Household Management*, London, Chancellor Press.

Bell, D. (1973) *The Cultural Contradictions of Capitalism*, London, Heinemann.

Bellamy, J. (1985) *Robin Hood: A Historical Enquiry* Beckenham, Croom Helm.

Benjamin, W. (1955) *Illuminations*, London, Jonathan Cape.

Benjamin, W. (1979) *One Way Street*, London, New Left Books.

Benjamin, W. (1983) *Charles Baudelaire: A Lyric Poet in the Era of High Capitalism*, London, Verso.

Bennett, T. (1983) 'A Thousand and One Troubles: Blackpool Pleasure Beach' pp. 138–55, in *Formations of Pleasure*, London, Routledge & Kegan Paul.

Bentham, J. (1988) *The Principles of Morals and Legislation*, New York, Prometheus.

Beresford, D. (1990) 'All the World's a Television Screen', *Guardian* 17.4.1990.

Berger, P., Berger, B. and Kellner, H. (1974) *The Homeless Mind*, Harmondsworth, Penguin.

Berman, M. (1982) *All That Is Solid Melts into Air*, London, Verso.

Bernheimer, L. and Kahane, C. (eds) (1985) *In Dora's Case: Freud, Hysteria and Feminism*, London, Virago.

Berridge, V. and Edwards, G. (1987) *Opium and the People*, New York, Yale University Press.

Bialeschki, D. and Henderson, K. (1986) 'Leisure in the Common World of Women' *Leisure Studies* 5(3) 299–308.

Bird, L. (1989) *Unbeaten Tracks in Japan*, London, Virago.

Birnbaum, S. (1988) *Walt Disney World: The Official Guide*, Los Angeles, Houghton Mifflin and Hearst Professional Magazines.

Birnbaum, S. (1989) *Disneyland: The Official Guide*, Los Angeles, Houghton Miffin and Hearst Professional Magazines.

Bishop, J. and Hoggett, P. (1987) *Organizing Around Enthusiasms*, London, Comedia.

Blake, R. (1982) *Disraeli's Grand Tour*, London, Weidenfeld & Nicolson.

Bloch, M. (1962) *Feudal Society*, 2 vols, London, Routledge & Kegan Paul.

Bloch, E. (1986) *The Principle of Hope, 3 vols*, Oxford, Blackwell.

Bogdan, R. (1988) *Freak Show: Presenting Human Oddities for Amusement and Profit*, Chicago, Chicago University Press.

Borzello, F. (1987) *Civilizing Caliban: The Misuse of Art, 1875–1980*, London, Routledge & Kegan Paul.

Bourdieu, P. (1986) *Distinction*, London, Routledge & Kegan Paul.

Braverman, H. (1974) *Labour and Monopoly Capital*, New York, Monthly Review Press.

Brinnin, J. and Gaulin, K. (1988) *Grandluxe: Transatlantic Luxury*, London, Bloomsbury.

Brodie F.M. (1967) *The Devil Drives: A Life of Sir Richard Burton*, Harmondsworth, Penguin.

Brohm, J.M. (1978) *Sport: A Prison of Measured Time*, London, Interlinks.

Buck-Morss, S. (1989) *The Dialectics of Seeing: Walter Benjamin and the Arcades Project*, Cambridge, Mass., MIT Press.

Burke, P., (1978) *Popular Culture in Early Modern Europe*, London, Temple Smith.

Burton, R. (1924) *The Anatomy of Melancholy*, London, Chatto & Windus.

Byington, M. (1909) 'The Family in a Typical Mill Town', *American Journal of Sociology*, 14, March, pp. 648–59.

Carnegie, A. (1903) *The Empire of Business*, London, Harper.

Carroll, J. (1980) *Sceptical Sociology*, London, Routledge & Kegan Paul.

Carroll, J. (1985) *Guilt*, London, Routledge & Kegan Paul.

Carroll, J. (1986) 'Sport: Virtue and Grace' *Theory, Culture and Society* 3(1).

Chambers, D. (1986) 'The constraints of work and domestic schedules on women's leisure', *Leisure Studies* 5(3) pp. 309–26.

Chaney, D. (1983) 'The Department Store as a Cultural Form', *Theory, Culture and Society*, 1 (3) pp. 22–31.

Chaney, D. (1990) 'Subtopia in Gateshead: The Metrocentre as a cultural form', *Theory, Culture and Society* 7(4) 49–62.

Clarenden Commission (1864) *Parliamentary Papers 186220, Report of H.M. Commissioners Appointed to Inquire into the Revenues and Management of Certain Colleges and Schools and the Studies Pursued and Instruction Given Therein*, London.

Critcher, C. and Clarke, J. (1985) *The Devil Makes Work*, London, Macmillan.

Clayton, P. and Price, M. (eds) (1988) *The Seven Wonders of the World*, London, Routledge.

Cohen, S. and Taylor, L. (1976) *Escape Attempts: The Theory and Practice of Resistance in Everyday Life* Harmondsworth, Penguin.

Connerton, P. (ed.) (1976) *Critical Sociology*, Harmondsworth, Penguin.

Corrigan, P. and Sayer, D. (1985) *The Great Arch*, Oxford, Blackwell.

Coward, R. (1984) *Female Desire*, London, Paladin.

Craddock, F. and Craddock, J. (1964) *The Bon Viveur Guide to Holidays in Europe*, London, Barker Books.

Crick, M. (1989) 'Representations of International Tourism in the Social Sciences', *Annual Review of Anthropology*, 18: 307–44.

Critcher, C. (1989) 'A communication in response to "Leisure and Status: A Pluralist Framework for Analysis"', *Leisure Studies*, 8(2) pp. 159–62.

Cunningham, H. (1980) *Leisure in Victorian Britain*, Beckenham, Croom Helm.

Cutten, G. (1926) *The Threat of Leisure*, New York, Yale University Press.

Dale, T. (1981) *Harrods: The Store and the Legend*, London, Pan.

Davidoff, L. (1973) *The Best Circles*, Beckenham, Croom Helm.

Davidoff, L. and Hall, C. (1983) 'The architecture of public and private life: English Middle Class Society in a provincial town 1780–1850' pp. 326–46, in Fraser, D. and Sutcliffe, A. (eds) *The Pursuit of Urban History*, London, Edward Arnold.

Davis, N. (1975) *Society and Culture in Early Modern France*, Stanford, Stanford University Press.

Debord, G. (1967) *Society of the Spectacle*, London, Rebel Press.

Deem, R. (1986) *All Work and No Play?* Milton Keynes, Open University Press.

Digby, A. (1989) 'Women's Biological Straitjacket', pp. 192–220, in Mendus, S. and Rendall, J. (eds) *Sexuality and Subordination*, London, Routledge.

Dingle, A.E. (1980) *The Campaign for Prohibition in Victorian England*, New Brunswick, Rutgers.

Dixey, S. (1988) 'Eyes Down: A study of Bingo', in Wimbush, E. and Talbot, M. (eds) *Relative Freedoms*, Milton Keynes, Open University Press.

Donnelly, P. (1986) 'The Paradox of the Parks: Politics of Recreational Land Use Before and After the Mass Trespasses', *Leisure Studies* 5(2), 211–32.

Donzelot, J. (1979) *The Policing of Families*, London, Hutchinson.

Dumazedier, J. (1967) *Towards a Society of Leisure*, London, Collier Macmillan.

Dumazedier, J. (1974) *The Sociology of Leisure*, Amsterdam, Elsevier.

Dunning, E. and Sheard, K. (1979) *Barbarians, Gentlemen and Players*, Oxford, Martin Robertson.

Durkheim, E. (1897) *Suicide: A Study in Sociology*, London, Routledge & Kegan Paul.

Durkheim, E. (1902) *The Division of Labour in Society*, New York, Free Press.

Durkheim, E. (1904) *Professional Ethics and Civic Morals*, London, Routledge and Kegan Paul.

Durkheim, E. (1912) *The Elementary Forms of Religious Life*, New York, Free Press.

Dutton, R. (1954) *The Victorian Home*, London, Bracken Books.

Eco, U. (1986) *Fatih in Fakes*, London, Secker & Warbourg.

Edson Evans, E. (1875) *The Abuse of Maternity*, Philadelphia, Lippincott.

Edwardian Etiquette Book (1902) *A facsimile reprint of Etiquette for Women: A Book of Modern Modes and Manners* by "One of the Aristocracy" published by C. Arthur Pearson Ltd in London in 1902, – facimile edition London, Allen & Unwin 1983.

Elias, N. (1956) 'Problems of Involvement and Detachment', *British Journal of Sociology*, 7. p. 226–52.

Elias, N. (1978) *The Civilizing Process, Vol. 1, The History of Manners*, Oxford, Blackwell.

Elias, N. (1982) *The Civilizing Process, Vol 2, State Formation and Civilization*, Oxford, Blackwell.

Elias, N. and Dunning, E. (1986) *Quest for Excitement: Sport and Leisure in the Civilizing Process*, Oxford, Blackwell.

Ewen, S. (1976) *Captains of Consciousness: Advertising and the Social Roots of Consumer Culture*, New York, McGraw-Hill.

Ewen, S. (1988) *All Consuming Images*, New York, Basic Books.

Ewen, S. and Ewen, E. (1982) *Channels of Desire*, New York, McGraw-Hill.

Fazio, J.R. (1979) 'Parks and other recreational resources', pp. 197–232 (in) Ibrahim, H. and Shivers, J. (eds) *Leisure: Emergence and Expansion*, Los Alamitos, Hwong.

Featherstone, M. (1982) 'The Body in Consumer Culture', *Theory, Culture and Society* 1(2) pp. 18–33.

Featherstone, M. (1991) *Consumer Culture and Postmodernism* London, Sage.

Feifer, M. (1986) *Tourism in History*, New York, Stein & Day.

Ferguson, H. (1990) *The Science of Pleasure: Cosmos and Psyche in the Bourgeois World View*, London, Routledge.

Finke, U. (1985) 'The Art Treasures Exhibition' pp. 102–26, in Archer, J.H.G. (ed.) *Art and Architecture in Victorian Manchester*, Manchester, Manchester University Press.

Fiske, J. (1987) *Television Culture*, London, Methuen.

Fiske, J. (1989) *Reading the Popular*, London, Unwin Hyman.

Flaubert, G. (1983) *Flaubert in Egypt* Steegmuller, F., (ed.) London, Michael Haag.

Flink, J. (1975) *The Car Culture*, Cambridge, Mass., MIT Press.

Forty, A. (1986) *Objects of Desire*, London, Thames & Hudson.

Foster, H. (ed) (1985) *Postmodern Culture*, London, Pluto.

Foster, H. (1985) *Recodings*, Washington, Bay Press.

Foucault, M. (1967) *Madness and Civilization*, London, Tavistock.

Foucault, M., (1973) *The Order of Things*, London, Tavistock.

Foucault, M. (1975) *Discipline and Punish*, Harmondsworth, Penguin.

Foucault, M. (1980) *Power/Knowledge: Selected Interviews and other Essays 1972–77*, Gordon, C. (ed.) Brighton, Harvester.

Foucault, M. (1981) *The History of Sexuality*, Harmondsworth, Penguin.

Freud, S. (1979) *Civilization and its Discontents*, Harmondsworth, Penguin.

Freud, S. (1984) 'A Disturbance of Memory on the Acropolis', *On Metapsychology*, Harmondsworth, Penguin.

Frisby, D. (1985) *Fragments of Modernity*, Cambridge, Polity.

Frisby, D. (1989) 'Simmel and Leisure' pp. 75–91, in Rojek, C. (ed.) *Leisure For Leisure: Critical Essays*, London, Macmillan.

Fussell, P. (1990) 'The Quest for Reality', *Guardian*, 8.10.1990.

Gardella, P. (1985) *Innocent Ecstasy*, New York, Oxford University Press.

Garfinkel, H. (1967) *Studies in Ethnomethodology*, New York, Prentice-Hall.

Garrett, R., and Garrett, A. (1879) *Suggestions for House Decoration*, London, Warne.

Gathorne-Hardy, J. (1979) *The Public School Phenomenon 1897–1971*, Harmondsworth, Penguin.

Gay, P. (1984) *The Bourgeois Experience Vol 1: Education of the Senses*, Oxford, Oxford University Press.

Gay, P. (1986) *The Bourgeois Experience, Vol 2: The Tender Passion*, Oxford, Oxford University Press.

Geras, N. (1983) *Marx and Human Nature: Refutation of a Legend*, London, Verso.

Gershuny, J. (1978) *After Industrial Society?*, London, Macmillan.

Gibbon, F. (1934) *William A. Smith of the Boy's Brigade*, Glasgow, Collins.

Giddens, A. (1981) *A Critique of Historical Materialism*, London, Macmillan.

Gilman, S.L. (1988) *Disease and Representation: Images of Illness from madness to AIDS*, Ithaca, Cornell University Press.

Glyptis, S., McInnes, H. and Patmore, A. (1987) *Leisure and the Home*, London, Sports Council/ESRC.

Goethe, J.W. (1962) *Italian Journey*, Harmondsworth, Penguin.

Goffman, E. (1967) 'Where the Action Is' pp. 149–270, in Goffman, E. *Interaction Ritual*, New York, Pantheon.

Goffman, E. (1974) *Frame Analysis*, New York, Harper & Row.

Gold, S.M. (1980) 'Future Leisure Environments in Cities' pp. 125–40, in Goodale, T.L. and Witt P.A., (ed.) *Recreation and Leisure*, State College, Venture Publishers.

Goldberger, P. (1990) 'Tours of Manhattan: The Facts and the Fiction' *New York Times* 12.8.1990.

Goldsmith, A.L. (1985) *The Glasgow International Exhibitions 1888–1930*, Glasgow, M.Litt Thesis, Strathclyde University.

Gorz, A. (1983) *Farewell To The Working Class*, London, Pluto.

Gorz, A. (1985) *Paths To Paradise*, London, Pluto.

Gosson, S. (1579) *The School of Abuse*, London.
Gray, E. (1986) 'Theme Park, USA', *Leisure Management*, (5) pp. 17–20.
Gray, R. (1981) *The Aristocracy of Labour in Nineteenth Century Britain*, London, Macmillan.
Green, E., Hebron, S. and Woodward, D. (1987) *Women's Leisure in Sheffield*, Dept of Applied Social Studies, Sheffield Polytechnic.
Griffin, C. (1985) *Typical Girls?* London, Routledge & Kegan Paul.
Hakluyt, R. (1986) *Voyages to the Colonies*, London, Hutchinson.
Hardyment, C. (1983) *Dream Babies*, Oxford, Oxford University Press.
Hamish-Fraser, G. (1981) *The Coming of the Mass Market*, London, Macmillan.
Hargreaves, J. (1986) 'Where's the Virtue? Where's the Grace? A discussion of the social production of gender through sport' *Theory, Culture and Society* 3(1).
Hargreaves, J. (1989) 'The promise and problems of women's leisure and sport', in Rojek, C. (ed.) *Leisure For Leisure: Critical Essays*, London, Macmillan.
Harvey, D. (1985) *Consciousness and the Urban Experience*, Oxford, Blackwell.
Harvey, D. (1989) *The Condition of Postmodernity*, Oxford, Blackwell.
Hayden, D. (1981) *The Grand Domestic Revolution*, Cambridge, Mass., MIT Press.
Hayner, N.S. (1928) 'Hotel Life and Personality' *American Journal of Sociology*, 33, 784–95.
Heath, S. (1982) *The Sexual Fix*, London, Macmillan.
Heeley, J. (1986) 'Leisure and moral reform' *Leisure Studies* 5(1) pp. 57–68.
Hegel, G.W.F. (1807) *Phenomenology of Spirit*, London, Oxford University Press.
Heller, A. (1978) *Renaissance Man*, London, Routledge & Kegan Paul.
Henry, I., and Bramham, P. (1986) 'Leisure, the local state and social order' *Leisure Studies* 5(2) pp. 189–210.
Herman, G. (1982) *Rock 'n' Roll Babylon*, London, Plexus.
Hewison, R. (1987) *The Heritage Industry*, London, Methuen.
Hill, C. (1975) *The World Turned Upside Down*, Harmondsworth, Penguin.
Hilton, C. (1957) *Be My Guest*, New York, Prentice-Hall.
Himmelfarb, G. (1984) *The Idea of Poverty*, London, Faber.
Hirst, P. and Woolley, P., (1982) *Social Relations and Human Attributes*, London, Tavistock.
Hobbes, T. (1651) *Leviathan* MacPherson, C.B. (ed.) Harmondsworth, Penguin.
Hobsbawm, E.J. (1964) *Labouring Men*, London, Weidenfeld & Nicolson.
Hobsbawm, E.J. (1969) *Industry and Empire*, Harmondsworth, Penguin.
Hobsbawm, E.J. (1975) *The Age of Capital*, Harmondsworth, Penguin.
Hobsbawm, E.J. (1987) *The Age of Empire*, Harmondsworth, Penguin.
Hollander, A. (1980) *Seeing Through Clothes*, New York, Avon.
Holmes, R. (1989) *Coleridge: Early Visions*, Harmondsworth, Penguin.
Holt, J.L. (1982) *Robin Hood*, London, Thames & Hudson.
Hopkinson, A. (1986) *Juliet Margaret Cameron*, London, Virago.
Horne, D. (1984) *The Great Museum*, London, Pluto.
Huizinga, J, (1924) *The Waning of the Middle Ages*, Harmondsworth, Penguin.

Huizinga, J. (1944) *Homo Ludens*, London, Routledge & Kegan Paul.

Hume, D. (1739) *A Treatise of Human Nature*, Harmondsworth, Penguin.

Hunt, J.D. (1982) *The Wilder Sea: A Life of John Ruskin*, New York, Viking.

Huysmans, J.K. (1884) *A Rebours*, Harmondsworth, Penguin.

Huyssen, A. (1986) *After the Great Divide*, Bloomington, Indiana University Press.

Jacks, L.P. (1932) *Education Through Recreation*, London, University of London Press.

Jameson, F. (1984) 'Postmodernism, or the cultural logic of late capitalism,' *New Left Review*, 146, pp. 53–96.

Jeffreys, S. (1985) *The Sexuality Debates*, London, Routledge & Kegan Paul.

Jeffreys, S. (1987) *The Spinster and her Enemies: Feminism and Sexuality 1880–1939*, London, Pandora.

Jencks, C. (1984) *The Language of Postmodern Architecture*, London, Academy Press.

Jenkyns, R. (1980) *The Victorians and Ancient Greece*, Oxford, Blackwell.

Jones, C. (1983) *State Social Work and the Working Class*, London, Macmillan.

Jones, D. (1990) *Dark Star*, London, Bloomsbury.

Jusserand, J.J. (1888) *English Wayfaring Life in the Middle Ages*, London, Fisher-Unwin.

Kabbani, R. (1986) *Europe's Myths of Orient*, London, Pandora.

Kaplan, F. (1988) *Dickens: A Biography*, London, Sceptre.

Kasson, J.E. (1978) *Amusing the Millions: Coney Island at the Turn of the Century*, New York, Hill & Wang.

Kellner, D. (1989) *Jean Baudrillard*, Cambridge, Polity.

Kellogg, J.H. (1888) *Plain Facts for Old and Young*, Iowa, Burlington Press.

Klein, V. (1971) *The Feminine Character*, London, Routledge & Kegan Paul.

Knight, D.C. (1986) *The Age of Science*, Oxford, Blackwell.

Kolakowski, L. (1972) *Positivist Philosophy*, Harmondsworth, Penguin.

Kracauer, S. (1975) 'The Mass Ornament' translated by B. Cowell and J. Zipes, *New German Critique*, 2, 1975, pp. 67–76.

Krafft-Ebing, R. (1886) *Psycopathia Sexualis*, New York, Putnam.

Kraus, R. (1979) *Recreation and Leisure in Modern Society*, Glenview, Scott, Foresman.

Kroker, A. and Cook, D. (1986) *The Postmodern Scene: Excremental Culture and Hyper Aesthetics*, New York, St. Martin's.

Lacey, R. (1986) *Ford: The Men and the Machine*, London, Heinemann.

Ladurie, E. (1981) *Love, Death and Money in the Pays D'Or*, London, Scolar Press.

Larner, C. (1981) *The Enemies of God: The Witch Hunt in Scotland*, London, Chatto & Windus.

Lash, S. (1990) *Sociology of Postmodernism*, London, Routledge.

Lash, S. and Urry, J. (1987) *The End of Organized Capitalism*, Cambridge, Polity.

Lawson, J. and Silver, H. (1973) *A Social History of Education in England*, London, Routledge & Kegan Paul.

Lea, H. (1913) *The Hardy Guides, 2 Vols: Touring Companion of Thomas Hardy*, Harmondsworth, Penguin.

Le Corbusier (1929) *The City of Tomorrow*, London, Architectural Press.
Lefebvre, H. (1976) *The Survival of Capitalism*, London, Allen & Unwin.
Lévi Strauss, C. (1955) *Tristes tropiques*, Harmondsworth, Penguin.
Lloyd, G. (1984) *The Man of Reason: 'Male' and 'Female' in Western Philosophy*, London, Methuen.
Locke, J. (1689) *Two Treatises on Government* Laslett, P. (ed.) Cambridge, Cambridge University Press.
Lovejoy, A. (1964) *The Great Chain of Being*, Cambridge, Mass., Harvard University Press.
Lowe, D.M. (1982) *The History of Bourgeois Perception*, Brighton, Harvester.
Lowenthal, D. (1985) *The Past is a Foreign Country*, Cambridge, Cambridge University Press.
Lukacs, G. (1923) *Soul and Form*, London, Merlin.
Lyotard, J.F. (1984) *The Postmodern Condition: A Report on Knowledge*, Manchester, Manchester University Press.
MacAloon, J.J. (1981) *The Great Symbol: Pierre de Coubertin and the Origins of the Modern Olympic Games*, Chicago, Chicago University Press.
MacCannell, D. (1973) 'Staged Authenticity: Arrangements of Social Space in Tourist Settings,' *American Sociological Review*, 79, pp. 589–603.
MacCannell, D. (1976) *The Tourist: A New Theory of the Leisure Class*, New York, Schocken.
MacCannell, D. (1990) 'Nature, Inc', *Quarterly Journal of Environmental Design* 6(3) 24–6.
MacIntyre, A. (1981) *After Virtue: A Study of Moral Theory*, London, Duckworth.
MacKay, J, and Thane, P. (1986) 'The Englishwoman' pp. 191–229, in Colls, R. and Dodd, P. (eds) *Englishness: Politics and Culture 1880–1920*, London, Croom Helm.
Mackenzie, J.M. (ed.) (1984) *Imperialism and Popular Culture*, Manchester, Manchester University Press.
Malthus, T. (1803) *An Essay on the Principle of Population, or a view of its past and present effects on human happiness*, 2nd edn, 2 vols, London, J. Johnson.
Manchester City Art Galleries (1987) *Parks for the People*, Manchester, Manchester City Art Galleries.
Mangan, J. (1981) *Athleticism in the Victorian and Edwardian Public School*, Cambridge, Cambridge University Press.
Mangan, J. (1985) *The Games Ethic and Imperialism*, New York, Viking.
Marcuse, H. (1964) *One Dimensional Man*, London, Abacus.
Marcuse, H. (1978) *The Aesthetic Dimension*, London, Macmillan.
Marin, L. (1977) 'Disneyland: a Degenerative Utopia,' *Glyph*, 1, 50–66.
Marriage Book (nd) *The Marriage Book: For Husbands and Wives and all Who Love Children*, London, Amalgamated Press.
Marsh, J. (1985) *Pre-Raphaelite Sisterhood*, New York, St. Martin's Press.
Marsh, J.(1986) *Jane and May Morris*, London, Pandora.
Marx, K. (1887) *Capital, Vol. 1*, London, Lawrence & Wishart.
Marx, K. (1964) *The Economic and Philosophic Manuscripts of 1844*, New York, International.
Marx, K. (1973) *Grundrisse*, New York, Random.
Marx, K. and Engels, F. (1848) 'The Communist Manifesto' in Marx, K. and Engels, F. (1968) *Selected Works*, London, Lawrence & Wishart pp. 31–63.

Mason, T. (1988) *Sport in Britain*, London, Faber.
Mathews, D.C. (1977) *Religion in the Old South*, Chicago, Chicago University Press.
Mayhew, H. (1861) *Mayhew's London* Quennell, P. (ed.) London, Bracken Books.
McLuhan, M. (1967) *The Gutenberg Galaxy*, London, Routledge & Kegan Paul.
McLuhan, M. (1973) *Understanding Media*, London, Abacus.
McRobbie, A. (1980) 'Settling Accounts With Subcultures: "A Feminist Critique"*, Screen Education*, 34.
McRobbie, A. and McCabe, T. (1981) *Feminism For Girls*, London, Routledge & Kegan Paul.
McRone, K. (1988) *Sport and the Physical Emancipation of English Women 1870–1914*, London, Routledge.
Melossi, D. and Pavarini, M. (1981) *The Prison and the Factory*, London, Macmillan.
Mendus, S. and Rendall, J. (eds) (1989) *Sexuality and Subordination*, London, Routledge.
Mennell, S. (1985) *All Manners of Food*, Oxford, Blackwell.
Meyrowitz, J. (1985) *No Sense of Place*, Oxford, Oxford University Press.
Mill, J.S. (1863) *Utilitarianism*, Glasgow, Fontana.
Mill, J.S. (1937) *Autobiography*, Harvard, Harvard University Press.
Miller, N.P. and Robinson, D.M. (1963) *The Leisure Age: Its Challenge to Recreation*, Belmont, Wadsworth.
Moorhouse, H.F. (1989) 'Models of Work, Models of Leisure', in Rojek, C. (ed.) *Leisure for Leisure*, London, Macmillan, pp. 15–35.
Mort, F. (1987) *Dangerous Sexualities: Medico-Moral Politics in England Since 1830*, London, Routledge & Kegan Paul.
Mosley, L. (1985) *The Real Walt Disney*, London, Futura.
Nairn, T. (1988) *The Enchanted Glass*, London, Radius.
Nash, J.B. (1953) *Philosophy of Recreation and Leisure*, Dubuque, Brown.
Nerval, G de (1851) *Journey to the Orient*, London, Michael Haag.
Nietzsche, F. (1986) *Human, All Too Human*, Cambridge, Cambridge University Press.
Nisbet, R. (1975) *Twilight of Authority*, Oxford, Oxford University Press.
Northbroke, J. (1579) *Spiritus Est Vicarius. Christi In Terra. A Treatise Wherein Dicing, Dancing, Vaine Plaies Or Enterludes With Other Idle Pastimes, Etc Commonly Used on the Sabbath Day, Are Reprooved by the Authoritie of the Worde of God and Ancient Writers*, London.
O'Brien, R. (1987) *Marriott: The J. Willard Marriott Story*, Salt Lake City, Desert Books.
O'Grady, R. (1982) *Tourism in the Third World: Christian Reflections*, New York, Orbis.
Oestereicher, E. (1979) 'The privatization of the self in modern society', *Social Research*, 46(3), pp. 600–15.
Oliver, R.B. (1980) *The Oceanliner: Speed, Style, Symbol*, New York, Smithsonian Institute.
Ossawska, M. (1956) *Bourgeois Morality*, London, Routledge & Kegan Paul.
Owen, D. (1982) *The Government of Victorian London 1855–1889: The Metro-*

politan Board of Works the Vestries and the City Corporation, Cambridge, Mass., Belknap.

Owen, R. (1857) *Life of Robert Owen By Himself*, London: Charles Knight.

Paine, T. (1792) *The Rights of Man*, Harmondsworth, Penguin.

Parker, S. (1981) 'Choice, Flexibility, Spontaneity and Self Determination in Leisure', *Social Forces* 60(2) pp. 323–31.

Parsons, T. (1951) *The Social System*, London, Routledge & Kegan Paul.

Pearson, G. (1983) *Hooligan*, London, Macmillan.

Pemble, J. (1987) *The Mediterranean Passion*, Oxford, Oxford University Press.

Perkin, J. (1989) *Women and Marriage in Nineteenth Century England*, London, Routledge.

Pfeiffer, I. (1851) *A Lady's Voyage Around the World*, Harmondsworth, Penguin.

Pirenne, H. (1936) *Economic and Social History of Medieval England*.

Polyani, K. (1944) *The Great Transformation: The Political and Economic Origins of Our Time*, Boston, Beacon.

Poole, R. (1983) 'Oldham Wakes', in Walton, J.K. and Walvin, J. (eds) *Leisure in Britain 1780–1939*, Manchester, Manchester University Press.

Poovey, M. (1988) *Uneven Developments: The Ideological Work of Gender in Mid-Victorian England*, Chicago, Chicago University Press.

Porter, R. (1982) *English Society in the Eighteenth Century*, London, Allen Lane.

Poster, M. (1990) *The Mode of Information*, Cambridge, Polity.

Pound, R. (1960) *Selfridge: A Biography*, London, Heinemann.

Price, R. (1971) 'The Working Men's Club Movement and Victorian Social Reform Ideology,' *Victorian Studies*, 15.

Ramazanoglu, C. (1989) *Feminism and the Contradictions of Oppression*, London, Routledge.

Riesman, D. (1958) 'Leisure and work in postindustrial society', in Riesman, D., (1964), *Abundance For What? And Other Essays*, London, Chatto & Windus.

Rigauer, B. (1981) *Sport and Work*, New York, Columbia University Press.

Ritvo, H. (1987) *The Animal Estate: The English and Other Creatures in the Victorian Age*, Cambridge, Mass., Harvard University Press.

Robinson, D. (1973) *World Cinema 1895–1980*, London, Eyre-Methuen.

Roberts, K. (1978) *Contemporary Society and the Growth of Leisure*, London, Longman.

Roberts, K. (1981) *Leisure*, 2nd edn, London, Longman.

Roberts, K. (1983) *Youth and Leisure*, London, Allen & Unwin.

Rojek, C. (1985) *Capitalism and Leisure Theory*, London, Tavistock.

Rojek, C. (1986) Problems of Involvement and Detachment in the Writings of Norbert Elias, *British Journal of Sociology* 37, p. 584.

Rojek, C. (1988) 'The Convoy of Pollution', *Leisure Studies* 7(1) pp. 21–32.

Rojek, C. (ed.) (1989) *Leisure for Leisure: Critical Essays*, London, Macmillan.

Rojek, C. (1992) 'The Field of Play in Sport and Leisure Studies', in Dunning, E. and Rojek, C. (eds) *Sport and Leisure in the Civilizing Process*, London, Macmillan.

Rousseau, J.J. (1974) *Emile, or Education*, London, Everyman.

Rousseau, J.J. (1974) *The Social Contract and Discourses*, London, Dent.

Rowbotham, S., Segal, L., and Wainwright, H. (1979) *Beyond The Fragments: Feminism and the Making of Socialism*, London, Merlin.

Rowling, M. (1971) *Everyday Life of Medieval Travellers*, New York, Dorset.

Russell, J.B. (1895) *The Evolution of the Function of Public Health Administration, As Illustrated by the Sanitary Condition of Glasgow*, Glasgow.

Ryan, A. (1984) *Property and Political Theory*, Oxford, Blackwell.

Said, E.W, (1978) *Orientalism*, London, Routledge & Kegan Paul.

Saisselin, R.G. (1985) *Bricabracomania: The Bourgeois and the Bibelot*, London, Thames & Hudson.

Samuel, R. (ed) (1988) *Patriotism, 3 vols*. London, Routledge & Kegan Paul.

Saxon, A.H. (1978) *The Life and Art of Andrew Ducrow and the Romantic Age of the English Circus*, Hamden, Archon.

Sayer, D. (1991) *Capitalism and Modernity*, London, Routledge.

Schivelbusch, W. (1980) *The Railway Journey: Trains and Travel in the Nineteenth Century*, Oxford, Berg.

Schivelbusch, W. (1988) *Disenchanted Light: The industrialization of light in the nineteenth century*, Oxford, Berg.

Scraton, S. and Talbot, M. (1989) 'A Response to "Leisure, Lifestyle and Status: A Pluralist Framework for Analysis' *Leisure Studies* (8(2) 155–8.

Scull, A. (1979) *Museums of Madness: The Social Organization of Insanity in Nineteenth century England*, New York, St. Martin's Press.

Segalen, M., (1983) *Love and Power in the Peasant Family*, Oxford, Blackwell.

Sennett, R. (1970) *The Uses of Disorder: Personal Identity and City Life*, Harmondsworth, Penguin.

Sennett, R. (1977) *The Fall of Public Man*, Cambridge, Cambridge University Press.

Shields, R. (1990) 'The "System of Pleasure"', *Theory, Culture and Society*, 7(1) pp. 39–72.

Shivers, J. (1987) *Introduction to Recreational Service Administration*, Philadelphia, Lea & Febiger.

Showalter, E. (1985) *The Female Malady: Women, Madness, and English Culture 1830–1980*, London, Virago.

Siegel, J. (1986) *Bohemian Paris: Culture, Politics and the Boundaries of Bourgeois Life 1830–1930*, New York, Viking.

Simmel, G. (1907) *The Philosophy of Money*, London, Routledge 1990.

Simmel, G. (1965) 'The Ruin' pp. 259–66, in Simmel, G. *Essays on Sociology, Philosophy and Aesthetics*, New York, Harper & Row.

Simmel, G. (1971) *On Individuality and Social Forms*, Chicago, Chicago University Press.

Skultans, V. (1979) *English Madness: Ideas on Insanity 1580–1890*, London, Routledge & Kegan Paul.

Slavson, S.R. (1948) *Recreation and the Total Personality*, New York, Association Press.

Smiles, S. (1859) *Self Help*, Harmondsworth, Penguin.

Smiles, S. (1894) *Character*, London, Murray.

Smith, D. (1983) 'Women, Class and Family', in Miliband, R. and Saville, J. (eds) *Socialist Register*, London, Merlin.

Soja, E. (1985) *Postmodern Geographies: The Reassertion of Space in Critical Social Theory*, London, Verso.

Soloway, R.A. (1982) *Birth Control and the Population Question in England 1877–1930*, Chicago, University of Chicago Press.

Springhall, J. (1977) *Youth, Empire and Society*, London, Croom Helm.

Stallybrass, P. and White, A. (1986) *The Politics and Poetics of Transgression*, London, Methuen.

Stedman Jones, G. (1971) *Outcast London*, Oxford, Clarendon Press.

Stone, L. (1972) *The Causes of the English Revolution 1529–1642*, London, Ark.

Stone, L. (1977) *The Family, Sex and Marriage in England 1500–1800*, London, Weidenfeld & Nicolson.

Stone, L. (1987) *The Past and Present Revisited*, London, Routledge & Kegan Paul.

Sussman, G.D. (1981) *Selling Mothers' Milk: The Wet-Nursing Business in France 1715–1914*, Urbana, University of Illinois Press.

Swaan, A. de (1981) 'The Politics of Agoraphobia: On Changes in Emotional and Relational Management', *Theory and Society* 10 pp. 337–58.

Tagg, J. (1988) *The Burden of Representation: Essays on Photographies and Histories*, London, Macmillan.

Talbot, M. (1988) 'Their Own Worst Enemy'? Women and Leisure Provision' pp. 161–76, in Wimbush, E. and Talbot, M. (eds) *Relative Freedoms: Women and Leisure* Milton Keynes, Open University.

Tartar, M.M. (1988) *Spellbound: Studies in Mesmerism and Literature*, Princeton, Princeton University Press.

Tawney, R.H. (1937) *Religion and the Rise of Capitalism*, Harmondsworth, Penguin.

Theobald, W. (1984) 'A History of Recreation Resource Planning: The Origins of Space Standards, *Leisure Studies*, 3, pp. 189–200.

Theweleit, K. (1987) *Male Fantasies, Vol 1: Women, Floods, Bodies and History*, Cambridge, Polity.

Thompson, E.P. (1963) *The Making of the English Working Class*, Harmondsworth, Penguin.

Thompson, E.P. (1967) 'Time, Work-Discipline and Industrial Capitalism' *Past and Present*, 38, pp. 56–97.

Thompson, E.P. (1978) *The Poverty of Theory*, London, Merlin.

Thompson, F.M.L. (1988) *The Rise of Respectable Society*, London, Fontana.

Tomlinson, A. (1989) 'Whose Side Are They On? Leisure Studies and Cultural Studies in Britain' *Leisure Studies* 8(2) 97–106.

Touraine, A. (1971) *The Post-Industrial Society*, New York, Random House.

Troubridge, Lady (1926) *Etiquette and Entertaining: To Help You on Your Social Way*, London, Amalgamated Press.

Turner, B.S. (1984) *The Body and Society*, Oxford, Blackwell.

Turner, B.S. (1987) *Medical Power and Social Knowledge*, London, Sage,.

Urry, J. (1990) *The Tourist Gaze: Leisure and Travel in Contemporary Societies*, London, Sage.

Vale, M. (1977) *The Gentleman's Recreations: Accomplishments and Pastimes of the English Gentleman 1580–1630*, Ipswich, Brewer.

Veblen, T. (1925) *The Theory of the Leisure Class*, London, Allen & Unwin.

Venturi, R., Scott Brown, D. and Izenour, S. (1972) *Learning from Las Vegas*, Cambridge, Mass., MIT Press.

Wall, J.F. (1970) *Andrew Carnegie*, New York, Oxford University Press.

Walton, J. (1983) *The English Seaside Resort: A Social History 1750–1914* Leicester, Leicester University Press.

Walton, J.K. and Walvin, J. (eds) 1983) *Leisure in Britain 1780–1939*, Manchester, Manchester University Press.

Walvin, J. (1982) *A Child's World: A Social History of English Childhood 1800–1914*, Harmondsworth, Penguin.

Wardle, D. (1970) *English Popular Education 1780–1970*, Cambridge, Cambridge University Press.

Waycott, A. (1983) *National Parks of Western Europe*, Southampton, Inklon.

Weber, E. (1986) *France: Fin de Siècle*, Harvard, Bellknap.

Weber, M. (1923) *General Economic History*, New York, Collier Books.

Weber, M. (1930) *The Protestant Ethnic and the Spirit of Capitalism*, London, Allen & Unwin.

Weber, M. (1968) *Economy and Society, 3 vols*, New York, Bedminster Press.

Weber, M. (1970) *From Max Weber* Gerth, H. and Mills, C.W., (eds) London, Routledge & Kegan Paul.

Whetman, C.D. (1909) *The Family and the Nation*, London, Longman and Green.

Wharton, E. and Ogden Codman Jr (1901) *The Decoration of Houses*, New York, Scribners.

Wiener, M.J. (1988) *English Culture and the Decline of the Industrial Spirit 1850–1980*, Hardmondsworth, Penguin.

Wigley, J. (1980) *The Rise and Fall of the Victorian Sunday*, Manchester, Manchester University Press.

Wilkinson, P.F. (1988) 'The historical roots of urban open space planning' *Leisure Studies* 7(2) pp. 125–44.

Williams, R. (1973) *The Country and the City*, London, Hogarth Press.

Williams, R. (1974) *Television: Technology and Culture Form*, Glasgow, Fontana.

Williams, R. (1981) *Culture*, Glasgow, Fontana.

Williams, R.H. (1982) *Dream Worlds: Mass Consumption in late nineteenth century France*, Berkeley, California University Press.

Williamson, J. (1978) *Decoding Advertisements: Ideology and Meaning in Advertising*, London, Marion Boyars.

Wilson, E. (1985) *Adorned in Dreams: Fashion and Modernity*, London, Virago.

Wimbush, E. and Talbot, M. (eds) (1988) *Relative Freedoms: Women and Leisure*, Milton Keynes, Open University Press.

Winstanley, G. (1973) *'The Law of Freedom' and other writings* Christopher Hill, (ed.) Harmondsworth, Penguin.

Winstanley, M.J. (1983) *The Shopkeeper's World*, Manchester, Manchester University Press.

Wood, J. (1982) *Show Windows: 75 Years of the Art of Display*, New York: Congdon & Weed.

Wouters, C. (1986) 'Formalization and Informalization: Changing Tension Balances in the Civilizing Process' *Theory, Culture and Society* 3(2) pp. 1–18.

Wouters, C. (1987) 'Developments in the Behavioural Codes Between the Sexes: the formalization of informalization in the Netherlands 1930–85', *Theory, Culture and Society* 4(2–3) pp. 405–27.

Wright, P. (1985) *On Living in an Old Country*, London, Verso.

Wright, W. (1975) *Six Guns and Society: A Structural Study of the Western*, Berkeley, California University Press.

Yates, F. (1975) *Astrae: The Imperial Theme in the Sixteenth Century*, London, Ark.

Yeo, S. (1976) *Religion and Voluntary Organisations in Crisis*, Beckenham, Croom Helm.

Yeo, E. and Yeo, S. (eds) (1981) *Popular Culture and Class Conflict 1590–1914: Explorations in the History of Labour and Leisure*, Brighton, Harvester Press.

Zukin, S. (1988) *Loft Living: Culture and Capital in Urban Change*, London, Radius.

Subject Index

Name Index